D1736382

Ballots of Tumult

Ballots of Tumult

A Portrait of Volatility in American Voting

COURTNEY BROWN

Ann Arbor

THE UNIVERSITY OF MICHIGAN PRESS

1994   1993   1992   1991   4   3   2   1

Distributed in the United Kingdom and Europe by
Manchester University Press, Oxford Road,
Manchester M13 9PL, UK

Library of Congress Cataloging-in-Publication Data

Brown, Courtney, 1952–
    Ballots of tumult : a portrait of volatility in American voting /
Courtney Brown.
        p.   cm.
    Includes bibliographical references and index.
    ISBN 0-472-10250-8 (alk. paper)
    1. Elections—United States—History. 2. Voting—United States—
History. 3. Political stability—United States—History.
I. Title.
JK1965.B74   1991
324.973—dc20   91-15599
                                                          CIP

British Library Cataloguing-in-Publication Data

Brown, Courtney
    Ballots of tumult : a portrait of volatility in American
voting.
    1. United States. Voting
    I. Title
    324.973

    ISBN 0-472-10250-8

Kwa Malkia wangu Wakiafrika,
nimpendaye
bila ya kiasi.

[To my African Queen,
whom I love
without measure.]

Acknowledgments

I am indebted to many people and a few institutions with regard to this book. Starting with the people, John Sprague introduced me to the type of analysis that I present here. I did not run into John by luck. I purposefully sought him out and went to study under him in 1977. My desire was to model dynamic change in social systems using deterministic mathematics. I was not disappointed, and I am grateful for his patience as a mentor.

Robert Huckfeldt and Robert Boynton were the manuscript readers for the University of Michigan Press. Their comments were particularly helpful in making final revisions to the manuscript. Colin Day, the Director of the Press, gave me some very valuable suggestions on focusing the "punch" of the book. Karen O'Connor gave me solid advice regarding the chapter on the 1920 extension of the voting franchise. Paul Allen Beck offered many helpful suggestions regarding the chapter on the 1928–36 Roosevelt realignment. Finally, there are many other people who helped me in countless ways. I am grateful to them all.

A number of institutions deserve thanks. Emory University, and to a lesser extent the University of California at Los Angeles, dedicated a large proportion of their mainframe computer resources to the estimations presented in these analyses. This was not a small commitment of resources. The vast majority of the estimations presented in this book were conducted at Emory University.

At Emory, running on a souped-up IBM 3090, I had to compete with numerically intensive users in the Physics department. The physicists were "creating" crystals, and I was "throwing" the masses into an interactive soup. But in the process of computing, we all got to know and appreciate one another's research. We were all keenly aware of how dependent we had become on supercomputer technology, social scientist and physicist alike. I thank the physicists for understanding when I needed more time.

The Emory mainframe computing staff were a tremendous help in these analyses. More often than I would like to admit, their top managers personally managed my estimation runs. Individual runs often took a day or more, and competition with other users who needed faster turnaround (like a second or two) required patient management and planning.

At UCLA in the mid-1980s, running on an IBM 8081, I was told my estimation programs were using 75 percent of all of the mainframe usage (and it was running at full capacity). That included all staff, teaching, and research users for eleven departments.

The Inter-University Consortium for Political and Social Research Summer Program had invited me to teach a course in formal theories of social systems for six summers, beginning in 1984. During that time I was able to refine the course and my own thinking about model building. Much of that refinement is reflected in this book. I am grateful to the Consortium, and especially to Jerry Clubb, Carolyn Geda, Hank Heitowit, and Chris Achen, who were instrumental in inviting me back.

The primary results and methods of chapter 4 of this book originally appeared as an article titled "Mass Dynamics of U.S. Presidential Competitions, 1928–36" in *American Political Science Review* 82, no. 4 (1988). These results and methods were recognized in the IBM Supercomputing Competition of 1989 and are also included in a volume of collected winning papers in a book published by MIT Press in 1991. I thank *American Political Science Review* for granting me permission to reprint the results both here and elsewhere.

I must thank the Inter-University Consortium for Political and Social Research for supplying me with all of the data used in these analyses. Of course, I alone am responsible for all interpretations, correct or incorrect, presented in this volume.

Special thanks are extended to Isaac Asimov. I have not yet met Dr. Asimov in person. Maybe I never will. But he nonetheless is the person who got me thinking about modeling the masses in the first place. He calls it *psychohistory,* and it is the science that structures the plot of his *Foundation* science fiction series. It was Asimov's influence that convinced me long ago that the modeling of mass behavior would be lots of fun. It is.

Finally, thanks to my wife, Isabella, for everything.

Contents

CHAPTER 1

Political Competition in a Volatile Electorate

"Compared with the politics of many, and perhaps most, other nations, American electoral politics are stable." In many respects, this sweeping though commonly believed statement disguises a greater yet opposite truth. It implies that electoral volatility is not a general characteristic of American elections.[1] It implies that volatility is atypical of the setting. It is an aberration. It contradicts the "systemic norm." It suggests that one should look for instability and volatility elsewhere, where it is more common, if one wants to study it systematically. Yet this conventional wisdom is as false as it is comforting.

This volume presents a portrait of American elections that sharply contrasts with the usual view of inherent stability. Indeed, the arguments presented here attack that view of stability with full vengeance, not simply as naive, nor merely as not true, but because it engenders an equally false scholastic view that American elections are "different" in some fundamental sense than elections held elsewhere. The view encourages a complacency about the study of American elections as a case of politics at or near equilibrium, unique to the setting, and not directly comparable to non-American democratic processes.

Indeed, the view encourages the study of American politics as a separate field. After all, if politics are stable in America, one need only study its stability. One need not compare it with, say, a democracy that collapsed, for American democracy is not that kind of democracy. One need not even compare it to a rapidly changing and evolving multiparty parliamentary system, for American democracy is not that kind of democracy either. Most important, American democracy need not be compared with any democracies that are experiencing dramatic change and/or instability, for they are different sorts of things, not applicable out of their context. Such things happen in Eastern Europe, in Latin America, and in historical places like the Weimar Republic. But they do not happen in America.

The arguments presented here suggest an alternative approach to the study of American elections, one that transcends some of the differences

---

1. Throughout this volume, *America* and *American* are limited in meaning to only those aspects of a subject that pertain to the United States; no wider context or meaning is intended or implied.

between stable and unstable democracies by reexamining electoral volatility in the American setting. The focus of this book is on volatile aspects of aggregate American voting in elections that have taken place during the last 100 years. The total scope of the analysis will, I hope, enable a reevaluation of the characterization of American politics as stable that is described above. This may enhance the more general study of mass electoral dynamics. And perhaps, by systematically investigating electoral volatility in the United States, it may help end the scholastic isolation of the study of American elections by revealing general characteristics of this volatility that can be examined elsewhere.

Thus, this study attempts to identify numerous dynamic components of electoral volatility in the United States. Within my discussions, some connections are made between these dynamic components of electoral volatility and non-American settings, but there are limitations to what can be accomplished in any single volume. A systematic review of electoral dynamics across a broad range of national settings is still needed as a next step, and it would greatly add to our understanding of electoral volatility generically conceived. Yet a systematic review of the dynamics of electoral change will be possible only after the case is made that American elections also display significant volatility, and when it is argued that this same volatility is comprised of clearly marked components that are, thus, potentially identifiable in non-American settings.

Why should there be a problem with assuming that U.S. elections are fundamentally stable? The problem lies with a lack of clarity in the meaning of the terms *stability* and *volatility*. It is important conceptually to separate questions regarding the stability of regimes and forms of government from electoral stability and the dynamics of electoral change. When people say that American elections are stable, they may be referring to the fact that there is little chance of a military coup or other such spectacular event following a particular electoral outcome. There is no king to dissolve parliament, and the government cannot collapse with a presidential call for new elections. Every two years there are elections for Congress, and every four years there are elections for president. Sometimes the Democrats may capture the White House, and sometimes the Republicans may do the same, but the basic structure of electoral competition between the parties remains unchanged. Thus, the case is made that American electoral politics is fundamentally stable. One has to closely examine this reasoning, and what one means by *stability*, to see why it is not true.

If one separates the concepts of *regime stability* and *electoral stability*, it is possible to accept that aggregate politics in the United States can change dramatically. It can change so dramatically that if a similar change happened in another national setting, say in a country with developing democratic institutions, the government could be thrown into a state of crisis. To use an example, consider the presidential election of 1912. Theodore Roosevelt split from the Republican party to form his own movement (the Bull Moose party) in his run for the presidency. At that time, there were basically two blocs of voters, Democrats and Republicans. The Republican party was, of course, the majority party. However, Roosevelt came in second in that contest, thus splitting the Republican party. This allowed Woodrow Wilson to capture the presidency for the Democratic party.

In terms of partisan dynamics, there is a significant degree of similarity between this election and the recent democratic election in South Korea in which there were two basic voting blocs, ruling party supporters and opposition supporters. The opposition forces were the majority. However, the opposition forces were split by two prominent opposition leaders, Kim Dae Jung and Kim Yong Sam, each forming their own party in a manner that was, in general, very reminiscent of the personal dispute between Taft and Roosevelt. The result was that the leader of the ruling party, Roh Tae Woo, was allowed to form a government. Few would quibble with a characterization of the South Korean election as being highly volatile and potentially unstable. But how many would say the same of the 1912 election in the United States? This ambiguity results from a failure to separate the concept of regime stability from dramatic electoral change.

The American electorate often experiences electoral change that would be considered unstable or volatile in other national settings. The strength of the democratic institutions and the failure of the American government to collapse are facts that should not cloud one's ability to recognize and to characterize the scope and magnitude of the mass electoral changes that do occur.

The matter is complicated by a confusion between *stability* and *volatility*. Electoral *volatility*, as used in this book, refers to dramatic, sudden, and large-magnitude shifts in aggregate electoral dynamics. In part, this definition of volatility is used in determining the choice of cases that are investigated and presented in later chapters. The volatility can occur for many reasons. For example, a powerful issue can suddenly emerge, or perhaps a charismatic candidate can run for office. Other more coalitionally dependent characteristics of party support can also govern the volatile electoral dynamics, such as when race begins to dominate class as the primary force structuring the electorate (see Carmines and Stimson 1989; as well as Huckfeldt and Kohfeld 1989).

Stability is another matter. Electoral *stability* refers to the consequences of the electoral dynamics of particular elections on the governing fortunes of particular parties. Thus, volatility can be destabilizing to an existing electoral balance. This, in turn, is different from the stability of the governing democratic institutions, weakness in which can lead to governmental collapse, a great potential in newly democratizing countries. Thus, this book is primarily about the dynamics of electoral volatility in the United States, as defined above. Secondarily, these investigations are concerned with the matter of electoral stability, since large-magnitude, sudden shifts in the electoral dynamics often have long-lasting consequences to the governing fortunes of the parties. Herein, through volatility, lies the conceptual access to understanding instability in the American electoral history of the last 100 years.

To show how important it is to resolve these distinctions in terms, consider another example, the election of 1920. In 1920, the American electorate virtually doubled with the universal extension of the voting franchise to women. Conventional wisdom has long asserted that the 1920 election was "simply" a "return to normalcy" election, in the sense that most of the early part of the century was a Republican-dominated period and the 1920 election returned the Republican party to power. However, the 1920 election was very far from anything that could be called "normal" for that time period. The electorate doubled! Moreover, only *one* party, the Republican party, registered any increase in mobilization. While it is true that 1920 witnessed the return of the Republicans to power, previous elections had, at least, been somewhat competitive. In 1920, the Republicans doubled their mobilization, producing one of the largest landslides in the history of the nation. Moreover, it was this victory and the spectacularly lopsided nature of the partisan mobilization that insured Republican dominance until 1932. Thus, the 1920 election contained lots of volatility, and it dramatically affected the stability of the electoral balance that followed. The "return to normalcy" interpretation obscures all this, and it minimizes the historical importance of a tremendously interesting electoral event.

Change as Signposts and Attempts to Control Change

When most people think of the history of a nation, they often review, in their minds, a sequence of major events, signposts of significant transformations of a nation's human experience. The same is true of electoral history. Often, electoral competitions between political parties become notable historical events. More often than not, the reasons behind the notability of the events rest with unusual changes in the behavior of the voting masses. Political parties sometimes die out. Partisan balances suddenly shift. Parties gain new support from different categories of voters. Third parties occasionally emerge. New voters, while a factor in all elections, sometimes participate in unusually large numbers, casting their ballots along lines that do not follow former electoral patterns. In short, change occurs rapidly. Headlines identify the winning party, but the stories below tell of fundamental alterations in the underlying political fabric. History is made when the sudden change establishes a new status quo, a new political game where the players abide by different rules.

While change occurs on the level of the masses, attempts to control such change emanate from politicians. To influence voters in the short term, politicians deliver speeches. In the long term, they channel the resources of the state to serve their own electoral needs. They offer jobs, allocate grants and loans, and support legislation. Many develop endless strategies to guide the masses. Some succeed for a while, and a few succeed through a great many elections. Most successful candidates for public office develop fine senses for detecting what the voters want. Recently, candidates have been spending large sums for survey research to determine what voters want with considerable precision. But even before the arrival of surveys, the success of candidates rose and fell on their abilities to read the public's mood, to sense when the voters wanted change and when they wanted continuity. Thus, as another commonly held wisdom asserts, politicians try to lead, but usually follow the masses. They achieve power and hold onto it dependent on their abilities to identify and satisfy the public's needs. They follow, and they serve. And when they no longer satisfy, they lose.

From the politician's perspective, when the masses are satisfied, they appear happy. They reward their leaders by voting for the same party time and again. The voters develop a "party habit." That is to say, they engage in patterned action, repeatedly supporting the same party, election after election. Thus, they become institutionalized partisan supporters. Moreover, much survey research of recent decades indicates that American voters build within their inner psyches an identification with a party that is characteristically stable, changing slowly, if at all, over periods spanning decades (Campbell, et al. 1960; Converse and Markus 1979; Nie, Verba, and Petrocik 1979). When good times are on a roll, it hardly seems that anything could disturb the existing balance of power. Politicians gain confidence, and some boldly suspect that they have become true "leaders."

But societies evolve, and history has taught us that the masses are fickle. Even authentically great leaders are subject to the peeves of these masses. Short-term control is difficult, at best. Long-term control may be impossible. In the United States, tracking the monthly popularity of presidents can be like watching a ride on a roller coaster. Moreover, such volatile and often surprising dynamics happen elsewhere. Recall that the British public tossed Winston Churchill and his party from office no more than two months following the successful conclusion of the world war through which Churchill so deftly guided his nation to victory. Again, while this is a book about the behavior of the masses during times of turbulent electoral competitions in the United States, some of the lessons drawn from this analysis can be directed toward understanding the mass dynamics of electoral politics in general. Indeed, these analyses were begun under the assumption that some things must be general to the way many masses vote. If we understand some of the common components of volatile electoral change, it makes perfect sense to muse over Churchill's fate in the same theoretical context that we examine an American politician's encounter with the masses.

The Masses as Superbeings

If we are to describe a Dionysian cult, we can hardly improve on the word the Greeks themselves used for the same purpose, *thiasos*. Yet technically, *thiasos* refers to "all kinds of sympathetic social bondings, from literary discussion groups to the kind of hysteria that turns crowds into raging super-beings" (Bagg 1978, 3). The current study is premised on an understanding that the voting masses are more than just a collection of voting individuals. Chapter 2 develops many of the theoretical concepts and definitions that are relevant here. Basically, the activities of groups, whether large or small, are seen as products of individuals within a social and political context. The individuals, within their context, produce a new social organism that runs by its own internal logic, the logic of mass behavior. As the reference to *thiasos* suggests, this is not a new idea.

It is the identification and exploration of this logic of mass behavior that dominates the explanatory motivations of the present analysis. This is an important point, for I am not concerned here with just an examination of the behavior of voters defined individually. While acting under their own motor and intellectual controls, voters are nonetheless responding to the pressures of their surrounding milieu. The story of how these pressures intermix to pro-duce diverse electoral outcomes that have few obvious surface similarities could be seen as grist for a wonderful plot. But it is more. It is the essence of understanding the masses as masses, the basis of generalization, and a prereq-uisite of any future attempt to transport theoretical findings regarding mass dynamics from American to non-American settings. Thus guided by theories of mass political behavior, these analyses are directed toward gaining causal insight regarding a number of particular events in the electoral history of the United States.

The Structure of Analysis

Chapter 2 introduces some important terms and concepts that are critical to the following analyses. In particular, these are the concepts of the time depen-dence of electoral change, voting within a social context, and electoral institutionalization.

Chapter 3 has a methodological orientation. It is not necessary to under-stand the details of the methodologies employed in these analyses in order to understand the substantive findings or their theoretical importance. However, I encourage the readers' persistence with regard to chapter 3. Many of the critical modeling strategies that are employed in subsequent chapters are introduced in an elementary fashion in this chapter. Most readers will find it fairly easy going, even those with little or no mathematical training. More-over, some persistence with chapter 3 may enhance the appreciation of the results presented later, and perhaps shorten the overall time needed to read this book with some degree of thoroughness.

Four types of mass electoral phenomena constitute the substantive focus of this study. They are (1) partisan realignment, (2) the rise and fall of third parties, (3) the impact of a major extension of the voting franchise, and (4) the long-term repercussions of recurrent electoral shocks to the institutionalization of mass political behavior with regard to congressional voting. These four types of phenomena are taken up in detail in chapters 4 through 7, respectively. However, in general, these types of events are closely connected in two respects regarding mass voter movements. Mass electoral change originates from two primary sources, partisan switchers and new voters. The implications of the source of change on the four types of electoral phenomena are different for each type of event, however, and deserve some elaboration.

Partisan realignment can refer to a surprising variety of events, depending on one's point of view (Eldersveld 1982, 386–88). Often the phrase is associated with work by V. O. Key (1955), in which a critical election initiates a process of a sudden and large-scale transfer of voters from one party to another. The process is usually associated with partisan shifts and, perhaps, coalitional change among the ranks of the already mobilized. A similar type of realignment, also characterized by partisan switchers but that occurs over a longer period of time, is referred to as a *secular realignment* (Key 1959). Sometimes a realignment is identified by a radical shift in the partisan balance, where the minority party (say, the Democrats before 1932) suddenly becomes the majority party.

New voters add an ingredient to the concept of realignment that has never been satisfactorily addressed in the literature on realignments. Some scholars suggest that new voters have had a major impact on the changes in partisan fortunes during periods of realignment (Andersen 1979a and 1979b; Petrocik 1981a) whereas others have argued that party switchers dominate the overall change (Sundquist 1983). The arguments usually revolve around the realignment of the 1930s in which the Democratic party was established as the new majority party. In this book, the various claims made by both sides of the argument are addressed in chapter 4 with regard to the entire 1928 to 1936 period. It is difficult to underestimate the importance of the resolution of the argument, since a shifting partisan balance caused by waves of new voters is an event with a fundamentally different character than one in which existing partisans bolt from one party and join another. Minimally, the implications of a resolution of the debate, extended to other electoral and historical contexts, address the connection between voting behavior and the stability and meaning of partisan identification on the level of the individual voter. Fundamentally, the debate's resolution will enhance our understanding of change in contemporary democratic societies, and, tangentially, the stability of electoral regimes during periods of political stress.

The rise and fall of third parties is a phenomenon that addresses a set of similarly complex questions. This is the focus of chapter 5. I begin with a puzzle. If, as much contemporary survey evidence indicates, partisan identification is as stable as it appears to be, which types of voters would vote in large numbers for a "flash in the pan" third party? Since the 1890s, there have been five occasions in which a third party received more than 6 percent of the vote (the highest being Theodore Roosevelt's Progressive—the Bull Moose—party in 1912 with 27 percent of the vote). In Roosevelt's case, conventional wisdom is that his party split the Republican party, and there can be little doubt that this was in fact true. But do third parties always rise at the expense of one of the mainstream parties? When Bryan carried the People's (Populist) party under the Democratic umbrella in 1896, was he re-recruiting former discontented Democrats who temporarily bolted from their traditional party's ranks to swell the ranks of the People's party in 1892? How many of these Populist/Democrats of 1896 were new voters, either in 1892 or 1896? Some of these types of questions can be addressed, in part, with survey information with regard to Wallace's presidential bid in 1968 and Anderson's challenge in 1980. However, especially for the earlier elections, these questions have never been answered, and even rarely asked.

The voting franchise in the United States was extended to women throughout all of the states in 1920. As a consequence, the number of votes for the Republican party in 1920 virtually doubled as compared with 1916 (from 8.5 million in 1916 to 16.0 million in 1920). Yet the number of Democratic votes hardly changed during that same time period (approximately 9.1 million in both 1916 and 1920). This is a truly remarkable phenomenon, given eight years of a Democratic presidency from 1912 to 1920. The campaign for women's suffrage prior to 1920 showed no signs of offering a distinct partisan advantage to the Republicans. Indeed, the Democratic president, Woodrow Wilson, offered his firm support to the passage of the Nineteenth Amendment to the Constitution (McDonagh and Price 1985, 418). This puzzle, explored as the central theme in chapter 6, addresses the causes underlying the channeling of the newly franchised voters into the Republican ranks. The event is characterized by a huge wave of new voters and a distinct partisan bias on the part of the new voters that dramatically altered the existing electoral balance between the parties. Identification of the factors associated with the mobilization of new women voters in 1920 will shed light on a more general understanding of the effects of other large-scale, new-voter activities.

The effect of multiple disturbances to the long-term characteristics of an electoral system is a topic that has been discussed from a theoretical perspective useful to the present analysis in an early work by McPhee and Ferguson (1962). Recurrent disturbances to an electoral system are conceptually different from isolated or one-time disturbances. For example, the appearance of a charismatic leader in an electoral competition, perhaps in combination with economic conditions favorable to his or her candidacy, may result in a large-scale movement of voters across party lines as well as the mobilization of many new voters. It is natural to wonder how long the effect of this event will be felt in the electoral competitions that follow. However, if the electorate experiences recurrent and regular influences of increased mobilization, would the impacts of these events have a cumulative effect, or would voters develop an immunization to the disturbances (the argument made by McPhee and Ferguson)?

The congressional mobilization cycle in the United States offers an especially valuable setting within which to approach this topic. Every four years, a presidential election increases mobilization for the congressional contests. In these contests, the winning presidential contestant's coattails often disproportionately increase his party's congressional vote as well. In the off-year elections between the presidential contests, overall congressional mobilization returns to a lower level that reflects the absence of the previous exogenous presidential influence. The magnitude of the up-and-down mobilization shifts are huge when viewed comparatively. In some areas of the United States, off-year mobilization can drop to approximately one-half of the on-year total. Were some other countries to experience even one such drop in a parliamentary election, the nation might be considered to be in a state of crisis. The regularity of the American electoral experience should not dull one's appreciation of its magnitude.

Different types of voters should react to the congressional mobilization cycle differentially, depending on the individual characteristics of the voters and the environments in which they live. It is crucial to note that the cyclical mobilization phenomenon allows for an examination of the mass dynamics of recurrent and regular electoral disturbances on future electoral competitions. In particular, it allows us to identify variations in that cycle that are linked to different social characteristics of the electorate. These are the types of questions that are raised and examined in the analysis of chapter 7 with regard to the congressional mobilization cycle during the period from the early 1950s to the mid-1980s.

A Defense of the Sample

The types of electoral events discussed above are all examples of politics under unusual, volatile, or stressed circumstances. Studying these topics within the framework of one book represents a purposeful effort to sort out some of the connecting and underlying components of the relevant mass electoral dynamics. Yet two questions arise immediately with regard to the topics included here. First, why are these topics examined instead of others? Second, what is the reasoning behind choosing the particular instances that have been chosen to represent these topics?

The first question is the easiest to answer. The types of electoral instances examined here are not an exhaustive list of all types of volatile electoral activity. Nonetheless, the examination of four such diverse types of electoral volatility in one volume broadens the spectrum of the analysis beyond that which exists in much of the extant electoral literature, and it encourages an attempt to draw generalizations relevant to other electoral events. From the author's perspective, this is an intellectual move in a potentially rich theoretical direction. Success with this effort, even if only partial, should encourage other investigations with regard to other types of volatile electoral events.

With regard to the second question, the topics covered here are represented by a sample of particular instances of volatile electoral activity. The type of sample is called a "purposive" or "guided" sample (see Nachmias and Nachmias 1987, 185). Its purpose is not to represent the universe of elections as a random sample would represent a population in, say, a cross-sectional survey of American voters. Rather, each instance examined in this volume has been chosen heuristically to cover, in combination with the other instances, a wide range of thematic types of electoral situations in which volatile voting has occurred.

Thus, in brief, the four topics discussed in this book are large-scale realignment, the appearance of a third party, the extension of the franchise, and the response of congressional mobilization to potentially destabilizing presidential elections. I investigate particular instances of electoral volatility for each of these topics. Yet, of course, more than one instance of electoral volatility has historically occurred in the United States with regard to each of these topics. For example, the pre–Civil War period experienced both multiple parties and a large-scale realignment, and congressional mobilization has been subject to the influences of the presidential competitions long before the 1950s.

The absence of a discussion of these and other instances in this book does not reflect a sense on my part of their lesser importance relative to the cases that are examined here. Rather, it is merely a consequence of the restrictions that are placed on any empirical study of this nature with regard to limitations in time and resources. Nonetheless, the cases examined here are very prominent examples of the general topics they have been chosen to represent, and the expectation is that lessons learned from these cases will be applicable to the study of other electoral events in other settings.

Indeed, it is probable that the types of events that are examined in this volume are the very types of phenomena that will reveal important dynamic components within a broader spectrum of electoral activity. While there are many parallels in the natural and physical sciences, the field of population biology seems the closest cousin to the approach of the current analysis. Population biologists often find themselves in a situation of trying to understand how an ecosystem is operating, in the sense of determining if it is stable, identifying the underlying food chain, and investigating the influences of variations in the environment (such as the effect of a reduction in tree habitat or an increase in pollution on certain species, etc.). Mathematical theorists in this field often attempt to model such ecosystems with interdependent systems of differential and difference equations. Structural changes in the equations and variations in parameter values allows them to test the effects of changes in one area of the ecosystem in terms of consequent effects on the overall environment. Often the results can lead to remarkable conclusions regarding what may have been thought to be a stable community. The following comment made by Robert May illustrates the potential volatility that can be inherent in many such systems. "Removal of one species can lead to a severe collapse in the overall trophic structure: thus Paine . . . has shown that removal of one species from an intertidal community of marine invertebrates led to its collapse from a 15-species to an 8-species system in under two years" (May 1974, 39).

In general, unusual phenomena often reveal subtleties that are hidden in our commonly observed world. Environmental stress reveals characteristics of the underlying dynamic interdependence of an environment to the population biologist. Similarly, electoral stress of the type examined in this volume should be expected to reveal otherwise hidden characteristics of an outwardly appearing stable political system. The electoral events examined here are approached on the level of their mass electoral dynamics with this idea clearly in mind.

With an understanding that all good contributions to our understanding of the world must be based on firm and often innovative foundations, readers should make special note of three aspects that have been purposely incorporated into these analyses. The first is the data that are analyzed. The entire set upon which this report is based is newly organized from extensive but scattered holdings that are available from the Inter-University Consortium for Political and Social Research. Their organization into a single usable data set required years of work and a heavy commitment of mainframe and microcomputer resources. Thus, the data, in terms of their present reorganization, are new.

The second aspect to be noted is the questions that are addressed. These questions have either not been asked before in a significant way (as with the chapter on the 1920 election), or they are being asked here from a different perspective, or perhaps a different view of politics, than that which is commonly encountered in the extant electoral literature. The possibility of fixed dynamic structures as characteristics of volatile mass electoral behavior differentially related to social context and evident across a wide range of events has not been extensively explored by any means.

The third aspect deserving special note is methodological. The methods used for these analyses are, in many respects, new applications to social scientific work. Many of the models explored here are formal in the sense that they are explicit mathematical representations of theories of mass voter-movements. The models employ both continuous and discrete time specifications that are not typical for the voting literature in terms of their functional forms and their estimation requirements (see the appendix). Indeed, the results in this volume could not have been obtained using a more commonly available but more restrictive statistical technology. Nonetheless, great effort has been invested in making this book thoroughly readable, on a substantive level, by all readers, regardless of previous mathematical training.

Finally, let me mention what this book is not. The analyses presented here do not attempt to trace voter movements longitudinally back to their initial intellectual or philosophical genesis. For example, chapter 4 contains an analysis of the 1928–36 realignment period. However, why begin the discussion in 1928? Could it be that some of La Follette's farm support in 1924 found its way into Roosevelt's winning coalition in 1932 (or perhaps 1936)? Going back further, perhaps some of Teddy Roosevelt's 1912 supporters became F.D.R. supporters in the 1930s. Further back still, it could be that some of F.D.R.'s 1932 support could be traced back to the political debates of the 1890s. Other scholars have made valuable attempts at such types of longitudinal tracings (e.g., Sundquist 1983). The current analysis is not an attempt to redo that work using a different methodology. This book is hunting different game.

The question of starting points for investigations into the longitudinal roots of almost all electoral phenomena rarely has a firm answer. Longitudinal tracings of sequences of events is a historical issue filled with the potential for interpretive controversy. Yet from the perspective of the goals of the current analysis, the farther back one goes in search of "rumblings in the distance," the farther away one gets from the critical period of greatest volatility. But it is the dynamics of the great volatility that are of interest here, not the historical connections to previous events.

The current analysis investigates the dynamics of rapid and large-scale change in the mass electorate of the United States. The primary point of the book is to look at the structure of these dynamics at the moments of greatest aggregate voter movement. It is from this perspective that the contribution of this analysis is to be located both theoretically and substantively. Perhaps others may find that what is learned from this investigation sheds light onto other electoral events, some of which may be connected historically. This would be a valuable next step, but it is beyond the scope of this single volume. Thus, this book is about the dynamic structures of explosive electoral politics in the United States. I am not concerned with the question of who lit a match, perhaps many years previously, that ultimately led to an explosion. My concern is the explosion itself, and its consequences to the electoral system in the aftermath of these ballots of tumult.

CHAPTER 2

Concepts of Change

This chapter develops some definitions and ideas that are used in the theoretical sections of later chapters. One such idea is the notion of time as an integral part of the structure of mass electoral dynamics. It is important to outline the general nature and broad scope of the time dependence of political phenomena, since these investigations identify this dependence within a diverse collection of social and historical settings, and because the time dependence of mass electoral politics is not always clearly defined in much of the extant literature on voting. Other aspects of mass political dynamics that are raised in this chapter are the influences of local social environments that condition the processes of change, electoral institutionalization (here viewed as a constantly evolving and stabilizing force that can contribute to the continuity of political systems), and partisan identification, which is often thought of as the enemy of political change.

These concepts lay the initial groundwork for what is to come. Yet it is important to note that this chapter is more than merely an introduction of terms. If the arguments in this volume are to challenge a scholastic orthodoxy claiming stability in American electoral politics effectively, it is crucial to establish an early recognition of concepts critical to the argument as well as to distinguish these concepts from concepts that are used elsewhere to argue the opposite.

Time

All political phenomena take place longitudinally. That is, the processes underlying the phenomena are dynamic in nature. Large aggregate movements may occur during particular elections, but the processes that cause each outcome occupy periods that span the time between elections. Voting is not instantaneous. Most voters typically do not have to wait until election day to know which party they tend to favor, even though there are often many "undecided" voters with respect to particular candidates, even late in some campaigns. Moreover, voters are people, and people are social beings who interact with other people. The process of making a vote decision is a process that takes place within an interactive social environment that is filled with the biases, prejudices, and thoughts of others. All this takes time.

We are looking at two levels of events that take place over time. The first is the individual vote decision, where the process leading to an individual's vote choice need not be independent of the individual's surrounding milieu. The second is the macrolevel electoral event, such as a realignment or the emergence of a third party. A central assumption of the present analysis is that the microlevel decision-making processes of individuals and the macroprocesses characterized in terms of the behavior of the masses are interconnected. Moreover, the macroprocesses are not merely a summation of vote choices, all made in individual isolation. Rather, a complex and reciprocal logic of mass political behavior is at work, with masses bending the individuals, and individuals shaping the masses.

Thus the micro- (individual) and macro- (electoral event) processes need not be linked by a one-way bridge, say, from the micro to the macro. Individuals making decisions can lead to increased votes for the Democrats, but the added Democratic strength can lead to an enhanced incentive for more individuals to vote Democratic. In its most elementary form, this is a common phenomenon that is often referred to as a campaign's "momentum." The important point to emphasize here is that both the micro- and macroprocesses are time dependent, and that both processes are in a continual state of interaction.

The time dependence of both micro- and macrophenomena takes two forms. The first is simply a result of the fact that events take place in time. For example, time is required for the spread of information, interactively or otherwise. This is true of individuals reading the newspaper as well as groups and larger societies interacting. This type of time dependence, called autonomous time dependence, does not require time to be an explicit explanatory variable in a description of the social process. Assumptions of this type of time dependence are typical in descriptions of social processes that are seen as consequences of existing social structures that are changing with time. The social structures themselves are the determinants of the rates of change of the processes being examined. This is the basic characteristic of all Markov dynamic processes (see Mesterton-Gibbons 1989, 175–79).

The second type of time dependence is called nonautonomous time dependence. This use of time explicitly structures descriptions of social processes as consequences of time, not just other variables that change with time. From a modeling perspective, this often takes the form of a variable, t (for time, of course), that is used as an exogenous factor (see Kocak 1989, 7–8). (This should not be confused with a subscript t attached to another variable.) Sometimes this is done to include a sense of history in a dynamic model. Thus, the model depends not only on existing social structures as determinants of change, but also on when the process takes place relative to some starting point (Mesterton-Gibbons 1989, 176–77).

In this volume, time-dependent processes of social and political change are described as autonomous. The main reason for this is substantive. Effort has been made, here, to identify determinants of rapid aggregate electoral change in terms of existing social environments. Thus, when an overall trend is discerned, the attempt is made to specify fully the process in terms of the explosive qualities of the milieu. This is not to say that an explicit time-control variable would not be helpful in other circumstances. But this volume presents results of investigations that have been guided, from the beginning, by the assumption that societies change because of their own internal social and political characteristics. The value of this assumption in structuring these analyses can be evaluated adequately only if the descriptive formalisms accurately correspond with the assumption, in the sense of adequate structural isomorphism between theory and mathematical form.

What, then, is meant by *time dependence* if social structure, not an explicit exogenous use of time, determines change in the phenomena under investigation? Is this not social structure dependence rather than time dependence? This is more than simply a matter of terminology. It is important to recognize that time dependence is a general characteristic of all phenomena that change with time, regardless of whether that change is autonomous or nonautonomous. For autonomous change, social structure determines the rate of change of the social processes, and that rate of change characterizes the time dependence. From the perspective of time dependence, it does not matter whether or not the rate of change is determined by social or other means. What does matter is that a pattern of change can be identified that corresponds with the passage of time. The goal of theory construction is to determine the underlying structure to that pattern of change.

The Environment of Change

Social scientists have long known that social and political environments affect individual behavior and attitudes. Since this book presents an elaborate set of arguments tying mass electoral phenomena to underlying social conditions, it is worthwhile to review some of what is already known about environmentally conditioned political behavior. Berelson, Lazarsfeld, and McPhee (1954) identified numerous collective influences on individuals that originated from friends and co-workers. Moreover, McPhee and Smith (1962, 129) have proposed a model of learning and information processing within a group context that captures both the structure of contextual influences and the associated dynamic considerations. Briefly,. an individual receives some stimulus from a political campaign. The stimulus can be in the form of direct contact between the voter and the candidate (or the candidate's representatives), or the stimulus can be the result of a voter listening to a news broadcast or paid advertisement. This campaign stimulus produces an initial response on the part of the individual receiving the stimulus. The person then talks to his or her friends (or co-workers, neighbors, etc.) about their response to the stimulus. If the consequent discussion with friends is positive, the voter's initial response to the campaign is reinforced and the vote decision begins to assume a concrete direction. If the discussion is negative (i.e., the friends reject the person's response to the campaign), then the voter withdraws from the discussion environment, formulates another response to the campaign, and tests this modified response with the friends again. A more positive evaluation from the group leads to a buttressing of the revised response.

For example, say a person sees a flag-waving commercial for Pat Robertson while on a trip to New Hampshire in February of 1988. Upon returning to New York, he attends a dinner party to which many of his liberal Democratic friends are invited. During the dinner, people ask him about his impressions of the campaign in New Hampshire, and he mentions that he did not get to see all that much of it due to his busy schedule, but he did see a commercial for Pat Robertson that moved him. He remarks that he never before realized how much America longed for that forgotten sense of patriotism. Following this remark, the dinner table grows deathly silent, with the spell broken finally by his closest friend asking him whether he is joking. The ensuing onslaught of verbal abuse is enough to force the New Hampshire traveler to reconsider his initial response to the Robertson commercial. A new response is formulated in time for the next encounter with his friends, this time guided by expectations of the group's reaction. Thus, in McPhee and Smith's learning model, the dynamic processes are biased in the direction of individual conformity to group norms.

The mechanisms by which groups enforce individual conformity to group norms can be quite complex. Gans (1962) has offered a detailed account of such group activity within the context of an Italian community in Boston's West End. Here, the group's arsenal for coercion includes the outright rejection of deviating individuals from the group and the administration of measured amounts of shame or guilt. More broadly, the groups have informational biases that feed these coercive pressures. It has been repeatedly shown that group members perceive real-world facts as if through an informational filter that either interprets or screens out external information to produce group-internal discussions that are consistent with established group norms (Berelson, Lazarsfeld, and McPhee 1954, 77–87; Garfinkel 1967; Gurwitsch 1962, 50–72; MacKuen and Brown 1987). Part of this is due to the manipulatory effects of leadership types within the group who act to control group conversations (Molotch and Boden 1985). But much of it also seems to be due to the influence of group "inertia," where the input of any one person's deviant views into the group discussions is necessarily only one view against an accepted group alternative. Consequently, deviant ideas must achieve some level of threshold acceptance before group norms could be successfully challenged.

Some evidence suggests that the acceptance of deviant ideas within a group is not a common occurrence. Huckfeldt and Sprague (1987 and 1988) argue that individuals with views in the minority are likely to encounter considerable resistance to their ideas from majority group members. These situations need not produce unanimous conformity across group norms. Indeed, a reverse threshold effect seems to operate as there are fewer members of a minority within the group. Such minorities can retreat from the group socialization process, further increasing their own sense of alienation.

Crucially, the coercive and informational biases of the group are directly influenced by the information available from the larger surrounding community, say, the neighborhood, town, or county (Blau 1977; Blum 1985; Simmel 1955). Heterogeneity within the larger environment produces within-group interactions reflecting that broader heterogeneity. Thus, memberships of social groups will tend to be mixed when the larger social environment is mixed. As well, between-group interactions also reflect that broader social heterogeneity in terms of the frequency and direction of the available informational cues. Putnam (1966) ties the influence of the larger community on individuals to the intermediating role played by smaller groups (secondary associations). Groups provide settings for individuals to interact socially with members of the larger community. Moreover, the internal expectations of the groups themselves rarely deviate strongly from the accepted norms of the larger community, lest the groups risk wholesale rejection by the community, together with all of the associated social costs for the individual members.

The general susceptibility of individuals to political influences originating from their environment is a finding with strong empirical support across a variety of cultures and societies. Much of the extant literature refers to these influences as "contextual," where the meaning points to the individual's social or political context or environment as a determinant in the structuring of attitudes and behaviors (usually voting). For example, Butler and Stokes (1969, 144–50) as well as Miller (1977) have found such contextual influences among the British electorate, and Langton and Rapoport (1975) have found similar effects among Chilean urban workers. In the United States, contextual influences on individual behavior have been observed nationally by Miller (1956), among migrants by Thad Brown (1981 and 1988), and within small neighborhood environments by Weatherford (1982).

Reported evidence of contextual influences on individual behavior have not always appeared to be of the same large magnitude and significance as was characterized by the findings of the early work by Berelson, Lazarsfeld, and McPhee (1954). One reason for this is that many contextual analyses have historically relied on cross-sectional data measured at one point in time. However, if the processes driving change within a complex society are dynamic, then cross-sectional studies are likely to miss the longitudinal traces that would appear as remnants of active social processes. This is an important theme of work by MacKuen and Brown (1987) as well as Huckfeldt and Sprague (1987 and 1988). In these studies, longitudinal evidence of contextually dependent social process is found to be very apparent. Indeed, the contextual influences, longitudinally measured, seem to be very powerful determinants of both attitudinal formation and voting behavior.

Institutionalization

An important concept from the perspective of the analyses presented in this book is that of electoral institutionalization. But to characterize electoral institutionalization in a meaningful fashion, we must first distinguish it from the varieties of meanings often associated with *institutionalization* in the social scientific literature.

Institutionalization is frequently used in the literature of political development to refer to a society's ability to absorb, direct, and even control change (Bill and Hardgrave 1973, 75–83; Eisenstadt 1966; Huntington 1968). The basic idea behind the usage is that the process of modernization in developing societies increases the demands that are placed on existing social and political institutions. Thus, citizen loyalty to the regime, the ability of political parties to represent population needs, the level of trust placed in the judicial system, and the developmental maturity of organized interest groups are all examples of institutional factors that can influence a society's ability to meet the rising demands of its citizenry. In large part, developed societies function smoothly because the citizens, the political elite, and most of those who hold intermediary positions have grown accustomed to working with the formal and informal rules that have evolved over many years in these societies. In this sense, the stability of a society is somewhat dependent on the level of accepted habitual participation among the populace. For example, if the people feel that the police are corrupt, the level of trust in that institution will be low and the overall level of institutionalization in that society will suffer. A consequence of this would be that the potential for instability within that society would be correspondingly higher.

Institutionalization is also a frequently discussed concept with regard to legislatures. In a seminal article, Nelson W. Polsby describes the U.S. House of Representatives in terms of an evolving, and institutionalizing, organizational body (Polsby 1968). The basic idea is that the members of the House develop behavioral routines that become increasingly more complex and habitual (i.e., "automatic"). The institutionalization of the House is said to be high when automated decision-making processes dominate over individual discretionary processes regarding the professional interactions among members. In short, the House members routinely "play along" with the norms and rules of the institution while advancing their own career goals within the institution. The discussion of institutionalization among legislatures has recently been extended to the British House of Commons by Hibbing (1988), with results suggesting lower levels of institutionalization within that body. In general, the role that legislative institutionalization plays as a stabilizing social force has spawned a lively and still expanding literature (see Eisenstadt 1964; Lowenberg 1973; Mishler and Hildreth 1984).

The concept of electoral institutionalization evolved out of the literature discussed above, with perhaps the larger contribution coming from the literature on political development. One of the early studies to establish a clear linkage between electoral behavior and institutionalization is by Przeworski (1975). Przeworski argues that high levels of electoral deinstitutionalization lead to lower levels of regime stability. In his work, deinstitutionalization is measured through voters withdrawing from their established patterns of electoral behavior (i.e., changing their long-term partisan preferences). Regime stability is represented by overall changes in vote share among competing parties in parliamentary democracies.

A similar use of the terms *institutionalization* and *deinstitutionalization* in the electoral sense is found in Brown (1987), a study that focuses on the dynamic patterns of mass electoral behavior in Germany during the Weimar period. In that analysis, a large wave of new voters who supported the Nazis was found to have destabilized the electoral environment in 1930 to such an extent that, in the following election in July of 1932, a large number of supporters of the other parties broke with their previous partisan affiliations. The theoretical focuses of that study are on the role of destabilizing electoral forces that lead to a deinstitutionalizing political environment, as well as the nature of the mass dynamics that transpire afterward.

In a related fashion, Sprague (1981) defines electoral institutionalization as a probability that describes the replicability of previous electoral behavior in current electoral behavior. Thus, "if everyone acts the same way in election t that they did in election $t-1$, with high probability, the system can be considered highly institutionalized" (Sprague 1981, 273). This characterization of institutionalization is particularly useful from the perspective of the analyses presented in this book, as the focus on repeated patterns of electoral behavior clearly adds to an understanding of that which is required to demonstrate a deinstitutionalizing process. If electoral institutionalization is the establishment of longitudinally consistent patterns of partisan support that are shown by repeated, over-time voting behavior for large segments of an electorate, then deinstitutionalization is evident in the disintegration of those patterns.

Thus, deinstitutionalization as a process is the mirror image of institutionalization. Presumably, electoral institutionalization takes place during times of relatively tranquil partisan competition. For example, high levels of reelection among incumbents in the U.S. House of Representatives would indicate a highly institutionalized voting environment on the congressional level as it has developed over recent years. Deinstitutionalization, as a process in which previously established patterns of partisan support are broken, should take place during more unsettled times, say, subsequent to a large economic depression. Thus, if large numbers of Republicans switch their partisan support to the Democratic party in 1932 following the onset of the Great Depression, then the process of deinstitutionalization begins when their previously established patterns of voting have been broken.

Partisan Identification

A great deal of the extant voting literature, especially that following the publication of *The American Voter*, has focused on aspects of voting that relate to an individual's partisan identification. One of the most widely held views of partisanship reflected in this literature is that it is extremely stable longitudinally. In other words, as generally perceived, partisan identification, once fixed, stays fixed for the large majority of American voters. Because of this, partisanship has typically been conceived of as the "enemy" of electoral change. Thus, it is important to distinguish the concept of electoral institutionalization (as it is used here) from partisan identification since instability in aggregate voting, and indeed, changes in institutionalized voting, may display little correspondence with changes in partisan identification.

Partisan identification is typically conceived of as a psychological commitment to a party, an expression of an individual's inner emotional and intellectual bonding to that party. It is often considered the best available predictor of a person's vote. Thus, if a person self-identifies with the Republican party (i.e., calling himself or herself a Republican), then it is likely that person will vote Republican in the next election. Moreover, individuals can often describe themselves in terms of the strength of their partisan bonding. Thus, someone may say that he or she is a "strong Republican" or, perhaps, a "weak Republican."

There has been a tremendous amount of argument in the American voting literature on the concept of partisan identification. Some of the arguments revolve around the number of psychological dimensions that voters have with regard to partisanship (Weisberg 1980). For example, identifying oneself as an independent does not necessarily mean that one has no partisan identification. On the contrary, *independence* can be viewed as a separate category of partisanship, with individuals feeling strongly bonded to this descriptive concept. Some of the other controversies that have revolved around the concept of partisan identification are the impact of partisanship on various forms of political activism (e.g., getting involved in a campaign), its stability in the United States as compared with other nations, associated degrees of political knowledge held by individuals, and methods of measuring partisanship (see Niemi and Weisberg 1984, 393–405). But the key point of partisan identification as it relates to the current analysis is that it is most often used as an explanatory predictor of an individual's vote.

Electoral institutionalization is also used as an explanatory predictor of an individual's vote. Electoral institutionalization is essentially the development of a consistent pattern of voting (i.e., patterned behavior, like a party "habit"). The social and individual determinants of the maintenance or deterioration of that behavior can be quite complex, and the aggregate structural determinants of such processes are, indeed, the subject of this book. Yet, how does electoral institutionalization differ from partisan identification?

To begin, electoral institutionalization and partisan identification are obviously interrelated. People who identify as partisans often tend to vote their partisanship consistently (although variation may be quite common). On the other hand, people who develop a consistent pattern of behavior in support of a party can identify themselves as partisans because of this consistency, that is, the vote causes partisanship rather than the other way around (see Holmberg 1981, 177; Thomassen 1976). But the two concepts are not the same.

Critically, electoral institutionalization refers to consistency in the way people vote, whereas partisan identification refers to the way people psychologically identify themselves. That they are not the same is evident in the difficulty that exists in attempting to use one concept to predict the other. In the United States, partisanship is by no means a perfect or even near perfect predictor of the vote. For example, there are many more Democrats than Republicans in the southern United States; yet in recent years, the Republicans have had much greater success at winning the White House because of a great number of Republican-voting southern "Democrats" (Asher 1988, 30). Moreover, in other countries, partisanship is sometimes found to be less stable as well as less useful as a vote predictor than in the United States, and there is some recent evidence suggesting that aggregate partisanship may not be so stable in the United States as well. A recent study by MacKuen, Erikson, and Stimson (1989) has identified a large degree of systematic longitudinal variation in aggregate partisanship among American voters. Thus, it serves us well to examine electoral institutionalization independently of partisanship. If we are interested in voting, we must study voting.

Yet associations with parties do have (minimally) two components. One component is a psychological bonding to a party, and we are correct to examine it when it is sufficiently strong to influence an individual's vote. However, the other component is consistency in voting. This is patterned behavior, not a psychological state. The dynamics that relate to one of these components need not be identical to the dynamics that relate to the other. For example, in chapter 4, evidence will be presented that strongly suggests that many Republican farmers switched to the Democratic party in 1932. This is an important finding in that the evidence relates to the dynamics of mass voting during an especially volatile period in the history of the United States. However, the evidence presented does not preclude the possibility that these farmers remained Republicans in terms of their psychological bonding to the Republican party, even though the consistency of their previous voting behavior had certainly suffered. Indeed, it is possible that, in 1940, or perhaps later, some of these formerly Republican-voting farmers drifted back to their previous political behavior and began voting Republican once again. (It may not be possible to ever resolve this question entirely, although speculations on these lines have been made by Petrocik [1981a].)

Finally, the focus of this book is on the mass dynamics of voting. The questions that are raised and to which answers are offered have to do with votes. Moreover, the aggregate data on which this study is based record vote activity. These data cannot be used to resolve questions relating to partisan identification. One needs surveys to answer such questions, since voters have to be asked about their psychological commitments. Nonetheless, the analyses that are offered here should be of significant interest, if only indirectly, to those who wish to study partisan identification. These analyses may be particularly relevant to the study of macropartisanship (see MacKuen, Erikson, and Stimson 1989). Both electoral institutionalization and partisan identification are critical components within the framework of mass participation in contemporary democracies. Indeed, if we wish to understand why some democracies maintain their balance while others falter, we must understand the underpinnings of both the voters' behavior and their psychology.

CHAPTER 3

An Algebra of Partisan Change

This chapter serves as a "bridge" to introduce some of the more essential mathematical forms that appear in the models presented in this book. In general, this is important since a model's algebra is so closely connected to substantive interpretation. The chapter begins with a discussion of this substantive-algebraic link. The later sections of the chapter deal with non-linearities and time, the matters of aggregate data, and in particular the ecological, individual level, and equilibrium fallacies, as well as more advanced concepts regarding the specification of dynamic processes.

Simple Models of Change

The simplest process of change at the level of mass behavior that is relevant to these discussions (other than no change at all) is constant growth or decay. Constant growth indicates that some group, say a political party, increases its membership at a constant over-time rate. In such a case, a certain number of new recruits join the party ranks during each time period, such as during an election. Constant decay implies the reverse, that is, the party loses some of its support (the same amount each time period).

The substantive application of constant gain or constant loss as a model is quite limiting with regard to most social processes (although a constant source of gain or loss can be an interesting component of a more complete characterization of a dynamic process). A few elementary mathematical symbols will enhance the explanation.

To represent change in the membership of some group (in this case, a political party), the term dR/dt is used to refer to the rate of change for that group. As an example, R stands for the level of support in an electorate for the Republican party. The term dR/dt is a derivative, and it is a function that describes longitudinal change in the level of Republican support within the electorate. To simplify this initial discussion, partisan change is characterized within a fictitious setting of a one-party electorate containing only Republicans and nonvoters.

If the Republican party neither recruits new members nor loses old members, then the derivative, dR/dt, would equal zero. If, on the other hand, the Republican party manages to recruit (or lose) a set number of members

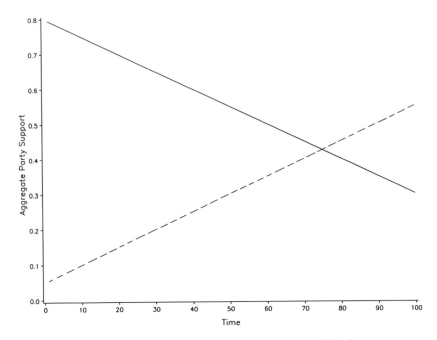

Fig. 3.1. Constant growth and decay as a proportion of the electorate

each election (a net gain or net loss), then the rate of change would be constant. A constant rate of change would be described mathematically as,

$$dR/dt = g, \qquad\qquad (3.1)$$

where g is a constant and a parameter in this simple model.

The over-time behavior of equation 3.1 is represented in figure 3.1. In figure 3.1, the horizontal axis represents time and the vertical axis represents the level of support for the Republican party. Two sample time paths (called *trajectories* of the model) are portrayed in the figure. In a situation of growth, the path moves upward as time advances (the dotted line). In a situation where the Republicans are losing support (i.e., decay), the path moves downward as time moves forward (the solid line). For this simple model, the over-time behaviors of the party's dynamics form straight lines. There are no other possible variations in the structure of this type of dynamic as long as parameter g is constant.

A more interesting characterization of partisan growth or decay could include a description of the rate of growth as dependent on the number of people in the electorate that are available for recruitment. If the recruitment drive is effective, then the fastest change in the level of the party's membership would be when there are the largest number of potential recruits available. As the recruitment drive continues, and the party's ranks swell, the rate of change of party membership should begin to decline as the drive runs into greater and greater difficulty finding people who have not yet been recruited. That is, change (as either a gain or a loss) depends on the size of the nonparticipating population. When the nonparticipating population is large, change in party membership is rapid. When the party is gaining, it gains more rapidly when there are more potential voters available. When the party is declining in membership, the decline is most rapid when the nonparticipating population is large.

A model characterizing change in support for the Republican party that is based on growth (or decay) from the available pool of nonvoters can be expressed as

$$dR/dt = e(1 - R), \tag{3.2}$$

where e is a constant parameter of the model. The level of Republican support, R, is measured as a proportion of the total electorate. When the level of Republican support is low, then the quantity $(1 - R)$ is high, and the magnitude of change, dR/dt, is high as well. When R is high (i.e., as R approaches one, a situation in which nearly all eligibles have been mobilized), then $(1 - R)$ is low, and the rate of change in Republican support is also low.

Figure 3.2 presents a graphic representation of the model expressed above as equation 3.2. Two example trajectories are displayed. As with figure 3.1, one trajectory represents growth in Republican party membership, and the other trajectory represents conditions of decay. Note that the trajectories correspond to our substantive expectations of the model's over-time behavior. With regard to the growth trajectory (the dotted line), the rate of change is highest (i.e., the curve is most steep) when the Republican party membership is low and, thus, there are many potential recruits. Growth slows when the party membership begins to approach unity, and there are consequently fewer people left to recruit. Similarly, decay in membership occurs most rapidly when the ranks are already diminished. This could be compared with a run on the banks, when increasing numbers of depositors withdraw their money when they see others doing the same. This model, while very simplistic and, thus, not realistic in describing most political processes of recruitment, nonetheless begins to capture some descriptive qualities of more complicated electoral phenomena.

Descriptive richness and dynamic flexibility on the part of the model is enhanced remarkably with the introduction of the simplest of nonlinearities to the mathematical form. If the growth of a party is dependent on personal interactions between partisans and nonpartisans, then a nonlinear interaction component is crucial to the specification of the social process (see Huckfeldt 1983; Przeworski and Soares 1971). An interaction term simply specifies the probability of a nonvoter becoming a voter (in my example, a Republican)

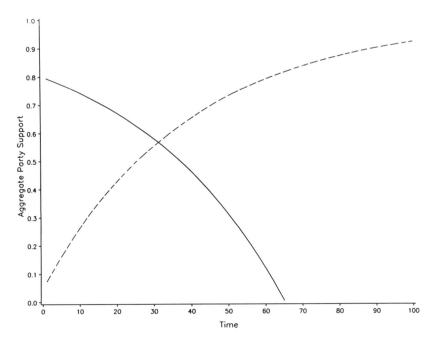

Fig. 3.2. Simple growth and decay as a proportion of the electorate

given the probability of a voter meeting a nonvoter (i.e., an interaction). Thus, if R is the proportion of the electorate in a given area that is Republican, and $(1 - R)$ is the proportion of the electorate that is not voting (in this simple, one-party case), then the multiplicative product $R(1 - R)$ represents the joint probability (assuming random mixing) of an interaction between the two. (The random mixing assumption is heuristically useful, but not necessary; see Mesterton-Gibbons 1989.) Some proportion of these interactions will result in a new Republican voter. This proportion, identified as the parameter b, captures the Republican mobilization rate that is due to such interactions.[1] The entire model can now be written as

$$dR/dt = bR(1 - R). \tag{3.3}$$

Some of the dynamic properties in equation 3.3 are presented graphically in figure 3.3. As with earlier graphs, conditions of both growth and decay are displayed. In both cases, the trajectories reveal logistic qualities, since Re-

---

1. Since there are two ways to achieve this outcome (i.e., by having a voter meet a nonvoter or a nonvoter meet a voter), the actual joint probability of the interaction is $2R(1 - R)$. It is customary, however, to ignore the two in this expression and to absorb the total change in parameter b.

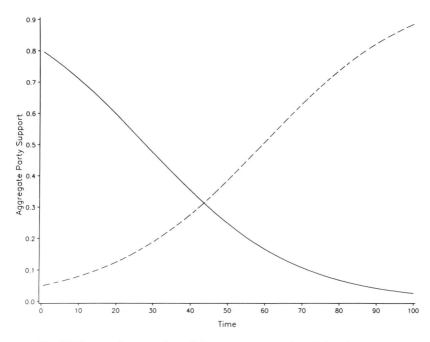

Fig. 3.3. Interactive growth and decay as a proportion of the electorate

publican growth slows as R approaches either unity (in which there are few left to mobilize) or zero (since interactions do not occur without a number of Republicans with whom to interact). The fastest growth occurs in the middle ground, when there are both many Republicans and many nonvoters.

Figure 3.3 contains trajectories for the level of Republican support over time. In order to see how fast the Republicans are mobilizing, one has to look at the steepness of the curves at different points in time. However, an alternative approach is to examine the derivative itself as it changes with respect to changes in the value of partisan support, R. Since the derivative *is* the rate of change, we have only to look at its value in correspondence with a given value for R. When the derivative has a high value, then growth is rapid. When it has a large-magnitude, negative value, then decay is rapid. When the derivative approaches zero, change is slight.

Such a portrayal of equation 3.3 is presented in figure 3.4. Figure 3.4 presents what is called a phase plane of the single-equation model given by equation 3.3 (Haberman 1977, 155–58). Here, the dynamic change in the derivative as R changes is clearly discerned. Returning briefly to figure 3.3, note that change is most rapid when the curves are steeply banked (near the center of the figure). Change is less rapid in the beginning and the end of the trajectories. In figure 3.4, the proportion of the electorate supporting party R is represented on the horizontal axis. Recalling that rapid change corre-

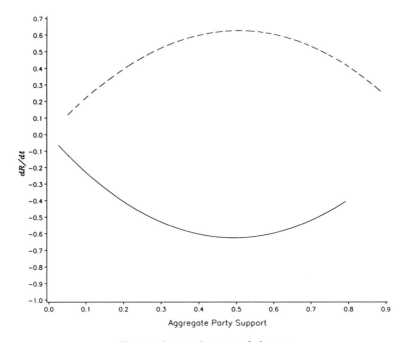

Fig. 3.4. Interactive rate of change

sponds to low (when negative) and high (when positive) values of the derivative, such change is found in the center of this figure for conditions with moderate levels of R.

One of the most important characteristics that is revealed in figure 3.4 is the symmetric quality of the interaction term. Note that when R is at moderate levels, then $(1 - R)$ is also at moderate levels. The quantity $R(1 - R)$ is greatest when $R = 0.5$. Thus, when either one of the two populations are low, change in the party membership is slight. Change occurs most quickly when there are high levels of both populations.

A model characterizing party growth can, of course, be written to incorporate many or all of the dynamic processes captured by the models discussed above. However, two of these processes have particular heuristic value with regard to the substantive analyses that follow in later chapters. I have discussed growth for the Republicans from the pool of nonvoters through both noninteractive and interactive paths (eqs. 3.2 and 3.3). It is quite possible that some nonvoters could be mobilized to vote for the Republican party without the necessity of encountering other Republicans face to face (i.e., noninteractively). On the other hand, other nonvoters could be mobilized because of interactive occurrences in their social environment. Thus, a more complete specification would include both avenues for Republican mobilization, as is contained in equation 3.4,

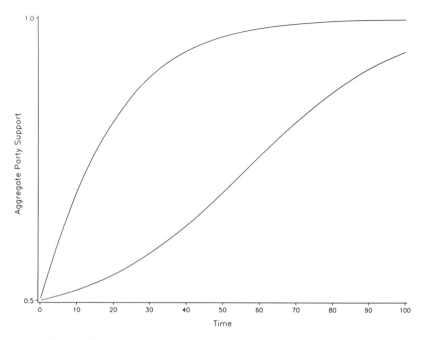

Fig. 3.5. Mixed growth and decay as a proportion of the electorate

$$dR/dt = g(1 - R) + bR(1 - R) \qquad (3.4)$$

or, rearranged,

$$dR/dt = g + (b - g)R - bR^2. \qquad (3.5)$$

The dynamic properties of equation 3.4 can be quite complex. Figure 3.5 presents two sample trajectories for such a model. Other trajectories, dependent entirely on the chosen parameter values and initial conditions, can be calculated to demonstrate different patterns of growth, no change in Republican support, or various histories of decay in Republican mobilization. Again, the characteristics of the trajectories depend on the initial conditions for R that are inputs in the derivative, as well as the values of the controlling parameters g and b.

Two Types of Nonlinearity

In general, things that are entirely linear are simple and easily understood. When things change, changes in the essential variables follow a line, and the specification of the line can be identified using addition, subtraction, and multiplication. Nonlinearity is everything else. However, there are two fundamental categories of nonlinearity. The first is *longitudinal nonlinearity*, and the second is *functional nonlinearity*. It is critical to appreciate their distinctness.

Longitudinal nonlinearity refers to behavior over time (in this case, behavior of the masses) with respect to essential variables. That is, over-time change in a variable does not follow a straight line. This has nothing to do with whether or not the equation that characterizes this change looks like the equation of a line. Indeed, all dynamic models except the most simple model of constant change (i.e., eq. 3.1) can produce nonlinear longitudinal trajectories for the essential variables. Even a functionally linear model can display nonlinear behavior when viewed over time.

What, then, is functional nonlinearity? Functional nonlinearity refers not to over-time behavior but, rather, to the algebraic structure of the model that represents the process of change. In the simplest of cases, this usually means that two or more of the variables appear jointly in a multiplication, or perhaps an exponential power or root is used with such a variable. While functional nonlinearity refers to algebraic form and not behavior, it is, nonetheless, true that functionally nonlinear models often display strong longitudinal nonlinearity as well. Yet the two forms of nonlinearity must never be confused. An example may be useful here.

By way of introducing the example, it is important to point out that, so far, we have been constructing differential equation models of mass behavior. Yet, everything that has been said with regard to differential equations is entirely consistent with regard to difference equations. The primary distinction between the two types of equations is the manner in which time is structured, continuously or discretely. Difference equations are, however, easier to work with since their behavioral characteristics can be examined using only simple arithmetic. The analyses in this book rely on both differential and difference equations. The choice of which type of model is appropriate within a given research setting is determined by the substance of the phenomenon being examined.

The sample model that I will discuss heuristically is a simple, first-order linear difference equation with constant coefficients. It is used to demonstrate potential nonlinear over-time characteristics of dynamic models under the conditions of a linear functional form. The algebra involved in the example is very simple and can be replicated with any calculator. A difference equation is used rather than a differential equation since the implications of its linear structure, when tied to its nonlinear over-time characteristics, are intuitive and easily demonstrated.

Consider the model in equation 3.6.

$$Y(t + 1) = aY(t) + b. \tag{3.6}$$

This model states that the relationship between the value of Y at any time point is linearly related to the value of Y at the previous time point. Indeed, this

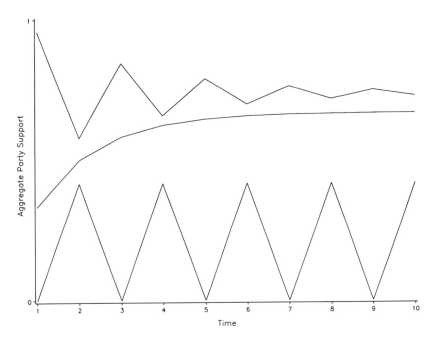

Fig. 3.6. Three examples of difference equation trajectories

linear relationship is clearly identified with a slope of a and an intercept of b. This form structures the relationship between each and every first difference (i.e., the change in Y from time t to $t + 1$), and, most important, this linear relationship is the same across all paired time points.

What is most interesting about the simple form of equation 3.6 is the large degree of variety that the model can produce when it is extended over many time points (i.e., not just two). What needs to be emphasized is that, while the relationship between any one time point and the next time point is the same and entirely linear, the relationship across all time points can be highly nonlinear. Figure 3.6 displays the general form of some of the possible over-time behaviors that are characteristic of equation 3.6. (Note that the three trajectories presented in figure 3.6 are arbitrarily chosen to illustrate some of the potential longitudinal variety in the equation.)

The type of longitudinal behavior of the linear first-order difference equation is entirely determined by the choice of the values of parameters a and b, and the initial condition for $Y(t)$. For example, if parameter a is negative, then the model's trajectory will oscillate, as do the top and bottom trajectories in figure 3.6. If the value of a is positive, then the movement will be smooth or monotonic, as is represented by the middle trajectory. If the absolute value of parameter a is less than one, then the trajectory of the model will converge to the equilibrium value Y^*, which is $b/(1 - a)$ (Goldberg 1958, 84–85). If the magnitude of parameter a is greater than one, then the trajectory will be "repelled" from this now unstable equilibrium value.

As this example demonstrates, functional linearity does not imply longitudinal linearity. Indeed, functional nonlinearity, as would occur if a power or interaction term were added to the model, merely increases the variety of longitudinal nonlinearity that is possible from the model. That is, the trajectories of functionally linear dynamic models have a fixed number of potential nonlinear longitudinal characteristics (e.g., oscillatory, divergent, convergent, etc.). Functionally nonlinear models of a similar order, depending on how they are written, potentially can display a wider range of such characteristics (i.e., they can "do more things," so to speak).

Multiple Observations at Each Time Point

So far, all of our modeling discussions have focused on longitudinal characteristics of various model specifications. By default, the implication has been that there were data for one "object" (say, a nation) moving over time. In such a setting, observations are defined as time points, with the essential variables being measured from the same object at sequential points in time, such as unemployment rates for one nation measured monthly. This is the typical setting of many time-series problems, and statistical approaches to such problems are well known (e.g., Judge et al. 1982; King 1989; Ostrom 1990).

However, the situation need not be limited to data from one object. A difficulty with many time-series problems is an all too common shortage of observations due to limitations in the historical records. But it is possible to have information for just a few time periods yet still have many observations if one examines data from more than one object. This is the situation encountered in my current investigations. The data base used here is for the approximately 3,000 counties in the United States. The time periods examined include numbers of elections ranging from two to approximately twenty. In situations with time periods spanning only two or three elections, there is still no shortage of information, since there are many objects for which there are measures despite the fact that there may be only two or three time points.

Typical statistical approaches for such problems with short time-histories yet with many objects (again, such as counties) measured simultaneously include pooling data and constructing dependent variables by computing differences in the essential variables. Thus, if we were interested in Democratic mobilization change, we could subtract Democratic mobilization at time t from Democratic mobilization at time $t + 1$, and this new measure would be our dependent variable in a multiple regression. In general, the analyses reported here do not use this approach. Indeed, computing such differences would have "erased" many (and sometimes all) of the longitudinal nonlinearities that have been discovered in my investigations. Regression equations can specify functional nonlinearities, but it is very difficult to "re-create" longitudinal nonlinearities with such a technology. The methods used here are a marked departure, both philosophically and mathematically, from commonly used, regression-oriented techniques, and are described in greater detail in subsequent chapters as well as in the appendix. But it is still useful to explain further why such a new technology is needed in the current research setting. Again, a few examples will serve the purpose.

To summarize before proceeding to the first example, in the subsequent discussion, there are two related matters of interest. The first to be addressed is the question of "erasing" longitudinal nonlinearities by creating a dependent variable by differencing between two elections. The second matter is the additional complication that arises when multiple objects are examined simultaneously.

To begin, consider the following scenario. Let us say that we are trying to understand a political mobilization process in which mobilization increases for a particular political party over a number of elections. Moreover, say we are interested in showing how we arrive at the high point in mobilization from a low point in mobilization that occurred years earlier. If we simply subtract the lower level of mobilization from the higher level of mobilization, thus producing the difference in mobilization between the two points in time, then the analysis could proceed using a multiple regression approach. Typical of much of the voting literature, the independent variables could be arranged in a linear form, although functional nonlinearities are easily employed by the inclusion of interaction and related terms.

We can usefully connect this scenario with the example of the first-order difference equation represented in equation 3.6. The scenario's strategy would be similar to using a first-order difference equation over two time points that could have spanned one or more additional elections. For example, let us say that we are studying Democratic vote mobilization from 1928 through 1936, a period in which the Democratic vote increased dramatically. Thus, for the purpose of analysis, 1928 would be t and 1936 would be $t + 1$. We ignore 1932 by pretending (for a moment) that we either do not think 1932 was important or perhaps because we do not have data for 1932. Subtracting the mobilization of 1928 from that of 1936 and using this difference as a dependent variable in a regression analysis would be the same as using a difference equation (such as eq. 3.6) to estimate the growth in mobilization between 1928 and 1936 (again, while ignoring 1932). Parameters a and b would be chosen to give us the correct mobilization value for 1936, given the comparable value for 1928. This would produce a linear connection between the earlier and later mobilization values.

But we know the reality that 1932 was an important election in the movement from 1928 to 1936. Moreover, there is no guarantee that the mobilization value for 1932 will lie on the same line that connects the 1928 and 1936 mobilization values. In short, a nonlinear, over-time trajectory for Democratic mobilization is missed when we look at the difference between

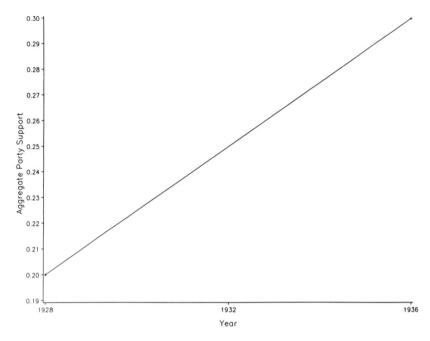

Fig. 3.7. Hypothetical difference trajectory, 1928–36, misses 1932 value

the two boundary time points. This is a general result that applies to all analyses that seek to explain a result at one time point based on an occurrence at a previous time point. The problem is given a graphic representation in figure 3.7. Nonlinearities that occur between the time points are not captured by the discrete analytical structure.[2]

The problem of overlooking nonlinear trajectories when examining time-dependent phenomena is a much more acute and complicated matter in cases in which there are many observations moving simultaneously over time, the situation encountered throughout my analyses. If there is only one object (say, national-level data for one country) moving longitudinally, then the question of whether or not a linear or a nonlinear trajectory joins two points may not be important, especially if one is interested only in getting from the first to the last point. In this case, one's concern for longitudinal nonlinearities can be determined by one's own substantive research interests.

However, if more than one object is moving over time (say, counties

---

2. Of course, this problem is not so important if one is using a difference equation to reconstruct a voting history that includes many elections as observations in a time-series. In this case, the nonlinearity over time between elections is typically not the focus of the analysis. Rather, the emphasis is on long-term change across many elections.

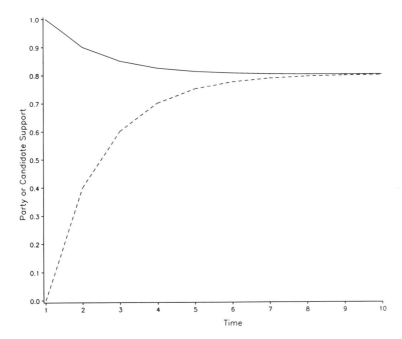

Fig. 3.8. Contrasting nonlinear trajectories with two different initial conditions

between time t and time $t + 1$), the ability to disregard longitudinal non-linearity among the observations is much more restricted. In such a situation, the degree of longitudinal nonlinearity in each trajectory for each object will depend on each object's initial conditions. This variation in longitudinal non-linearity will have a great impact on the predicted values (i.e., the end points) of the model. Thus, the ultimate fit of the model to the data (and, conse-quently, the optimized choice of the parameter values) will depend on the nonlinearities in the trajectories for each observation, each uniquely deter-mined by the associated initial conditions. To force a longitudinally linear trajectory across all observations distorts the descriptive characterization of the situation's dynamics and adds an unnatural constraint to the estimation process. This would be an example of longitudinal misspecification in a model. The result would be dubious estimated parameter values and a mea-sure of fit suggesting too low an association between the dependent variable and the exogenous variables.

These ideas relating to multiple observations moving simultaneously across time can be portrayed graphically. Figure 3.8 presents two trajectories obtained using the same linear first-order difference equation model with identical parameter values. (These trajectories are computed over many time periods, not just two.) The two trajectories correspond to two separate observations (i.e., objects) with different initial conditions. Both trajectories are extended through an equal number of time points.

Note that for each time period, the two trajectories come to rest at different values of Y (with the exception of an eventual arrival at equilibrium). In a case in which there are many objects moving longitudinally, the chosen trajectories (and consequently, the final values) would be determined by some evaluative criteria that are likely to maximize the overall fit of the model across all observations (e.g., counties). Linearizing the trajectories across observations between only two time points (which could span nonlinear time paths) would act to distort the longitudinal movements as well as to distort the determination of the predicted end points, thereby reducing the model's fit to the data. More important, linearizing the trajectories would act to misrepresent, through oversimplification, our characterization of history.

In general, when there are only two time points but many objects, differential equations will capture the potential longitudinal nonlinearities the best. In such situations, the partisan trajectories between the two elections more closely represent an analytical re-creation of the electoral battle on a continuous-time basis. If a dependent variable were constructed by subtracting an earlier partisan total from a later partisan total (thus computing the difference between elections), then that potentially nonlinear over-time history between the two elections would be lost. This would be true whether or not the model itself is functionally linear or nonlinear. The degree of nonlinearity in the trajectory between elections would depend on the initial conditions in the early election. If there are many observations (as with 3,000 counties), then there are many initial conditions, and the range of these initial conditions is probably quite large. On the other hand, in situations with many time points, difference equations are probably the better choice, since nonlinearities across the many time points will not be lost.

When Both Processes and Properties Matter

There are times when both the processes of the mass electoral dynamics and the various properties of the electorate are theoretically important in the causality of an electoral phenomenon. For example, one may be interested in who voted for the Nazis during the decade of the Weimar Republic. If the answer is Protestant peasants, then religious, class, and occupational characteristics of the electorate are the focus of the study. The question of how to phrase a problem in terms of properties and processes that may be causally linked to a phenomenon is a critical consideration of empirical analysis in general (see Nachmias and Nachmias 1987, 131–52). The strategic consequence of the choice of focus is usually a different methodological approach to the analysis. If the focus is on the properties of the electorate and not the process of electoral competition, then some researchers find that it makes more sense to use a traditional type of multivariate regression analysis. In such a situation, the dependent variable measuring the level of partisan change might logically be constructed by subtracting an earlier partisan total from a later one. Moreover, nonlinearities that occur over time and are causally connected to possible underlying dynamic processes are, in this case, considered to be small or nonexistent.

The differences between an analysis that focuses on processes and one that focuses on properties are discussed here in order to emphasize to the reader that the overall process orientation of this book is not the result of a particular view that all political phenomena can or should be understood in procedural terms only. One's choice of focus depends on the type of event and the underlying characteristics of the phenomenon. Moreover, in the analyses that follow, it will be clear that even dynamic processes are often conditioned by various social properties. For example, it would not be surprising that partisan competitions in urban areas would be different in many respects from those occurring in rural areas, since the social environments in both areas are mutually distinct, and since many governmental policies affect cities and rural areas differently.

Thus, I caution the reader to keep an open mind toward the variety of perspectives that arise with regard to the particular electoral events discussed in subsequent chapters. Many of the events are clearly dominated by a process of partisan competition, the specification and analysis of which can lead to a significant increase in our understanding of the relevant politics. However, processes are sometimes conditioned by social properties. Properties and processes are the yin and yang of mass political behavior. Sometimes one eclipses the other in dominance, but more often there is a moving balance of both that changes from event to event.

The Ecological, Individual Level, and Equilibrium Fallacies

Nearly all of the analyses presented in this book rely on the use of aggregate data. The aggregate data are all county level for all of the United States. The entire data set, newly collected and organized, is unusually rich and complete. Both census and aggregate voting data have been merged for all counties in the United States from the 1890s to the 1980s. A more complete description of these data is presented in chapter 4. Such a large and complete set of data has never before been available to examine the types of questions that are addressed in this study. Indeed, in the absence of these data, no investigation similar to the current one would be possible. Nonetheless, these data, as valuable as they are, are not without controversy, and it is worthwhile to explain this controversy, to more fully appreciate what we can expect from the data.

From the beginning, my goal has been to investigate the mass dynamics of volatile electoral movements in the United States that have occurred since the 1890s. In the situations examined here, survey-level data either do not exist, are of questionable reliability, or have inadequate sample sizes to answer particular questions. In these cases, aggregate-level data are all that are available for such an examination. Thus, many researchers have relied on and encouraged the use of aggregate data of the same type used here when conducting historical analyses (see Barrilleaux 1986; Brown 1982, 1987, and 1988; Campbell 1986; Irwin and Lichtman 1976; Parent, Jillson, and Weber 1987; Powell 1986; Sprague 1976).

The primary controversy that surrounds the use of such aggregate data focuses on a debate found in the methodological literature about the "ecological fallacy." The basic idea is that it is difficult to know (for certain) what individuals are doing if a researcher only has aggregate-level data available. For example, let us say that we notice that, in a particular election, Republican votes are greater in counties that are predominantly Protestant. Can we then say that individual Protestants are voting for the Republican party? Well, it could be. But some social scientists would question whether something else is going on. Perhaps Catholic minorities in Protestant areas are voting predominantly Republican as a response to some dynamic interaction with the generally Democratically voting Protestants. This is the basic dilemma of the ecological fallacy problem.

Yet, readers should be cautioned from frantically waving the flag of ecological fallacy. It is not just that aggregate data are the only data available, and thus we must resolve ourselves to be content with them. Our knowledge of the characteristics of ecological data is now more complete than it was when the ecological fallacy was first raised. Indeed, there are situations in which aggregate-level data are superior to cross-sectional survey-level data, and it is useful to understand clearly why.

The initial comments presented here on the use of aggregate-level data are designed to be intuitive in nature. Useful formal mathematical treatments of these ideas have been offered by Kramer (1983) and Sprague (1980). But the intuitions behind the ideas themselves are quite easy to understand. To begin, let us examine a potential problem with cross-sectional survey data.

Again, a picture is often better than a thousand words. Thus, let us return to figure 3.8. We will be using this figure for a different purpose than that for which it was used earlier. Recall that both of the trajectories in the figure are computed using the same equation. The only differences between the trajectories are their initial conditions. For the present purpose, the vertical axis will measure the probability that a given individual will vote for a particular political party. The range of this variable is from zero to one, as is indicated on the figure. Consider that the horizontal axis is measured in weeks leading up to an election, and that the election takes place at the end of week ten. Consider also that a cross-sectional survey is taken during week one and some measure of probability to vote for the party in question is established.

Let us say that the two trajectories presented in figure 3.8 represent the real probabilities over the course of the campaign for two voters who are surveyed. (Again, we survey them in week one, but the probabilities later change during the campaign.) Initially (in week one), one voter has a low probability of voting for the party and the other voter has a high probability. A statistical analysis is then conducted by the researchers, and the measures of probable vote for each of the two respondents constitute a dependent variable. Ignoring the problems of degrees of freedom and measurement error, the statistical analysis would likely include a set of independent variables that would be found to be causally linked to the different probabilities of voting for the party that are associated with each of the respondents. Thus, slopes are computed to indicate that individuals with such-and-such measures for the independent variables tend to have low probabilities to vote for the party and individuals with this-and-that measures for the independent variables tend to have high probabilities to vote for the party.

Now, consider that the survey is conducted later during the campaign, say, in week seven. In this week, the two respondents have almost identical probabilities of voting for the party. New slopes are computed indicating completely different results. Now the analysis finds that such-and-such measures for the independent variables predict that the individuals have similar probabilities to vote for the party. At this point, the crux of the problem should be clear. The problem is that the cross-sectional survey is being taken at one point in time, but it is being used to measure a moving process. The cross-sectional survey could have results that might seem almost random, depending on the week that the survey is taken. Slopes could oscillate in sign and vary dramatically in magnitude and significance from time period to time period. In fact, such surveys are the most useful when the dynamic processes involved in voter choices are in equilibrium, which means that they are not moving.

A superb way to resolve this problem is to conduct wave after wave of panel surveys. In this way, a researcher can measure the change in voter attitudes from election to election as well as during the campaigns. The 1980 NES panel is an excellent example of such a design. The problem is that these studies are terribly expensive, and thus are terribly rare. Yet even if we could afford to conduct these surveys regularly, there is no guarantee that we would measure everything without bias. There is the worry that repeated contact with the same voters may bias their responses, for example, by making them more interested in the campaign than they might otherwise be due to their awareness that the interviewer is coming soon and they might not want to appear stupid.

Before one concludes that the only problem with cross-sectional survey data is the absence of a longitudinal component, let me hasten to add that there is an additional problem with such data, a problem that is sometimes referred to as the "individual-level fallacy." This problem is the converse of the ecological fallacy. In its essence, it is sometimes difficult to explain the behavior of aggregates from individual survey information. An interesting way to explain this problem is through an example. Beginning in large part with an early piece of research by Kramer (1970–71) that focused on an individual-level analysis, skepticism was raised in the social scientific community regarding the value of party canvassing in affecting individual vote choices. This modified a conclusion found within an earlier tradition of analysis using aggregate data (see, especially, Katz and Eldersveld 1961) in which party activities were seen as aiding vote mobilization.

Recently, however, using an extraordinarily rich body of survey and aggregate data, Huckfeldt and Sprague (1989) have found that an analysis based on only individual-level data can lead to a misspecification of the political process regarding party activities. Huckfeldt and Sprague find that party contacting efforts generally do not influence the vote of the individuals who are contacted (the result found using survey data). However, the party contacts act as catalysts to further activity on the part of those contacted. Contacted people tend to be people who are already on party lists, and these people give money, place bumper stickers, and hang up yard signs after they are asked to do so. These contacted people, in turn, help to mobilize their neighbors, both directly and indirectly, through a classic set of contagion and diffusion processes. Thus, if one surveys a community, it is likely that there will be little evidence that direct party contacts change voters' minds about their candidate choice. But aggregate data will reveal the effect of party canvassing on the overall partisan mobilization in the community.

The individual-level fallacy problem is quite general and can work in tandem with a longitudinal misspecification. This more complex setting has recently been reported with regard to partisan identification. MacKuen, Erikson, and Stimson's report on large magnitude and systematic variation in aggregate partisanship (1989) draws into serious question both the stability of party identification and the specification of partisan change. The important point is that they made their discovery because they examined longitudinal variation across short time-intervals (i.e., quarterly) and because they examined aggregate rather than individual partisanship. They do not show that investigating individual partisanship is wrong; it is not. However, they do show that investigating aggregate partisanship is important, and that it is not the same as examining individual partisanship.

In brief, cross-sectional and panel surveys are extraordinarily valuable. But they are not a panacea, and their absence in historical analyses need not cause us to bite our nails. Aggregate data are equally valuable in their own way.

What do we get from aggregate data that may be of help? First, it is important to understand that the problem of ecological fallacy is a real one, just as the problems of misinterpreting survey data, such as when a static measure is taken of a longitudinal process or when individuals are extracted from a context-dependent process, are real as well. There is no substitute for sensible interpretations of all data. But in the absence of large-sample panel data combined with aggregate community measures, ecological data by themselves do capture the longitudinal movement of aggregate voter choices in a very desirable fashion. They also enable a potentially broad range of specifications of contextually dependent processes.

Thus, mathematical models, be they formal or statistical, can capture the essential characteristics of these longitudinal movements if they are adequately specified. The important point is not the type of data used, for we use what is available. If survey and aggregate data were both available in all situations, it would be advisable to find correspondence between analyses that rely on the two data types. It is important for researchers to expend considerable effort in developing their model's specification with regard to variables and longitudinal processes regardless of the type of data used. This includes more than simply collecting a complete set of relevant independent variables on the right-hand side of an estimation equation. It also involves the determination of whether or not that which is being measured is a dynamic process, which in turn addresses the matter of the functional form of the specification.

An Elegant Algebra of the Equilibrium Fallacy

The following algebra, developed by John Sprague (1980), puts a bit more formal "meat" on the intuitive "bones" that I have presented here. It also helps to identify further the problem of extracting individuals from a dynamic process as an equilibrium fallacy that can have striking consequences. In particular, the algebra demonstrates that cross-sectional slopes (typical products of regression analyses using survey data) can potentially be wildly misleading if there is a longitudinal component in the data.

Consider a most simple case in which two people are surveyed. Two measures are taken of each individual. It is thought that one of the things that is measured has a causal relationship with the other thing that is measured. Let us say that we suspect that a person's income is related to their ideology. Thus, our two variables are (1) each individual's income (call that variable X), and (2) a measure of their ideology (measured with a feeling thermometer scale, call that variable Y).

Now, let us identify the relationship between ideology and income by determining the slope $\Delta Y / \Delta X$. That is, we divide the difference between the two individuals' scores on Y by the difference between the two individuals' scores on X, which is, of course, the change in Y divided by the change in X. Yet what if Y has both a static and a dynamic component to it? That is, what if there is a longitudinal change in Y that is taking place at the time we do the survey? Perhaps some new conservative charismatic leader has taken the attention of much of the media and people are reevaluating their attitudes toward conservativism as the weeks progress and as they are exposed to more of the media coverage of this charismatic figure. Yet the static component of Y still exists. Let us say that rich people still tend to be more conservative than not-so-rich people.

Thus, let us write variable Y as $Y = y_t + y_s$, where y_t is the time-dependent component of Y and y_s is the static component of Y. Substituting this expression for Y into the numerator of the slope, we have

$$\Delta Y/\Delta X = [(y_{1t} + y_{1s}) - (y_{2t} + y_{2s})]/\Delta X, \tag{3.7}$$

where the subscripts 1 and 2 for y represent each of the two people (respectively) who are sampled in our very small survey.

Furthermore, for simplicity, let us describe the time component of Y as the first-order linear process

$$y_t = ay_{t-1} + b, \tag{3.8}$$

where a and b are constant coefficients. (The time subscripts are arbitrary, and t and $t - 1$ are used here rather than $t + 1$ and t simply to neaten the algebra of the substitution that follows.) Substituting equation 3.8 into the numerator of equation 3.7, we have

$$\Delta Y/\Delta X = \frac{[(ay_{1(t-1)} + b) + y_{1s}] - [(ay_{2(t-1)} + b) + y_{2s}]}{\Delta X}. \tag{3.9}$$

Simplifying and rearranging (noting that parameter b cancels), equation 3.9 reduces to

$$\Delta Y/\Delta X = \frac{a[y_{1(t-1)} - y_{2(t-1)}] + y_{1s} - y_{2s}}{\Delta X}. \tag{3.10}$$

From equation 3.10 it is easy to see that the slope relating X to Y can be enormously influenced by the value of parameter a as well as the initial difference between the two individuals' ideology score at time $t - 1$. Yet the estimations using cross-sectional data assume only static components in the calculations.

Substantively, the effect of the dynamic components in equation 3.10 can be very marked. Consider the following example. Let us say that our variable Y stands for a feeling thermometer response for George Bush rather than ideology. Recall that in the spring of 1988 there was tremendous tension between the Bush and Robertson campaigns. In some places, such as in Michigan during the primary season, fistfights even broke out between the two groups of Bush and Robertson supporters. Pat Robertson supporters, in particular, tended to be drawn from the Protestant fundamentalist communities, and those communities tended to be less well-off financially than many of those in the mainstream of Republican circles. At the time of the conflict, many Robertson supporters voiced resentment over what they perceived to be an attempt by the Republican "establishment" (by and large, Bush supporters) to exclude them from the rule-making party hierarchy.

Now, compare this setting with that which occurred in the fall of 1988. The primary battles were over, and Robertson supporters had the choice at that time between Bush and Dukakis. Bush was maintaining a strong stance against abortion, an important issue for the fundamentalist community, whereas Dukakis was strongly pro choice. It is not hard to imagine that Robertson supporters felt more warmly about Bush in the fall of 1988 than in the spring of 1988. Indeed, the difference between a Bush and a Robertson supporter in the spring could be very large, and this would be reflected in the dynamic components at time $t - 1$ in equation 3.10, assuming that the survey is taken in the spring and that one of the two voters surveyed was a Bush supporter and the other was a Robertson supporter. Thus, one could expect income to relate to feelings toward Bush. But, if the survey is taken out of equilibrium, then it is likely that the estimated slope will be severely "contaminated" by the dynamically related initial conditions in the numerator of equation 3.10.

To take this one step further, let us assume that the dynamic component of the numerator in equation 3.10 is at equilibrium. That is, $y_{1(t-1)} = y_{2(t-1)} = y^*$. Then equation 3.10 becomes

$$[a(y^* - y^*) + y_{1s} - y_{2s}]/\Delta X = \Delta y_s/\Delta X, \tag{3.11}$$

where y_s is again the static component of the measure of conservatism. Here we recover the simple slope assumed in the cross-sectional analysis. Note that this only occurs when the dynamic component is in equilibrium. If that is not the case, then one has encountered an equilibrium fallacy.

To summarize, these results suggest that estimated cross-sectional slopes can be very misleading if the dependent variable is involved in a longitudinal process at the time at which the cross-sectional measures are taken. It is only when the process has reached equilibrium that a cross-sectional slope will yield the desired result. Since surveys are typically conducted in the "heat" of political campaigns, to assume the arrival at equilibrium may, to say the least, be a very large assumption. The use of aggregate data in this study unravels this problem by allowing for an explicit identification of the longitudinal processes between elections.

This section and the previous section identify both the individual-level fallacy and the equilibrium fallacy. They are, respectively, the danger of (1) extracting individuals from a context dependent process, and (2) extracting individuals or aggregates from a dynamic process. These fallacies generate problems at least as severe as the traditional bogeyman, the ecological fallacy. The antidote to all of these fallacies is in the substantive specification of the social and political processes.

CHAPTER 4

Mass Dynamics of U.S. Presidential Competitions, 1928–36

Arguably, the most dramatic, important, and significant example of an electoral realignment in the United States this century occurred between 1928 and 1936. Those were years of great political change, the Great Depression, and the years of Franklin D. Roosevelt's New Deal. The Republican party lost control of the White House for 20 years following the 1932 election. The Democratic party actually gained seats in the U.S. House of Representatives in the off-year elections in 1934, despite their control of the White House and a historical pattern predicting a "normal" off-year loss for that year. Charismatic and sometimes radical leaders such as Father Caughlin, Huey Long, Dr. Townsend, and Father Divine demanded major social changes and often developed huge followings. Those were unusual years for society, for the nation, and for electoral politics. The mass dynamics of the electoral politics of those years are authentically unique in this century, and they are the subject of this chapter.

More specifically, in this chapter I begin developing an inventory of the mechanisms of mass electoral volatility in earnest. I compare the roles of new voters and partisan switchers (former Republican supporters) as actors in the volatility that lead to the dramatic rise in Democratic presidential support between 1928 and 1936. This phenomenon is examined here with an eye toward enhancing our understanding of the processes of institutionalization and deinstitutionalization. This is approached by investigating the relative influences of socially interactive and noninteractive mechanisms of mass mobilization.

As recalled from the discussion of institutionalization presented in chapter two, the institutionalization of partisan behavior is identified by the existence of enduring, patterned partisan support and is viewed as a function of time and the frequency of repeated electoral experiences among voters. Deinstitutionalization refers to the process by which voters break these former partisan behavioral habits.

Reprinted, with additions, from *American Political Science Review* 82, 4 (December 1988): 1153–81. A similar version of the original article was recognized in the 1989 IBM Supercomputing Competition, and included in the volume of winning papers published by MIT Press, 1991, titled *Computer Assisted Analysis and Modeling on the IBM 3090*.

There are two factors crucial to the process of deinstitutionalization as it is characterized here. First, the assumption is made that influences that disturb partisan ties (i.e., deinstitutionalize voters) affect voters differentially, depending upon the force of the political appeals on particular groups in the population and the strength of the each group's previous ties (a central theme in Nie, Verba, and Petrocik 1979). Second, previous electoral experiences for certain groups can produce resistance to these appeals. This second factor addresses the concept of political immunization as it has been described by McPhee and Ferguson (1962). Major social and political disturbances of sufficient magnitude to cause large-scale changes in partisan attachments among many groups should more strongly affect those who are the least immunized to alternative partisan appeals.

Critical to the dynamics of the deinstitutionalizing process is the role played by new voters, a totally noninstitutionalized and nonimmunized sector of the electorate. A number of questions on the general impact of new voters on electoral systems bear particular relevance to this analysis. When new voters enter the electorate in substantial numbers in response to a major social disturbance (such as the depression), do they do so equally across all subgroups in the population? In terms of the timing of their entry into the electorate, do they begin to participate at moments when there are large partisan shifts as well? Alternatively, are they drawn into the electorate following a previous election in which there was significant excitement generated by large partisan shifts? Or, perhaps, do the new voters enter the electorate in massive waves due to exogenous social and political conditions, subsequently destabilizing the existing partisan alignment and precipitating a full-scale realignment? Answers to these questions are viewed here as central to an understanding of realigning processes and are addressed with regard to the 1928–36 realignment period in the United States.

In characterizing the dynamic processes involved during periods of volatile electoral change, this analysis distinguishes between two separate mechanisms by which such mass movements may occur. The first concerns the ability of nationally distributed political appeals to effectively channel the shifting partisan and new voter movements. The second addresses the ability of localized political forces to act as a mediating factor in determining the magnitude and direction of the electoral changes. For example, in the case of the new voters, this asks the question of whether new voters are activated by national political forces as presented to them, say, by the national media or whether they are drawn into the participatory setting by other voters and localized partisan campaign forces. Here, questions associated with the identification of the relative impacts of these two different political mechanisms of the mass dynamics focus on their independent effects on the new voter and shifting partisan populations.

This analysis begins with a consideration of the conversion versus new voter hypotheses with regard to the 1928–36 electoral period in the United

States. It presents a baseline description of the partisan strengths for the Unites States during the period from 1920 through 1936. The analysis also presents and investigates a formal model capturing the dynamics of the partisan competitions and new voter fluctuations and uses the model to identify contrasting patterns in roles played during the 1928–36 realigning period by certain groups in the U.S. population. Then, the magnitudes of the national as well as the more localized political influences are compared to determine the relative strengths of the underlying components of the mobilization and conversion processes.

The Conversion and New Voter Hypotheses

The literature focusing on the conversion versus new voter hypotheses is quite divided. Sundquist (1983, 229–39) uses selective aggregate data to argue that Republican-to-Democratic conversion was the dominant type of electoral activity for the period. Further support for the conversion hypothesis comes from Erikson and Tedin (1981)—who use the *Literary Digest* "straw poll" data—as well as from Key (1964, 523–35), Burnham (1970), Ladd and Hadley (1978), and others. The most prominent proponent of the new voter hypothesis has been Kristi Andersen (1979b), with support for the hypothesis also coming from Converse (1975), Campbell et al. (1960, 153–56), Petrocik (1981a, 55–57), and others.

Arguments supporting the conversion hypothesis typically suggest that the steadily worsening national economic conditions of the time produced widespread discontent with the Republican administration. Moreover, Roosevelt was able to mobilize many of these discontented former Republicans. Indeed, he developed a "natural" constituency among the working class, especially coming from the economically hard hit industrial urban areas (Sundquist 1983, 214–23). The new voter proponents argue that partisan attachments were probably as firm (or nearly as firm) then as they have been found to be in later years (e.g., as reported in Campbell et al. 1960). Thus, the new Democratic support probably came from a generation of new voters rather than disenchanted Republicans. Many of these new voters were young, and perhaps also immigrants or descendants of immigrants (see Andersen 1979a, 39–52; Petrocik 1981a, 55).

Arguments concerning virtually all of these hypotheses have relied on data around whose quality and completeness there are controversies. Andersen's use of the 1952–72 Survey Research Center/Center for Political Studies data to reconstruct the partisan voting habits of the respondents in terms of how they voted in the 1920s and 1930s has been seriously challenged by Erikson and Tedin (1981), Sundquist (1983, 229–39), Niemi, Katz, and Newman (1980, 648), and Reiter (1980). Erikson and Tedin (1981) have tried to address this problem by using the only available survey data for the period. However, they acknowledge that the "straw poll" data collected by the *Liter-*

ary Digest is of a "tarnished sort" (Erikson and Tedin 1981, 952). Problems of sampling technique abound, and the authors disagree with Shively's characterization of the nature and direction of the various biases (see Erikson and Tedin 1981, 953; Shively 1971–72, 62). To date, users of aggregate data have hardly fared better. Previous studies have typically limited their analyses to particular geographic areas. The widespread use of "heuristic" samplings of aggregate data to study realignments goes back to Key 1955. For example, Key uses data for various towns in five states, and Sundquist (1983, 236-37) uses selected county and town data from five states. Yet there is no guarantee that the selected areas are representative of the nation as a whole. In sum, there are no reliable survey data for the period under study, and until now there has never been available for analysis a single complete set of electoral and census data for all of the Unites States using (the relatively small) county-level aggregations.[1]

Table 4.1 presents the aggregate electoral strengths for the Democratic and the Republican parties in the presidential contests from 1920 through 1936. All of the results in table 4.1 are written as proportions of the eligible electorate and thus can be understood as measures of mobilization. These measures differ from those commonly presented elsewhere. Typically, the electoral outcomes of the period are represented either as vote shares (i.e., as proportions of the total vote) or as partisan vote totals. For example, vote shares are used by Ladd and Hadley (1978, 43) and Key (1964, 523–40), while partisan raw totals (i.e., actual votes) are presented by Andersen (1979a, 29).

There are problems with the vote share and raw totals methods however. Vote shares can produce a misleading interpretation of over-time aggregate change in situations in which the total vote is also changing. For example, it is possible for a party's share of the vote to decrease due to an expansion in the denominator (i.e., the total vote) while at the same time the party has not lost any of its previous support in the population. In a situation in which new

---

1. There are three basic reasons for the previous unavailability of a usable complete collection of U.S. county-level aggregate data. First, the electoral data are available from the Inter-University Consortium for Political and Social Research data collections in what amounts to a scattering of over 200 separate data files. County-level returns for all states and all years have not been organized into a few accessible large data files. Second, the available data sets, although scattered, are still terribly complete. There are data for literally hundreds of parties, covering all U.S. congressional, presidential, and many state elections. The bottom line is that the variable names in the separate data sets are not comparable. One cannot simply merge the data sets, since the variable names do not correspond in year or party. Third, the information that is necessary to merge the various data sets is contained in the variable labels. There are often hundreds of variable labels for the many data sets, each of which needs to be read individually, and from which new variable names need to be constructed. Thus, the process of identifying particular partisan returns for all counties in the United States has been unusually difficult, given normal constraints of staff, budget, and personal wear and tear.

TABLE 4.1.   U.S. Presidential Vote as a Proportion of Total Eligibles, 1920–36

	1920	1924	1928	1932	1936
Democratic	0.15	0.130	0.210	0.300	0.350
Republican	0.26	0.240	0.300	0.210	0.210
La Follette	—	0.080	—	—	—
Total Vote[a]	0.44	0.450	0.520	0.530	0.570
New Voters	—	0.004	0.079	0.006	0.045

[a]Partisan proportions, when summed, do not equal total vote because of two reasons. First, typically there are a substantial number of minor parties competing in all U.S. presidential elections. Second, the rounding of proportions contained in this table results in some minor deviations from the totals.

voters are suspected of playing a pivotal role in determining the direction of a shifting partisan balance, a vote share measure can indicate partisan shift when there may have been only new voter movement. The use of actual votes, or raw totals, instead of vote shares encounters a related problem. Comparing raw partisan totals at different times makes most sense when the size of the electorate is stable. Such a longitudinal comparison can be misleading in situations in which the electorate (i.e., total eligibles) is expanding or contracting. Thus, a party may receive 15 million votes in one election and 16 million votes eight years later, but if the eligible population has increased as well, the increased partisan total need not indicate increased partisan "power" relative to the other parties or the overall electorate. Indeed, the party's support relative to the size of the total electorate could have decreased. Both of the problems mentioned above regarding the vote share and the raw vote measures are unraveled by using the mobilization measure.

The data in table 4.1 indicate that both the Democratic and the Republican parties increased the level of support they received from the pool of total eligibles from 1920 through 1928. However, from 1928 to 1932, the positions of the two parties relative to each other virtually reversed. While the Democratic party increased its share of the total electorate from 21 percent to 30 percent, the Republican party's support fell from 30 percent to 21 percent. Note also that the total vote relative to the electorate increased only slightly from 1928 to 1932. Between 1932 and 1936, however, the total vote increased substantially (more than four times the 1928–32 increase); at the same time, Democratic strength continued to increase and Republican strength remained approximately constant. Conclusions about partisan shifts can barely qualify as tentative with such large aggregate measures. On the surface at least, these results seem to suggest that new voters may not have played as crucial a role in the 1932 election as they did in the election of 1936 and that there indeed may have been an actual realignment in 1932, defined in terms of partisan conversions. The analysis that follows pursues these points more directly.

The Structure of Party Competition

The model of partisan competition developed here is a time-dependent system of three interconnected differential equations, which, in combination, address expectations of change in aggregated partisan electoral totals.[2] Such models have been successfully exploited in the social science literature by Coleman (1964 and 1981), Simon (1957), Przeworski and Soares (1971), Przeworski and Sprague (1986), Sprague (1981), Tuma and Hanna (1984), Luenberger (1979), and Huckfeldt, Kohfeld, and Likens (1982), as well as others, and have been notably useful in modeling the dynamics of military spending in competitions between nations (see Gillespie et al. 1977; Ward 1984). This type of modeling is also similar to that employed to characterize time-dependent ecological systems of biological populations within fixed environments (see May 1974). The mathematical theory underlying the analytic and dynamic properties of all such systems, both linear and nonlinear, is complete (Hirsch and Smale 1974; Kocak 1989; Luenberger 1979; Mesterton-Gibbons 1989). Here we are interested in modeling the population fluctuations of three groups in the political environment, Democrats, Republicans, and nonvoters. We want a mathematical statement that corresponds to each group and describes change as a function of existing voter support for all other groups. Thus, we desire three statements that, when taken together, describe the voter movements among parties as well as shifts between parties and nonvoters, all of which take place simultaneously at each point in time.

I begin by developing a model of the mass electoral dynamics for the Democratic party. In this analysis, I differentiate between two types of dynamic processes that could lead to growth or decay in the various partisan populations. The first type to be developed is labeled the "uniform" component of aggregate partisan movements. It is likely that many voters throughout the nation were energized through a national appeal to the electorate's broad social sensibilities in 1932. For example, widespread discontent with the Republican handling of the economy could have led to the development of a generalized sympathetic ear for the Democratic message across the electorate. Moreover, this increased attentiveness for the Democratic appeal could have affected many voters independently of their localized partisan environment (i.e., "uniformly" across the nation); that is, it may not have mattered whether or not there existed a strong Democratic presence within the voters' localized milieu. Rather, a certain number of Republicans, based only on the number of Republicans available within a given area, would have weighed their electoral

---

2. The model developed here is different from a typical econometric specification in the sense that it has imbedded within its algebraic structure an explicit and theoretically driven formal representation of aggregate electoral dynamics. In this sense, the model allows us to investigate some critical "why" questions about causal components of these dynamics. These questions are addressed throughout this chapter and book, but are particularly evident in the section of this chapter labeled The Relative Impact of Mechanisms for Change.

options and decided to switch their support from the Republican party to the Democratic party.

If we use the proportion of the localized electorate that supports the Republican party as a measure of the size of the Republican population (theoretically available for conversion to the Democratic party), then we can express the change in support for the Democratic party as

$$dD/dt = fR. \qquad (4.1)$$

Here, R is the proportion of the electorate supporting the Republican party, D is the proportion of the electorate supporting the Democratic party, and f is a parameter of the model that corresponds to the probability of the occurrence of a Republican-to-Democratic conversion within the population at an instant in time. Throughout this analysis, this type of dynamic process is referred to as the "uniform" component of the model, due to the sense of the voter calculations assumed, and the independence of the mathematical statement in equation 4.1 from the strength of the localized Democratic presence, which might have conditioned, through social interaction with the existing Democratic environment, the rate of conversion to the Democratic party.

Yet this suggests another way in which partisan conversions may take place. The rate at which the national Democratic appeal produces new Democratic converts could have a social (i.e., contextual) component as well; that is, voters may see how others in their local environment react to the Democratic message. In areas in which there exists at least a moderate Democratic presence, pro-Republican sentiments on the part of some voters might be more difficult to defend. The availability of accepted alternative partisan perspectives within politically heterogeneous neighborhoods, combined with the institutional strength of a locally stronger Democratic party's electoral apparatus, should be enough to loosen the grip of the Republican party on some voters and, thus, allow for a higher level of conversion to the Democratic ranks. Thus, we wish to capture the effects of interacting partisan populations in producing electoral change in our modeling efforts.

This argument can be included in the model for change in the support for the Democratic party over time by rewriting equation 4.1 as

$$dD/dt = fR + bRD,$$

where b is a parameter in the model and expresses the probability of a Republican-to-Democratic conversion at an instant of time due to the conditional strengths of both partisan populations interacting simultaneously. This is the second type of dynamic process to be included in the model, and it is subsequently referred to as the *social* component. It addresses the dynamics of locally interacting partisan populations, and its inclusion here reflects the lessons of some recent research indicating that the impact of such localized social forces on voter responses to electoral battles can be substantial and crucial to the specification of the properties of aggregated partisan movements (Beck 1974; Brown 1987; Huckfeldt and Sprague 1987 and 1988; MacKuen and Brown 1987).

All such interaction terms, as specified above, are symmetric in the sense that interactive growth for the Democrats is low when either there are (1) few Democrats interacting with few or many Republicans or (2) few Republicans interacting with few or many Democrats. Interactive growth is greatest when there are sizeable Democratic and Republican populations, which is both an expected and desirable property of my characterization of the partisan competitions. This specification of such an interaction is well represented in extensive social science literature on communication, contagion, and diffusion modeling (Coleman 1964; Huckfeldt 1983; Huckfeldt, Kohfeld, and Likens 1982; Koppstein 1983; McPhee 1963; Przeworski and Soares 1971; Rapoport 1963 and 1983; Simon 1957; Sprague 1976). Such terms are also common in ecological models of interspecies interactions within contained biological ecosystems (Danby 1985; Haberman 1977; May 1974; Rosen 1970).

Democratic party electoral strengths can also improve due to an infusion of new voters to the party ranks. This addresses the hypothesis that the mobilization of new voters was a crucial factor in the changing Democratic fortunes between 1928 and 1936. It is possible for the new voters to be mobilized due to a national appeal to their potential partisan sensibilities, thus attracting new voters in correspondence to the size of the localized nonvoting population. Struck by the declining national economic fortunes and the possibility of change given by a new Democratic leadership, perhaps many former nonvoters made the decision to begin to participate in partisan contests.

However, new voter movements need not have been limited to a response to a national appeal, the "uniform" component of the model. Previous nonvoters could also be motivated to vote due to interactions with partisans. Such interactions can be both direct and indirect. The effectiveness of an established partisan apparatus in mobilizing the vote by establishing direct contact with potential voters is a result that was reported long ago in Gosnell 1927 and demonstrated repeatedly since. Partisan interactions with the nonvoting population leading to the mobilization of new voters can also be indirect, however. By themselves, nonvoters can witness the partisan characteristics of their communities. In some areas in which Republican norms are very strong or, perhaps, where overall voting activity in either partisan direction is very slight (i.e., turnout is traditionally low), it may be that nonvoters lack the relevant localized partisan cues that would cause them to initiate the internal processes of becoming politically involved. However, in areas in which Democratic partisan activity is already established, some nonvoters may follow the lead of their local political environment (following the Jones's, so to speak) and begin their trek to the polling booths. This addresses the "social" component of the new voter mobilization for the Democratic party.

Both the uniform and the social components of the new voter mobilization dynamics for the Democratic party can be included in the model as

$$dD/dt = fR + bRD + mN + aND, \tag{4.2}$$

where N is the proportion of the electorate that is nonvoting, and m and a are parameters of the model. Parameters m and a, respectively, reflect the probability of mobilizing a Democratic supporter at an instant in time from within the localized pool of nonvoters due to the nonvoters' consideration of the appeal of the national campaign independent of local partisan traditions, as well as to the interaction between the nonvoting population and the local Democratic partisan environment.

Finally, it is possible that none of the components of the model describing fluctuations in Democratic partisan populations will completely capture the aggregate movements between Republicans and Democrats as well as between nonvoters and Democrats. This addresses the realistic considerations involved in mapping any model to a body of data. Thus, it is important to include a constant term in equation 4.2 that allows for Democratic population change independent of the included components. Equation 4.2 can now be rewritten as

$$dD/dt = fR + bRD + mN + aND + k, \tag{4.3}$$

or, for economy,

$$dD/dt = R(f + bD) + N(m + aD) + k, \tag{4.4}$$

where k is the constant element of the derivative and a parameter of the model.

It is important to note that, while the analysis here refers to components of the model in terms of voters moving from one group to another, the components are actually capturing the net movements between groups. Thus, parameter b captures the net interactively determined change between the Democratic and Republican parties. This "net" is, of course, the difference between the total of Republican to Democratic conversions and the simultaneous Democratic to Republican conversions. This is a characteristic of all models, both statistical and formal, that rely on aggregate-level data. There is no way for independent estimates to be derived that capture the changes in both directions.

However, the question remains about whether this potential crisscrossing movement would seriously bias one-way interpretations that one might like to draw from the analysis. This depends on the degree of crisscrossing that actually occurred. The data used in this analysis clearly suggest that any potential interpretive bias would be extremely small. Using U.S. county-level aggregations, only 8 (0.3 percent) of the approximately three thousand counties experienced a decrease in the Democratic vote combined with an increase in the Republican vote in 1932. If there had been a significant degree of crisscrossing, this surely would have been more detectable on the national level, ecological considerations notwithstanding. The situation is similar regarding Democratic and nonvoter crisscrossings in 1932. Only 2.4 percent of the counties experienced a decrease in the Democratic vote combined with an increase in the nonvoter populations. In 1936, there were larger numbers of counties experiencing decreases in the Democratic vote combined with increases in the Republican and nonvoting populations (34 percent and 22 percent respectively). However, all of these cases occurred in farm areas, which are accurately accounted for in the conditioning analysis for these areas presented below. Thus, the one-way movements of the electorate clearly seem to dominate these data. Moreover, this closely corresponds to a historical reading of the politics of the times as it is presented in the vast related extant literature. Thus, while a discussion in terms of net movements among parties and between parties and nonvoters more closely fits the technical realities of any model that utilizes aggregate-level data, interpretations that phrase these movements in one or another direction probably do no injustice to a historical analysis of the politics of those years.

The model describing longitudinal change in the Republican party population can be developed in a manner that is similar to that for the Democratic party. Republican defections to the Democrats (or, in some cases, gains from the Democrats) will occur either uniformly across the nation, independently of the strength of the local Democratic presence, or through the process of local competition in which the strength of the Democratic traditions within each community will condition the rate of partisan change (again, the uniform and social components of the model). Furthermore, gains or losses for the Republicans due to nonvoter volatility can be similarly directed. Given the weak economic conditions of 1932, some Republicans may have simply stopped voting, thus joining the ranks of the uninvolved. Yet some nonvoters with Republican tendencies may have felt that it was time to get involved when their favorite party was under attack. These potential gains and losses for the Republican party could have taken place uniformly throughout the United States, dependent only on the availability of nonvoters in a given community. Alternatively, the nonvoter-Republican shifts may have been dependent upon the interactive effects of the nonvoter and Republican populations. All such partisan and nonvoter trade-offs with regard to the Republican party can be captured with the statement

$$dR/dt = D(q - bR) + N(s + wR) + j, \qquad (4.5)$$

where q, b, s, w, and j are parameters of the model. Here, parameters q and s control the uniform inputs to changing Republican support, whereas parameters b and w govern the social inputs. Note the negative coefficient for parameter b. This results from its appearance in the statement for change in Democratic support over time (i.e., eq. 4.4). The negative coefficient for parameter b maintains the accounting compatibility of both models and has implications for the procedures used to estimate the parameters. Parameter j is the constant term of the derivative and is included to identify Republican partisan change that cannot be captured by the other components of the model.

Changes in the nonvoter population of the United States are due to new voter movements to or from the Democratic and Republican parties. New voters can be carried toward a particular party on a wave of national excitement, again, independently of existing local partisan strengths. However, new voters also can be drawn toward a party due to the influence of the local party apparatus or led by the partisan directional cues sensed from the surrounding environment. These two paths address the uniform and social components of the models and can be incorporated directly in a model describing longitudinal fluctuations in the nonvoter population. Thus we have

$$dN/dt = D(g - aN) + R(v - wN) + y, \tag{4.6}$$

where g, a, v, w, and y are parameters of the model, and are linked to the uniform and social components of the model as are the corresponding components in equations 4.4 and 4.5. Parameters a and w have occurred elsewhere and are included here to preserve the population compatibilities of the overall system. Parameter y is the constant element of the derivative and describes change in the nonvoting population that cannot be isolated by the partisan-directed components of the model.

Equations 4.4 through 4.6 constitute an interdependent system of three nonlinear differential equations that together describe the mass electoral dynamics between the Democratic and Republican parties as well as between both parties and the nonvoting population. Throughout, the system includes both the uniform and the social components of population trade-offs between the three electoral groups (Democrats, Republicans, and nonvoters). The system has general properties and is entirely symmetric in tracing aggregate population shifts from any one group to all other groups. (Some characteristics of these models, written in reduced form, are presented in the appendix to this chapter.)

While the system can be used to estimate the partisan and nonvoter trade-offs for the entire United States without modification, additional leverage can be gained by identifying different social conditions that could change the magnitude or direction of the partisan and nonvoter shifts. For example, we may be interested in how the system of electoral competition differed in urban areas in comparison with rural areas. This can be done by conditioning the system with respect to a separate variable of interest—specifically, by writing each parameter as a linear function of this additional variable (referred to as the *conditioning* variable). Thus, using parameter f as an example, we can rewrite the parameter using the form

$$f_0 + f_1 X.$$

Writing all parameters in this fashion restructures the dynamic characteristics of the overall system with respect to the conditioning variable, X (see also Jackson 1987).[3] The unconditioned parameters are recovered under the conditions where $X = 0$. The complete system is now

$$dD/dt = R[(f_0 + f_1 X) + (b_0 + b_1 X)D] + N[(m_0 + m_1 X) + (a_0 + a_1 X)D] + (k_0 + k_1 X);$$

$$dR/dt = D[(q_0 + q_1 X) - (b_0 + b_1 X)R] + N[(s_0 + s_1 X) + (w_0 + w_1 X)R] + (j_0 + j_1 X);$$

$$dN/dt = D[(g_0 + g_1 X) - (a_0 + a_1 X)N] + R[(v_0 + v_1 X) - (w_0 + w_1 X)N] + (y_0 + y_1 X).$$

The Data and Estimation

Estimating the parameters in this system is a nontrivial problem. However, an extensive literature does exist that addresses these problems as well as an entire class of related issues. Standard approaches using regression techniques are of no utility here. It is not possible to solve for D, R, and N explicitly. Tuma and Hanna (1984) as well as Coleman (1981) offer linearizing techniques that are useful for analyzing simpler models. These techniques are pursu' d primarily to recover known statistical properties of the estimators but require algebraically approachable systems allowing the uncoupling of equations. Rather, the model must remain in derivative form and estimations must be obtained using numerical techniques to obtain longitudinal population trajectories for each group. In the social sciences, examples of the use of such techniques include estimations of systems of difference and differential equations addressing concepts of partisan competition (Brown 1987; Przeworski and Sprague 1986) as well as systems of equations modeling arms race competitions (Ward 1984). The procedures are commonly described in the engi-

---

3. Writing each parameter in this fashion is different than simply estimating the nonconditioned system separately, using select subsets of the aggregate data for each estimation. Writing the parameters as a linear function of a conditioning variable allows the use of all of the data, as well as an interpretation of the system based on progressive changes in characteristics of the social environment.

neering literature and are often used to solve practical problems employing systems of interdependent differential equations. A lucid summary of such techniques, as well as an introduction to the broad literature on the subject, can be found in Hamming 1971 as well as Dennis and Schnabel 1983. A more complete description of the techniques as they are used in this analysis is contained in the appendix to this volume.

The data used to estimate this system are the electoral returns for all counties in the United States from 1928 to 1936.[4] There are approximately 3,000 counties in the United States. All population measures for each group (Democrats, Republicans, and nonvoters) are written as proportions of the eligible electorate (21 years of age and older). Census information for all counties has been merged with the electoral data to produce an unusually complete collection of U.S. data for that time period.[5]

Three conditioning variables are used in this analysis. They are (1) urbanization (the total urban population as a proportion of the total population); (2) the level of farm activity, measured as the total county acreage under farm cultivation; and (3) the average number of wage earners in manufacturing industries during 1929, measured as a proportion of the total population. These three conditioning variables are defined as in the 1930 U.S. Census, and are included here because their significance to the politics of the period has been repeatedly addressed (not always with parallel interpretations) by the topical literature (Clubb 1978, 75–79; Ladd and Hadley 1978, 66; Lubell 1965, 57; Petrocik 1981a, 57; Sundquist 1983, 217; also see Clubb, Flanigan, and Zingale 1980).

While other conditioning variables could be used (and others were used in analyses that are not reported here), these three variables seem of particular heuristic value in identifying major differences in the nature of partisan competitions. For example, contemporary Democratic support is located, in large part, in urban settings. However, prior to the 1930s, Republicans depended heavily on urban support. How that transfer from Republican to Democratic urban strength took place, and under what dynamic settings, is a question of substantive importance. For example, it is of interest to inquire whether the onset of the depression sparked a realignment of existing urban voters in 1932 or, rather, whether it caused an upsurge in new voters to swell the Democratic

---

4. The data utilized here were made available by the Inter-University Consortium for Political and Social Research. Neither the original collectors of the data nor the consortium bear any responsibility for the analyses or interpretations presented here.

5. The problem of organizing the data described in n. 1 was accomplished by first printing (on magnetic disk) a listing of the many data sets. A BASIC program was then constructed that "read" each of the listings. This program also wrote computer code in SAS based on the information from these listings. The result was a program written in SAS that recoded all variables in all data sets to have common names containing embedded information that had been extracted from the original variable labels. All of the data sets were then merged to produce the manageable set used here.

ranks in such areas. Similarly, farmers were among the first groups to be affected by the depression. An examination of the dynamic characteristics of partisan competitions in farm areas will address questions of whether large sectors of the farm-related population saw the 1932 and 1936 elections as times to abandon the Republican ship, or as times to join the Democratic movement from the quiet land of the previously uninvolved. The working populations fill a similar role in this analysis. Comparing the nature of partisan competitions in both working and farm areas allows for an examination of crucial differences between diverse populations both in the timing and the manner of their movement to the Democrats. While both the working and farm populations were heavily affected by the depression, it is of interest to know whether differences with the economic, social, and political conditions for each group encouraged dissimilar partisan dynamics.

All of the conditioning variables are standardized to a mean of zero and a standard deviation of one before being entered into the analysis. The transformation inspires the intuitive interpretation of the conditioning variables as measures of the social milieu, recognizing that small changes in a social environment (subjectively detectable as a shift in local ambience) can result in more dramatic electoral consequences (see Blau 1977; Blum 1985; Simmel 1955).

The period from 1928 through 1936 is broken into two separate time spans. Thus, the model is evaluated based on its ability to explain longitudinal, county-level population fluctuations for the Democrats, Republicans, and nonvoters for the period from 1928 through 1932 and from 1932 through 1936. We are, of course, anticipating that the model will detect and reveal underlying systemic patterns from within the data. However, the system evaluated here measures change between and among partisan and nonvoter populations. In situations in which little systemic change has occurred nationally, the model should have a poor goodness of fit. In such a case, local noise would dominate. On the other hand, in those cases in which the model does discern a significant national trend in terms of the voter and nonvoter trade-offs, the goodness of fit should reflect the system's success in characterizing the period's mass dynamics. Throughout all of the analyses, each case (i.e., county) is weighted by its eligible population.

My analysis examines the mass dynamics of the electoral movements during an unusual time in U.S. history. To repeat briefly what was discussed at the end of chapter 3 regarding the use of aggregate data, since available survey data for this period are of questionable reliability, aggregate measures have been extensively used in the extant realignment literature in an attempt to unravel some of the electoral mysteries of those years. My analysis pursues an unusual treatment of the same type of data analyzed elsewhere. This analysis finds correspondence with results by Kramer and others that suggest that the analysis of dynamic aggregate data can be superior to cross-sectional survey data in determining individual-level behavior when the examined behavior involves a systematic longitudinal component (Kramer 1983; see also Barri-lleaux 1986; Campbell 1986; Irwin and Lichtman 1976; Parent, Jillson, and Weber 1987; Powell 1986; Sprague 1976). The present analysis is formulated from the perspective of aggregate population trade-offs between groups. The expectations of the model rest with the direction of change in aggregate group memberships. Where aggregate relationships are strong, the corresponding expectations regarding individuals are buttressed from the perspective of the characterization of the mass dynamics.

Results

The results of the parameter estimations for the system are contained in tables 4.2–4.5. The estimates are separated by time periods as well as by the conditioning variables used in the analysis. On the left sides of the tables are the estimates for the 1928–32 period, and the estimates for 1932–36 are displayed on the right sides of the tables. The goodness of fit of the models for each group (Democrats, Republicans, and nonvoters) are also included in the tables. The chi-square statistics test the statistical significance of each esti-mate in terms of its influence on the predicted values generated by the overall system and are explained more thoroughly in the appendix.

  Substantive interpretations of the system's characterization of the mass

TABLE 4.2. Unconditioned Parameter Estimates

Parameter	1928–32		1932–36	
	Estimate	χ^2	Estimate	χ^2
f	0.17663	552,344	0.16550	261,216
b	0.28495	210,164	0.00220	15
m	0.05874	202,611	0.04801	78,357
a	0.21841	218,718	0.08603	44,440
g	0.06158	39,570	−0.07332	115,710
q	−0.04302	34,852	0.05017	94,374
s	−0.02308	32,020	−0.00871	4,170
w	−0.18302	154,735	0.04190	4,571
v	−0.11234	129,542	−0.14990	200,499
k	−0.00918	22,113	−0.00349	2,369
j	−0.01609	70,537	−0.00461	6,737
y	−0.02275	79,659	−0.00806	11,773
	Goodness of Fit			
Republican	0.72210		0.10401	
Democratic	0.70980		0.46233	
Nonvoter	0.29513		0.59062	

Note: Chi-square $df = 2$.

TABLE 4.3. Urban-Conditioned Parameter Estimates

Parameter	1928–32 Estimate	χ^2	1932–36 Estimate	χ^2
f_1	−0.041184	73,638.4	0.016983	6,436.4
b_1	−0.013620	1,035.9	0.007756	447.3
m_1	0.006823	6,293.5	0.017480	19,756.1
a_1	0.003570	154.7	0.009544	1,354.1
g_1	0.012993	4,157.1	−0.013117	9,240.0
q_1	0.045386	89,041.7	−0.018512	31,892.4
s_1	−0.014611	27,723.4	0.007009	5,468.0
w_1	0.008769	949.4	0.001171	10.6
v_1	0.009201	2,043.3	−0.005351	638.6
k_1	−0.001442	1,323.4	0.000179	13.5
j_1	−0.000850	445.5	−0.000590	254.3
y_1	−0.003496	4,321.9	−0.001291	699.7

Goodness of Fit

Republican	0.75175	0.16159
Democratic	0.73101	0.53219
Nonvoter	0.30703	0.61885

Note: Chi-square *df* = 2.

TABLE 4.4. Workers-Conditioned Parameter Estimates

Parameter	1928–32 Estimate	χ^2	1932–36 Estimate	χ^2
f_1	−0.056730	50,843.8	0.018393	2,814.2
b_1	−0.025263	1,153.9	0.008776	197.6
m_1	0.004884	994.3	0.025507	13,335.3
a_1	−0.003974	57.8	0.011860	611.7
g_1	−0.007105	380.4	−0.014155	3,175.2
q_1	0.081014	82,174.5	−0.030970	26,567.4
s_1	−0.018781	13,699.8	0.010886	4,112.4
w_1	−0.034929	5,483.0	0.002252	14.8
v_1	0.030527	8,471.5	−0.007042	402.6
k_1	−0.002115	908.5	0.000393	21.1
j_1	−0.001122	241.1	−0.000650	98.1
y_1	−0.003614	1,518.3	−0.001862	460.6

Goodness of Fit

Republican	0.76030	0.17262
Democratic	0.74926	0.52578
Nonvoter	0.32356	0.61129

Note: Chi-square *df* = 2.

TABLE 4.5. Farm Density–Conditioned Parameter Estimates

Parameter	1928–32		1932–36	
	Estimate	χ^2	Estimate	χ^2
f_1	0.049522	5,045.8	−0.055609	4,333.1
b_1	0.035395	256.4	−0.022492	183.7
m_1	−0.003735	259.9	−0.012324	1,572.3
a_1	0.012268	227.9	−0.013577	392.4
g_1	−0.039536	3,149.1	0.031656	4,860.7
q_1	−0.074097	20,940.7	0.032871	9,013.1
s_1	0.017093	5,855.5	−0.019620	6,467.1
w_1	−0.032939	1,168.3	−0.002274	3.6
v_1	0.038948	1,789.7	0.018547	447.5
k_1	0.001887	215.5	−0.003577	602.0
j_1	−0.000359	8.5	0.001869	265.2
y_1	0.003798	506.7	0.001154	58.7
	Goodness of Fit			
Republican	0.78489		0.15693	
Democratic	0.73126		0.54827	
Nonvoter	0.31185		0.63657	

Note: Chi-square *df* = 2.

dynamics of the period are difficult to obtain solely from an examination of tables 4.2–4.5. However, while the parameter estimates are used to produce graphic analyses of the overall system, an interpretation of a few of the estimates is heuristically useful as an introduction to how the graphs are produced. Note that, in tables 4.2–4.5, the estimates for parameter b between both periods (in the unconditioned case) change dramatically. Recall that parameter b represents gains for the Democrats due to interactive losses (i.e., the social component of the model) from the Republicans. These results suggest that the Democrats gained heavily from the Republicans in this fashion during the 1928–32 period but not nearly so heavily during the later period. Similarly, the estimate for parameter q changes substantially from the first to the second period. In this case, the magnitude remains approximately the same but the sign changes. Again, parameter q represents the uniform component of the model describing aggregate group change from the Democrats to the Republicans. These results suggest that uniform Republican losses corresponded with Democratic gains in 1932 but not in 1936. Indeed, this parameter value (examined in isolation from the remainder of the system) seems to indicate that there were some uniform gains for the Republicans from the Democrats in 1936. (The subsequent graphic analysis will show that some reverse movement did, in fact, occur in farm areas in 1936.)

An examination of the goodness of fit for the unconditioned cases similarly provides some useful initial interpretive guidelines with regard to the entire system. For the period from 1928 to 1932, note that the models account for a considerable amount of variance in the longitudinal population fluctuations for the Republican and Democratic parties. Note also that the model that characterizes change in the nonvoting population does less well during that time period. Compare these results with those obtained using the unconditioned system for the period from 1932 to 1936. While the model describing change for the Democratic party continues to account for a reduced (but still substantial) degree of variance in the aggregate Democratic outcomes, the model for Republican change now performs poorly. On the other hand, the model for change in the nonvoting population does very well. These initial results can only offer very tentative guidelines for the interpretations of large-scale aggregate movements. However, they do suggest that during the 1928–32 period, the greatest aggregate movement on the county level was between Republicans and Democrats, as the model for nonvoter change encounters relatively less national trend and more local noise for that period. But in the 1932–36 period, the situation seems to have reversed. These results suggest that it is activity between the Democratic and nonvoter population groups that dominates the later period.

A more comprehensive description of the characteristics of the estimated system under the influence of the various conditioning variables can be obtained using graphic analysis. The simplest form of such an analysis is a straightforward longitudinal plot of support for a particular party. Figure 4.1 presents such a plot for the Democratic party. There are four model-generated time paths presented in figure 4.1. The path labeled national is the longitudinal trajectory for the Democratic party using the unconditioned estimates from table 4.2. This path is included in figures 4.2 and 4.3 as well and serves as a baseline from which to evaluate the other trajectories. The time paths labeled farm, urban, and worker represent the system's predicted level of voter support for the Democratic party in areas that can be described as primarily farm oriented, totally urban, and heavily working class in character.

Note that, from 1928 through 1936, the Democratic party's strength continued to grow nationally (i.e., as seen using the trajectory labeled national). However, the greatest growth for the Democratic party between 1928 and 1932 was in the farm areas of the country, and there seems to have been no additional growth in Democratic support from such areas after Roosevelt's initial election. However, Democratic support coming from heavily urban and working-class areas exhibits an opposite pattern. Between 1928 and 1932, such areas contributed less to Roosevelt's first victory than did many of the other sections of the nation. Indeed, areas with high concentrations of workers produced the smallest growth in Democratic support in 1932. These results are of interest considering the focus of much of the realignment literature for the United States on the urban and working-class basis of the Roosevelt coalition (see Degler 1971, 141; Petrocik 1981a, 53). However, note that,

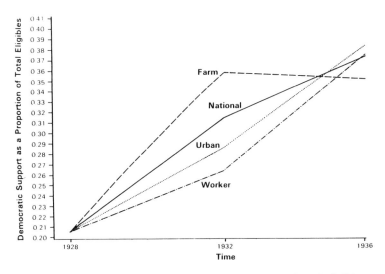

Fig. 4.1. Democratic support, 1928–36, as a proportion of total eligibles

after the 1932 election, Democratic support from urban and working-class areas increased dramatically, marginally surpassing the overall national strength of the party and completely eclipsing the now stagnant growth from the farm areas. These results for 1936 seem to support arguments by Sundquist and some others (Sundquist 1983, 218–19; see also Lubell 1965, 57–63) that the urban and working-class elements of the Roosevelt coalition did not emerge in their full form until after 1932. However, the trajectories in figure 4.1 suggest surprising differences in the manner and timing in which various groups turned to the Democrats. In particular, the magnitude of the differences between the farm areas, when compared with the urban and working-class areas for 1932, is quite striking, given the claims by some authors that the growth in Democratic support in 1932 was primarily affected by a broadly based sense of dissatisfaction (cutting across all groups) with the previous Republican leadership (Ladd and Hadley 1978, 87). Moreover, the dramatic reversal of these patterns after 1936 is noteworthy in terms of its magnitude and deserves further examination.

A problem with figure 4.1 is that it does not allow for an examination of the relative trade-offs between groups; that is, it is not clear whether the growth in Democratic support coincides with an increase in new voter strengths or a decrease in local Republican fortunes. These trade-offs can be seen more clearly in an analysis of a type of graph called a *phase diagram*. Figure 4.2 is a phase diagram representing change in Democratic and Republican support from 1928 through 1936. As with the other phase diagrams described below, each curve on the plot represents simultaneous change in two separate populations. In figure 4.2, the horizontal axis identifies Republi-

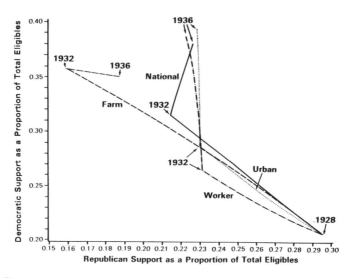

Fig. 4.2. Democratic and Republican trade-offs, 1928–36, as a proportion of total eligibles

can support from the pool of eligibles while the vertical axis represents Democratic support.

Note that each line on the plot is labeled with respect to whether it is an unconditioned (national) or a conditioned (farm, urban, or worker) trajectory. Also note that each line on the figure is labeled with regard to the three election years 1928, 1932, and 1936. As one follows any one of the lines (all beginning in 1928 and originating in the lower right-hand corner of the figure) upward and to the left, it is possible to examine the voter trade-offs between the two groups over time. For example, follow the line labeled national diagonally up from its starting point in 1928 until its sharp bend upward in 1932. This part of the line indicates that from 1928 to 1932 there was a large drop in national Republican support combined with an approximately equal gain in Democratic support, all computed using the entire estimated system (thus simultaneously controlling for all partisan-nonvoter shifts as well). Continuing up the line from 1932 to 1936, there appears to be very little movement in Republican support (shown by the nearly vertical nature of the line after 1932) and a substantial increase in national Democratic support. When a line cuts a dramatic diagonal across a plot, this indicates a substantial simultaneous movement between the two populations represented on the figure's axes. When a line is placed horizontally or vertically in the figure (or nearly so, relative to the other lines), this indicates little or no aggregate movement between the two populations (i.e., one population stayed constant while the other either increased or decreased).

While the line for the national-level trade-offs is included in all phase diagrams for reference, the other lines tell the more interesting story. In figure 4.2, note that the line representing the system of competition as it occurred in predominantly farming areas marks a very dramatic diagonal sweep across the plot from 1928 to 1932. This suggests that a great deal of formerly Republican support coming from farm areas in the United States abandoned the Republican party and joined the ranks of the Democratic voters. Moreover, the magnitude of the Republican loss in farming areas, combined with that of the Democratic gain, surpasses those for urban or working-class areas, as well as the national average. Such a strong movement away from the Republicans and toward the Democrats in farming areas probably had its origins in historical conditions reaching back more than ten years. Recall that the La Follette movement in 1924 registered marked discontent with Republican farm policies (Sundquist 1983, 182–91) and that Calvin Coolidge did once say, "Well, farmers never have made money. I don't believe we can do much about it" (White 1965, 344). It seems that the onset of the Great Depression was the last straw for many farmers. While the Republicans may have maintained a substantial degree of farmer support throughout the 1930s, they do seem to have lost a good part of that support in 1932. However, note that the Republicans did bounce back somewhat in the farm areas after 1932. This suggests that many of the switching farmland folks of 1932 stayed Democrats in 1936, but a few returned to their Republican roots.

The pattern between the Democrats and the Republicans in farm areas differs remarkably from that in urban and working-class areas. Figure 4.2 suggests that, among urbanites, there was a substantial Republican loss combined with a large Democratic gain, primarily in 1932. However, in areas in which there were large numbers of workers, Republican support dropped between 1928 and 1932 with less than an equivalent Democratic gain. After 1932, Democrats seemed to have scored heavily from such areas without a Republican loss of comparable magnitude. This raises the question of what these working-class voters did in 1932. While they seemed to have abandoned the Republican party in large numbers in 1932, they do not seem to have been a fundamental component of the Democratic gains until after 1932.

This puzzle regarding working-class trade-offs between the Democrats and the Republicans is answered, in large part, in figure 4.3. Figure 4.3 contains the longitudinal trade-off population trajectories for Democrats and nonvoters. The horizontal axis represents the nonvoting population, measured as a proportion of the total electorate, and the vertical axis represents support for the Democrats (as in fig. 4.2).

Note that the line labeled worker moves upward and somewhat to the right after its beginning in 1928. From 1932 to 1936, the line makes a marked change and moves diagonally upward and to the left. These results suggest that voters in heavily working-class areas experienced no increase in mobilization in 1932 (and perhaps a degree of demobilization).

This result, interesting in comparison with the magnitude of the shift

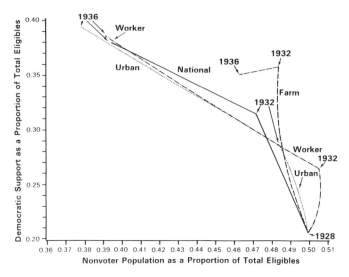

Fig. 4.3. Democratic and nonvoter trade-offs, 1928–36, as a proportion of total eligibles

from 1932 to 1936, is not completely without interpretation guided by some of the extant realignment literature of the period. Recall that the 1932 election was not a radical departure from other elections in the 1920s with respect to Roosevelt's campaign rhetoric (Ladd and Hadley 1978, 38; Lubell 1965; Sundquist 1983, 208–10). Indeed, it was not until Roosevelt came to power that the shape of the future was so clearly directed in New Deal terms (Petrocik 1981a, 53–54). While the depression made the Republicans an unpopular party in 1932, the Democrats were not clearly identified as a party of economic and social salvation (Key 1964, 523–24).

The results shown in figure 4.3 suggest that workers did not initially rise up and attempt to throw the Republicans out of the White House, regardless of whether or not they blamed that party for their own depression-related economic misfortunes. Rather, they remained inert, and some may have even stopped voting, withdrawing from political participation just as they had begun to withdraw from their participation in the national economy. This may have been tied to the dramatic decrease in the unionized work force at the time. They may have been struck by anger at their plight, but all were not motivated (or perhaps organized) to register their anger at the polling booths. One can only suspect that they did not really know where to turn for assistance in 1932. Conceivably, they were more interested in their own domestic situations than in politics, and they were perhaps unsure of what any government could do for them, given decades of Republican political dominance and a previously widespread public acceptance of the principle of nonintervention in the private economy. But in 1936 they saw the difference between the parties, and partisan politics in the United States experienced a massive infusion of new as well as formerly demobilized voters from working-class areas.[6]

Figure 4.3 suggests a related story for urban voters (of whom many were workers). There was little overall movement to the Democrats from the pool of nonvoters in urban areas between 1928 and 1932, as is indicated by the near vertical course of the line labeled urban through 1932 (although there was certainly variation between many particular urban areas, of course). Yet after 1932, the diagonal movement for the line indicates that the urban areas experienced heavy Democratic mobilization among new voters. Voters in farm areas acted in an entirely different fashion. The Democrats managed to mobilize some new voters in 1932 from such areas. However, the Democrats had no comparable success from the farming areas in 1936. Indeed, a fraction of their 1932 farmland supporters failed to turn out at all.[7]

The argument suggesting that rural switchers dominated the dynamic activity of the 1928–32 period and urban new voters were more critical in the 1932–36 period is usefully supplemented with a presentation of some rural and urban data that would not depend on the analysis of the model that is developed in this chapter. The rural and urban components of the argument may seem somewhat controversial given the amount that has been written elsewhere suggesting that the New Deal realignment was fundamentally a working-class and urban phenomenon. This is true if the time frame under discussion is limited to the 1932–36 period. If the argument is extended to include the 1928–32 period as well, then it is not true, since the current analysis clearly finds that the early part of the realignment took place predominantly in farm areas.

Two plots help to demonstrate the dramatic difference in the demographic shift from rural to urban realignment activity between the two peri-

---

6. It seems unlikely that the results for the worker populations would be influenced to a large degree by an ecological aggregation effect, although such a possibility does exist with any analysis of aggregate data. The farm and urban results would appear less susceptible to such aggregation effects due to the relative homogeneity of these areas. However, the areas with large worker populations also tend to be heavily urban, and the results for the workers tend to have similar dynamic properties to that of the urban areas. Moreover, subsequent checking with alternative statistical strategies ranging from simple weighted correlations to more complicated logistic structures indicates that the present description of worker behavior is not a product of the particular model specification used here, but rather a real structural characteristic of these data.

7. A similar conditional analysis was also performed to test for differences in the partisan and new voter dynamics for the southern states as compared with the nonsouthern states. This analysis is not included in the body of the text only for reasons of space. However, the basic result is that there were no large differences in the directions of partisan and nonvoter change between southern and nonsouthern states (see also Shively 1971–72). This is not to say that the magnitudes of the static partisan totals for each election were similar, for obviously they were not. But the characteristics of change did not vary according to this regional division. In the southern states as well as the nonsouthern states, vote switching from the available pool of Republicans (admittedly small in the South) to the Democrats still dominated the 1932 election, whereas the new voters had their greatest impact in the 1936 contest.

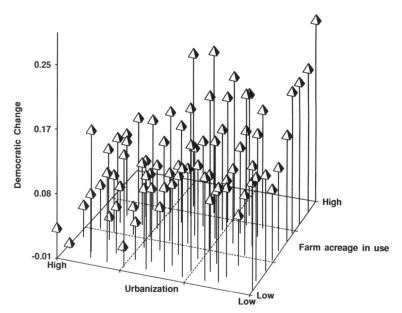

Fig. 4.4. Urban, farm density, and Democratic change as a proportion of total eligibles, 1928–32

ods. Figure 4.4 is a three-dimensional scatterplot that allows the simultaneous comparison of Democratic change in both farm and urban areas. The data presented in figure 4.4 is for the 1928–32 period. Figure 4.5 is a similar scatterplot for the 1932–36 period.

In both figures 4.4 and 4.5 the "floor" axes are measures of urbanization and farm activity. These variables are defined exactly as they are used in the rest of the chapter. Urbanization is a population density measure and farm activity is the proportion of each county's acreage that is engaged in farming. Both variables have been standardized with a mean of zero and a standard deviation of one. In both figures, each floor variable has been broken up into deciles. Given that there are two axes, each broken up into ten units, there are 100 floating points above the floor. Pyramids are used to represent each data point for the early period; balloons are used for the later period. In both figures the vertical axis is the change in support for the Democratic party measured as a proportion of adults 21 years of age or older (i.e., the eligibles).

The reader should be cautioned from trying to find a one-dimensional interpretation of the floor of the figures. The two floor axes measure different things, and one cannot simply assume that low urban means high farm for there are low population areas in the United States in which farming is not a primary occupation.

Figures 4.4 and 4.5 are best examined sequentially. Note that the pyramids in figure 4.4 rise highest off of the floor in areas in which urbanization is

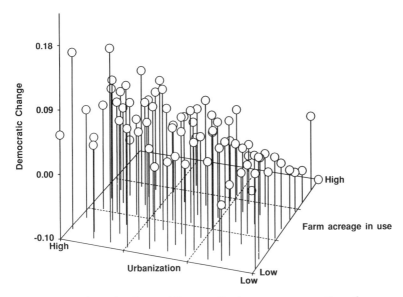

Fig. 4.5. Urban, farm density, and Democratic change as a proportion of total eligibles, 1932–36

generally low and farm activity is high. This indicates that Democratic change was highest in these rural farm areas between 1928 and 1932. However, figure 4.5 suggests an opposite pattern for the 1932–36 period. In figure 4.5, the balloons rise highest off of the floor in high-population urban counties with low levels of farm activity. This supports the conclusion that Democratic gains in the later period came mostly from these high-density areas.

While neither figure 4.4 nor figure 4.5 changes the results presented in the rest of the chapter, they do add a sense of descriptive realism when compared with the more abstract qualities of phase plane diagrams. They also help in supporting the idea that the early and later periods of the realignment were fundamentally different in character.

With this said, however, it is important to add one caveat to the interpretation of these findings. The word *realignment* is used because of the long-term impact of the 1932 and 1936 elections on the electoral history of the United States. It should be noted, however, that since this analysis focuses on the period from 1928 to 1936, some questions regarding some of the long-term aspects of the realignment remain unanswered. It is not clear whether the vote-switching realignment in 1932 implies a permanent reorientation of what would be thought of as the "normal vote" for many voters. Some have suggested that many of the switchers of 1932 returned to their earlier Republican habits by 1940 (Petrocik 1981a, 57). Survey responses (were they available) could have been used to query the voters' inner psychological commitments to particular partisan labels and attachments. However, in the absence of such data, I rely here on an examination of the voting patterns of the early period, identifying vote switching and nonvoter interactions but leaving open the question of whether or not both the 1932 and the 1936 elections represented a deviating electoral period for some voters in which previous partisan allegiances were subsequently reestablished in 1940 or beyond.

The Relative Impact of Mechanisms for Change

Figures 4.6–4.9 change the focus of this analysis to ask a question based on the structure of the model explored. Within each mathematical statement characterizing growth and decay for the partisan and nonvoter populations, there are both uniform and social components. It is descriptively useful, as well as analytically important, to evaluate the relative impact of the two components.

Figure 4.6 displays the *Simon bounds* for aggregate partisan change for the Democrats from the ranks of the Republicans. Figure 4.7 contains a similar representation for partisan change for the Democrats from new voters. Both figures 4.6 and 4.7 are drawn with respect to the urban-conditioned environment. Figures 4.8 and 4.9 are a similar representation for the farm-conditioned environment. The term *Simon bounds* refers to an early work by Herbert A. Simon (1957), in which substantive meanings were explicitly tied to formal mathematical expressions of social change of the type used here. In all figures, time is on the horizontal axis and Democratic support as a proportion of the total eligibles is on the vertical axis.

It is useful to pause for a moment and explain the reasoning behind this analysis of the Simon bounds of the estimated system. In multiple regression analysis (which, of course, this is not), standardized parameter estimates could be computed to allow for relative comparisons in the influences of each of the independent variables of the regression equation in causing change in the dependent variable. Thus, we could see which variables have greater influence in determining change in the Democratic vote by comparing the magnitudes of these estimates, with larger magnitudes implying larger influence. In the current analysis, this would indicate which of the components of the model (i.e., social or uniform) are most influential in changing partisan mobilization. This would help in determining the mechanisms behind the mass dynamics with greater precision. Unfortunately, standardized parameter estimates are not easily computed for the type of dynamic systems investigated here. But the analysis of the Simon bounds is an alternate method of answering these questions of relative influence among social and uniform model components that does work with such dynamic systems.

To interpret figure 4.6, note that the lines labeled combined represent the total longitudinal gains for the Democrats in urban areas and are identical to the urban-conditioned trajectories presented under the urban label in figure 4.1. The lines labeled uniform and social are computed using only the sys-

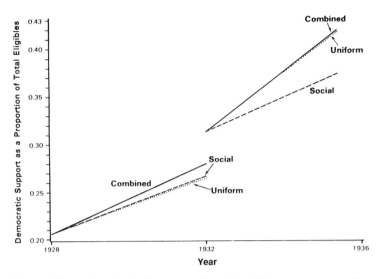

Fig. 4.6. Simon bounds for Democrats from Republicans—urban conditioned

tem's uniform or social components (respectively) as inputs to the joint Democratic and Republican totals. For example, to compute the Democratic vote represented by the lines labeled uniform in figure 4.6, parameter *b* was set to zero. This parameter represents the probability of recruiting a Republican for the Democrats at an instant in time due to the interactive influences of the two

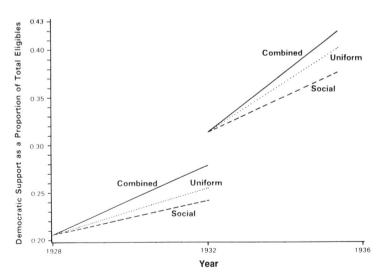

Fig. 4.7. Simon bounds for Democrats from new voters—urban conditioned

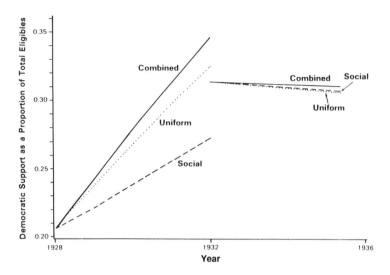

Fig. 4.8. Simon bounds for Democrats from Republicans—farm conditioned

existing partisan populations. Setting this component to zero leaves only Democratic gains due to nationally uniform Republican defections (i.e., parameters f and q mediating the uniform components of the expressions for Democratic and Republican change). Alternatively, the lines labeled social are computed by setting the uniform components between the Republicans and

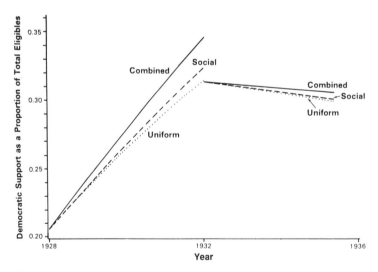

Fig. 4.9. Simon bounds for Democrats from new voters—farm conditioned

the Democrats to zero, leaving only the social component in the model. To summarize, the lines labeled uniform in figure 4.6 use only the uniform components of the model as inputs to the nationally changing partisan totals, whereas lines labeled social use only the social components. These lines represent the mobilization that would have happened historically if only that type of mobilization had occurred.

For urban environments during the period from 1928 to 1932 in figure 4.6, note that the social component of the model contributes only a slightly larger share of the national Democratic vote gain than the uniform component. This is indicated by the height of the social time path relative to the height of the uniform time path. Both the uniform and the social paths are lower than the combined path since they both contributed to the national totals, and the absence of either would produce a lower outcome. This suggests that Democratic gains from the Republicans in 1932 in urban areas were approximately equally dependent on the localized abilities of the Democratic party to compete (i.e., converting more Republicans where the Democrats are strong and fewer Republicans where the Democrats are weak) and on a more uniformly distributed sense of dissatisfaction with the Republicans.

The time paths on the right of figure 4.6 (for the period from 1932 to 1936) indicate that the uniform component was largely responsible for any further Democratic gains from the Republicans in urban areas. This is shown by the much greater height of the uniform time path relative to the social time path. Recall from figure 4.2 that there were very few Democratic gains from the Republicans in urban areas in 1936. The results in figure 4.6 suggest that the Democrats did not have to rely on their own localized partisan strengths in order to maintain those gains.

Figure 4.7 contains the Democratic time paths identifying the Simon bounds with respect to Democratic gains in urban areas from new voters. Comparing 1928–32 with 1932–36, note that the relationship between the uniform and social time paths is similar in both periods. Democratic gains from the new voters were relatively independent of local Democratic party strengths. Apparently these new voters (fewer in 1932 than in 1936) were driven by the national sense of crisis and (especially in 1936) the overall Democratic appeal. In other words, Democratic mobilization of new voters in urban areas was relatively less dependent on existing local Democratic partisan strengths.

Recall from the discussion of figures 4.2 and 4.3 that Democrats gained a great deal of Republican support as well as a substantial amount of new voter support from farm areas in 1932. Figures 4.8 and 4.9 present the Simon bounds for Democratic gains from the Republicans and the new voters within farm-conditioned environments. The trajectories on the left side of figure 4.8 indicate that the Republican-to-Democrat defections in 1932 were not a result of locally dependent partisan competitions. This is shown by the much greater height of the uniform trajectory relative to the social trajectory. Following

1932, there was much less difference between the separate components of the competition. But the Democrats did not gain much from the farm-based Republicans in 1936 (in fact, they seem to have lost support there).

Figure 4.9 reveals an interesting difference from the pattern presented in figure 4.8. From the new voters in 1932, the dominant component of the Democratic gains came from the local partisan competitions in areas where existing Democratic organizations could successfully mobilize former nonparticipants. In this figure, the social component has a substantially higher trajectory than the uniform component. The same pattern exists after 1932, but the relative impact of farm-based new voters on Democratic gains in 1936 was slight overall (from fig. 4.3).

In summary, figures 4.6–4.9 present an interesting and contrasting picture of the dynamics of partisan competitions in urban and farm environments. In the urban areas, the movement toward the Democrats by new voters was a phenomenon that occurred, in large part, uniformly throughout these areas, relatively independent of existing Democratic strengths. Among Republican-to-Democratic conversions in 1932, the effects of the uniform and social components were more-or-less equal. In farm areas, the situation was also complex. Uniform movement dominated among Republican-to-Democratic conversions. However, new voters from farm areas were most easily brought into the Democratic ranks when the local Democratic presence was relatively strong.

The nature of this recruitment corresponds to findings reported by Beck (1974) regarding the environmental properties of county-level partisan competitions during periods of realignment. In farm areas, the early Democratic success came from former Republicans across-the-board (i.e., uniformly) who were fed up with Republican farm policies (or perhaps the lack of them) and some new voters in locations in which there was an existing Democratic presence. Thus, Roosevelt's relatively "gentle" campaign, filled with farm-oriented themes, aided local Democratic mobilization efforts among new voters in rural areas. But the already mobilized former Republicans did not need the party contact. They jumped ship uniformly, and their impact on the early Democratic success was much greater than that of the new voters.

It was only after 1932 that the New Deal coalition began to form around identifiable centers of Democratic strength in urban areas. When this occurred, the movement was relatively less dependent on local partisan competitive abilities than on the national momentum of the times. The campaign of 1936 did not represent the politics of the former status quo. The Democrats had a new and coherent message, a message that had direct appeal to the urban masses. It seems that the radical nature of the message transformed the campaign from one where local party organizations were a major factor in the processes of converting Republicans (as in 1932 for urban areas) to one in which the party benefited from the windfall resulting from the newly energized and volatile electorate.

These results for farm and urban areas suggest that, during periods of rapid change in mass voting patterns, party organizations are more likely to be victims or beneficiaries than causes of the mass movements. When the movements are of smaller magnitude, the activity of the party organizations has much greater impact. However, large aggregate movements, especially involving new voter activity (as with the Democrats in 1936), could also be seen as the beginning of the renaissance of local party apparatus, reenergized by the masses after years of decay with little national-level guidance. When partisan politics settled down, the enhanced organizational strength of the Democratic party was certainly a factor in the dominance of the party in national politics until the 1950s.

Remarks

This chapter develops and explores a model of mass political behavior with respect to the realigning period in the United States from 1928 to 1936. The analysis suggests that vote switching from the Republicans to the Democrats dominated the 1932 part of the realignment. However, discontent with the Republicans was not distributed equally or even nearly equally across social groups in the nation. Voters in farm areas—both former Republicans and some new voters—joined Democratic ranks in large numbers. But urbanites responded to the Democratic appeal with less enthusiasm in 1932. Republican urban voters converted at a rate lower than that for the nation as a whole, and the nonvoters in these areas generally stayed put. Moreover, these results suggest that some workers may have even withdrawn from active participation in the electorate in 1932 rather than be drawn toward an emergent Democratic party that had not yet developed a clear identity.

The election of 1936 changed the character of Democratic politics. Some voters from the farm areas returned to the Republican fold. But urbanites and workers flooded the Democratic party's ranks. Moreover, these new Democrats of 1936 were also predominantly new voters.

The model developed here characterizes the nature of the partisan competitions as a dynamic process containing both nationally uniform and locally interactive partisan ingredients (the uniform and social components of the model). In a situation of national crisis combined with large-scale mass movements, the uniform components often dominate, especially given weaknesses in the local party structures of at least one party. But when the mass movements are less severe but the political climate is favorable, the social components of partisan mobilization can yield substantial gains as well. In either case, the rejuvenation of the party organization as linked to the resurgence of its national fortunes must certainly enhance the party's long-term prospects for securing the attachments of these newly oriented partisans.

In brief, we can now begin to assemble our initial inventory of structural characteristics of mass electoral volatility. The mass dynamics of realignment politics are dependent on social context in a variety of ways. In the most basic sense, the dynamics are differentially structured across various social groups. Group-defined partisan coalitions (e.g., farmers, workers, etc.) change due to the behaviors of both switchers and new voters.

However, the switchers need not switch at the same time as the new voters begin to vote. Each group responds to its own particular set of stimuli independently. Issues count, but mobilization efforts on the part of the gaining party are critical as well. The fact that new voters in urban areas did not come out strongly to support Roosevelt in 1932 despite their desperate needs tells this very forcefully. This suggests that new voters are particularly dependent on partisan mobilization efforts. Switchers, on the other hand, already participate in politics, and may be more easily swayed by traditional appeals driven by social crises. Metaphorically, it seems easier to get someone in a canoe to paddle in a different direction than it is to persuade someone on the banks to get in and push off. In this sense new voters and switchers do not respond equally to identical political stimuli. Moreover, the types of stimuli that affect new voters and switchers are clearly structured by both socially interactive and noninteractive partisan efforts. We will return to these ideas in the context of subsequent chapters.

APPENDIX TO CHAPTER 4

All of the models (i.e., the entire system) can be rewritten in reduced form. For purposes of explanation (since all three derivatives have similar structural forms), the present discussion is limited to the mathematical statement for dD/dt. Taking advantage of the identity $D + R + N = 1$, solving for N and making the substitution into equation 4.4 produces

$$dD/dt = fR + bRD + m(1 - R - D) + aD(1 - R - D) + k.$$

This simplifies to

$$dD/dt = (k + m) + D[(a - m) + (b - a)R - aD] + (f - m)R$$

or, in reduced form,

$$dD/dt = \beta_0 + D(\beta_1 + \beta_2 R - \beta_3 D) + \beta_4 R. \tag{A4.1}$$

All of the right-hand side components of equation A4.1 are standard features of many such reduced form models that are described in the literature on dynamic modeling (e.g., Danby 1985; Haberman 1977; Hirsch and Smale 1974; Huckfeldt, Kohfeld, and Likens 1982; Luenberger 1979; Nisbet and Gurney 1982). In reduced form (thus in the complete absence of the original structural equations), substantive interpretations might be proposed as follows: β_0 represents a term characterizing constant growth; β_1 describes growth based only on existent levels of D (exponential growth or decay); β_2 controls the interactive input to the model as either growth or decay; β_3 is a logistic limitation to growth, where growth in D slows as D approaches an upper bound; and β_4 represents noninteractive gain (or loss) dependent on existent levels for R.

The problem with the reduced form expressions is that these interpretations do not characterize the more complex social processes such as those revealed through the imbedded (i.e., nonreduced) parameters found in the original structural equations. This problem is characteristic of all reduced form models, which leads to the natural desire to estimate complex systems in their structural representation. Hanushek and Jackson offer the following interpretation of the two forms. "The reduced form equations summarize the entire structural model in terms of the total changes expected in each endogenous variable from a change in any one of the exogenous variables. The structural model on the other hand 'explains' how those changes occur and describes the behavioral process underlying the predicted changes" (1977, 227).

It is not necessary to estimate the models in their reduced form. Indeed, for estimation purposes, the models are best left in their original structural form (with all of the model-to-model parameter interdependencies left explicit), thus allowing statistical tests for all of the original (nonreduced) parameters. This is a general problem of nonlinear parameter estimation toward which is directed a sizable body of literature in both the engineering and econometric fields (Bard 1974; Dennis and Schnabel 1983; Hamming 1971; Judge et al. 1982, 773–74; SAS Institute 1990, chap. 19). The precise methods of parameter estimation as they are used in this analysis are explained in the appendix to this volume.

CHAPTER 5

Third-Party Dynamics

Third parties, when they arise, make for exciting political seasons. Questions abound about whether the new party is attracting a new set of voters who have never been motivated to support either of the two major parties, or whether the third party is benefiting from the "hide" of one or both of the major parties. The presidential nominees of both parties often try to persuade voters that the third-party candidate has no chance, and thus the voters should not throw away their votes on someone who is not capable of winning the election. The fear is that the third party just may take away some of the strength of the major party candidates. On the other hand, citizens seem to like the added excitement that the third party brings to the election. Third parties often raise issues that seem radical for their day. Major parties sometimes adopt these positions as their own after a time. Thus, the third parties often raise controversial issues that the major parties sometimes try to avoid. However you look at it, the presence of a third party on the ballot excites the voters, worries the major party leaders, and brings the potential for significant levels of volatility to the electoral battle.

This chapter is about major third-party movements in the United States since the 1890s. The theoretical focus is on mechanisms of mass mobilization and electoral volatility that are specifically tied to third-party movements. Substantively, I concentrate on those third-party movements that received more than 6 percent of the total presidential vote. There were five such third-party movements since the 1890s. The candidates who led these movements (together with their party names and popular vote percentages) are James B. Weaver (the People's party; 8.5 percent) in 1892, Theodore Roosevelt (the Progressive party; 27.4 percent) in 1912, Robert La Follette (the Progressive party; 16.6 percent) in 1924, George Wallace (the American Independent party; 13.5 percent) in 1968, and John Anderson (Independent; 6.6 percent) in 1980.

The third-party movements mentioned here are of sufficient magnitude to allow for a general examination of such movements with regard to the destabilizing influences of the movements on voter institutionalization. If, for example, voters who support third-party movements tend to be new voters who vote only in one election and then leave the electoral arena after their candidate fails, then there should be little destabilizing influence on the electoral system as a whole. The previous partisan balance should remain approximately intact, and competitions between the two main parties should resume in a normal fashion after the third party leaves the scene. However, if new voter supporters of the third party decide to return to the ballot box in future elections, their allegiance to one or the other of the major parties could tip the electoral balance in a critical fashion. Indeed, if the increase in mobilization is sufficiently significant and enduring in the direction of one party, the change may represent a political realignment.

It is possible, however, that third-party movements may "steal" voters from one or both of the two main parties. If that happens, the question of what those voters will do once the third party disappears remains. If the voters come primarily from one of the two major parties, then that party would suffer in future elections if those voters cease voting, or worse, begin to support the other major party.

The analysis presented in this chapter was initiated under the assumption that some things about the dynamics of third-party movements must be general. My goal is to explore those dynamics with regard to the five cases mentioned here, extracting those generalizations that do apply to such movements and noting some of the idiosyncracies that remain characteristic of particular contests. Of special concern are general characteristics of such third-party movements that may have implications for voter deinstitutionalization, such as whether third-party movements act as catalysts of realignment.

There is no shortage of published analyses of third parties in the electoral literature. An extensive (and annotated) bibliography of third-party movements has been compiled recently by D. Stephen Rockwood and his colleagues (1985). Much of this literature is descriptive of particular movements (see especially Hesseltine 1948 and 1962; and Nash 1959). Some of this literature focuses on particular types of third-party movements, such as Walton's analyses of African-American political parties as well as the role of African-Americans with other third parties (Walton 1969 and 1972). However some of the analyses and underlying theoretical approaches to the subject are quite general. Moreover, there are some common themes that appear in the relevant literature that are of particular interest to my analysis.

A particularly interesting empirical analysis of third parties is by Rosenstone, Behr, and Lazarus (1984). These authors find empirical support for a theme that is often repeated elsewhere in the third-party literature, namely, that third parties arise when voters are disenchanted with the major parties' abilities to address critical issues. Voters who are attracted to third parties are those with particularly low levels of partisan institutionalization. Great numbers of such voters are available for third-party recruitment during times of dealignment, periods typically preceding major realignments.

An analysis less empirical in nature than that of Rosenstone, Behr, and Lazarus (1984), but nonetheless rich in its theoretical perspective, is that by Daniel A. Mazmanian (1974). Of particular interest from the view of my current analysis is that Mazmanian notes that third-party movements are usually not associated with increases in turnout among voters in general. Indeed, third parties tend to form when interest in the major parties declines, and, thus, overall turnout remains stable or even decreases moderately. This implies that third parties either attract voters who are already mobilized supporters of the major parties, or that third parties attract new voters at a time of demobilization with regard to the major parties. This point has not yet been resolved in the extant third-party literature.

The commonly raised connection between third-party movements and partisan realignments has been given an interesting interpretation by McRae and Meldrum (1960). Analyzing county-level data for the state of Illinois, they find that third parties can act as instruments for voters to ease the transition between the two major parties. They find this result particularly strong with regard to La Follette's Progressive movement in 1924, where some voters appeared to be shifting from the Republican to the Democratic parties during the period from 1920 to 1928.

The analysis that follows addresses many of these issues by evaluating such ideas with regard to a formal model and a complete national collection of county-level data of the same type that was exploited in the previous chapter on the 1928 to 1936 realigning period. Of particular importance are questions focusing on the source of third-party support, that is, from the existing two major parties or from the ranks of the previously nonmobilized. Moreover, do third-party movements act as springboards for partisan realignments? Thus, once the institutionalized bond between voters and their party has been broken (through the attraction of a third party), are such voters then more likely to switch major parties after the third party vanishes? Finally, the analysis addresses the implications of the research to the potential for deinstitutionalization and subsequent large-scale electoral volatility.

The Parties

We begin with a very brief description of the third parties that are analyzed in this chapter. The descriptions are included here to remind readers of the basic issues that the third parties supported as well as of the general political scene at the time of the third party activity.

Populism

Populism was a term used to describe the political philosophy of supporters of the People's party. At its first national convention in 1892, the party nominated James B. Weaver for president of the United States. As with James Weaver, most of the leaders of the party tended to come from the ranks of the then defunct Greenback party. The first People's party platform was quite wide-ranging in its issue content, but its primary concerns were the welfare of farmers concentrated in the South and the Midwest. Their main issue was the support of the free coinage of silver, symbolic of their discontent with a shrinking money supply and depressed farm prices. Unhappy with high railroad freight rates, they also advocated government ownership of the railroads. The party was basically absorbed by the Democratic party when that party nominated the free silver candidate, William Jennings Bryan, in 1896.

The Bull Moose

The Bull Moose party is the popular name for the Progressive party that formed in 1912 as a result of a personal and ideological split between two Republican leaders, former president Theodore Roosevelt and then president William Howard Taft. Roosevelt was displeased with Taft's conservative philosophy. He challenged and nearly defeated the incumbent Taft for the Republican nomination for president in 1912. Soon after the Republican national convention, Roosevelt was nominated for president by the Progressive party. It became known as the Bull Moose party because of a statement by Roosevelt that he felt as fit as a bull moose. The party's convention drew many middle- and upper-class supporters, mostly from small towns. The platform reflected the party's roots in an earlier progressive movement, advocating issues such as government involvement in social, labor, and antitrust reform.

La Follette Progressivism

Wisconsin Republican Senator Robert M. La Follette led a newly created Progressive party in the 1924 presidential contest. The party had only a partial resemblance to the Progressive party led by Theodore Roosevelt. The 1924 Progressive party primarily supported government action to thwart the power of corporate monopolies. However, the party also supported a variety of issues aimed at gathering farm and labor support. La Follette carried only Wisconsin in the general election, despite his respectable national showing. Most of his strength seemed to come from voters in farming areas west of the Mississippi River. The party collapsed as a result of La Follette's death in 1925.

The Wallace Reaction

Alabama Governor George C. Wallace sought the Democratic nomination for president in 1964, 1968, and 1972. However, in 1968, he split with the Democratic party after failing to receive the nomination and ran as an independent, calling his movement the American Independent party. The party gained support among lower- and middle-class whites, and especially blue-collar workers, who were angry with the civil rights movement of the 1960s, the open opposition to the Vietnam War expressed by many young people, and President Johnson's social programs. Wallace's support came to be known as a "white backlash," a conservative reaction to the volatile and changing society of the time. Wallace carried five southern states. While running for the Democratic nomination in 1972, he was partially paralyzed as a result of an assassination attempt. The American Independent party nominated two John Birch Society members that year, but failed to regain a national presence.

Anderson's Dissenting Voice

John Anderson ran for the Republican nomination in 1980. He made an initially favorable impression among many people due to his outspoken nature in the televised debates held during the Republican primaries. His popularity in the news polls soared, and he decided to form an independent movement to continue his drive for the presidency after he lost the Republican nomination. His public visibility during the summer months was diminished due to his preoccupation in putting his name on the ballot in a large number of states. When his public campaign was restarted in September, voter attention seemed to have shifted from him to the two major party candidates, Ronald Reagan and Jimmy Carter. His independent movement fell apart after 1980, and he endorsed the Democratic nominee for president, Walter Mondale, in 1984.

The Question of Overall Mobilization

The mobilization totals for these third-party movements give some initial guidance to the current analysis. Table 5.1 contains mobilization proportions for the two major parties as well as for the third parties. Proportions are given both for the election in which the third parties participated as well as for the previous and subsequent elections. These mobilization figures are computed as proportions of the total eligible populations at the time of the third-party competitions. Thus, the numbers are comparable across elections as well as across third-party movements.

From table 5.1, first note that none of the elections in which there were large third-party movements were associated with major increases in the overall turnout (found by comparing "total vote" across elections for each of the five third-party competitions). Indeed, only in 1924 was there an increase in turnout at all, and this increase was quite small. An initial reading of this result suggests that third parties do not attract many new voters, and, thus, one or both of the major parties suffer as a consequence of third-party mobilization success. However, the potential for interpretive error with figures of such a large level of aggregation is not at all remote. These initial results do not rule out the possibility that the third parties did attract new voters while the major parties suffered a demobilization of their previous support. Indeed, if third parties arise when voters are discontent with the two major parties, the potential for demobilization among major party supporters is quite high. Nonetheless, table 5.1 does reconfirm the suggestion, made elsewhere in the third-

TABLE 5.1. Mobilization as a Percentage of the Eligible Electorate for Third-Party Movements

	Weaver			Roosevelt[a]			La Follette[a]			Wallace[b]			Anderson[a]		
	1888	1892	1896	1908	1912	1916	1920	1924	1928	1964	1968	1972	1976	1980	1984
Democratic	35	31	34	25	23	31	15	13	21	38	26	21	27	22	21
Republican	34	29	37	30	13	29	26	24	30	24	26	33	26	27	31
Third party	0	6	0[c]	0	15	0	0	8	0	0	8	0	0	5	0
Total vote	71	68	72	58	54	63	44	45	52	62	61	55	54	53	53
Nonvoter	29	32	28	42	46	37	56	55	48	38	39	45	46	47	47

Note: The percentage of the total vote includes votes for other minor parties that did not gain at least 6 percent of the vote.
[a] Third-party candidate was formerly associated with the Republican party.
[b] Third-party candidate was formerly associated with the Democratic party.
[c] Votes for the People's party included in the Democratic percentage.

party literature, that elections with large-scale third-party activity are not associated with large increases in aggregate turnout (Mazmanian 1974).

From table 5.1, note also that in all cases except those of Wallace and Anderson, the third-party movements coincide with a decrease in the mobilization of both of the major parties. Moreover, in the cases of Wallace and Anderson, Republican mobilization increased only slightly while Democratic mobilization decreased more dramatically. Combined with the observation that third-party movements generally arise during elections in which there is little or no increase in overall turnout, this result again tempts the initial interpretation that the third-party supporters are coming from the previously mobilized ranks of the major parties.

Finally, the data in table 5.1 suggest that there may be something to the idea that third-party movements precipitate subsequent large-scale realignments. Note that, in all cases except those of Wallace and Anderson, the elections following those with third-party competitions experienced both an increase in total mobilization as well as an increase in the mobilization of both of the major parties. Again, in the cases of Wallace and Anderson, the Democratic party continued to suffer a decline of mobilization, but the Republican party increased its mobilization markedly. The problem with interpreting these results is that it is difficult, at this stage, to say whether the third-party supporters are moving to support one or both of the major parties in combination with an increase in new voter activity, or whether the third-party supporters become disenchanted with their party's loss and subsequently decline to vote at all in the next election. The latter interpretation would require that all or most of the increase in mobilization following the third-party activity would be due to new voter activity. If, however, at least one of the major parties moves to adopt some of the policy positions held previously by the third parties, a suggestion made by Mazmanian (1974), it is likely that many of the third-party supporters would shift their support to one of the accommodating parties. Nonetheless, these results suggest that there is the potential for two types of realigning processes sparked by third-party movements. The first is that partisan switching is involved from a major party to a third party and then back to a (potentially different) major party. The second is that a realignment characterized by large-scale new voter activity is common to periods following third-party activity. These questions are explored more thoroughly in the next section.

The Competitions

My analysis of third-party competitions utilizes a formal model very similar to that used in chapter 4 for the 1928–36 realignment. The primary difference is that there is now an equation characterizing longitudinal change in third-party support as a function of competition with the two major parties. Also, for economy, change in the nonvoting population is now expressed in terms of change in the identity $N = (1 - R - D - L)$, where R and D represent the proportions of the eligibles supporting the Republican and Democratic parties, respectively, and L represents the proportion of the eligibles supporting the third party. The entire system is now

$$dR/dt = D(q - [bR]) + N(s + [wR]) + L(y + [cR]) + j; \qquad (5.1)$$

$$dD/dt = R(f + [bD]) + N(m + [aD]) + L(g + [vD]) + k; \qquad (5.2)$$

$$dL/dt = D(x - [vL]) + R(e - [cL]) + N(u - [zL]) + p; \qquad (5.3)$$

$$N = (1 - R - D - L). \qquad (5.4)$$

Since the system is so similar to the system developed for competition between two parties, the current discussion proceeds directly to the analysis of the estimations of the system. As with the dynamic system developed earlier, note that there are both social and uniform components to the change between the parties and the nonvoting population. Moreover, the system is estimated both nationally and within conditioned environments. Here, the conditioning environments are urbanization (again, a population density measure is used) and farm activity (the proportion of county acreage used in farming). The estimates of the entire system are presented in the appendix to this chapter as tables A5.1 through A5.15.

The analysis of the system with regard to each of the third-party movements is organized in terms of some of the effects of the third parties on the major parties rather than chronologically. I begin with a case in which the third party simply splits the vote of only one of the major parties (Roosevelt). This is done to ease the presentation of subsequent results for the other third-party movements, since clear expectations can be advanced for this case. The analysis then turns to a case in which the third-party activity coincides with a minor realignment between the major parties (Anderson). These cases are placed back-to-back because they are similar in their initial setting (i.e., two Republicans splitting from their party) but different in the types of voters that they attract. To show the variety in the possible mass dynamics for third-party movements, the next case is one in which a very complex set of dynamics affected the voter movements between all three parties (La Follette). This is followed by an analysis of two cases in which one of the major parties positioned itself to absorb the third-party supporters (Weaver and Wallace).

The Party Cracker: A Third Party Divides
One Major Party

I begin with a case for which our expectations are relatively straightforward: Theodore Roosevelt's candidacy for the presidency in 1912. In this case, the historical record would strongly suggest that Roosevelt and Taft split the

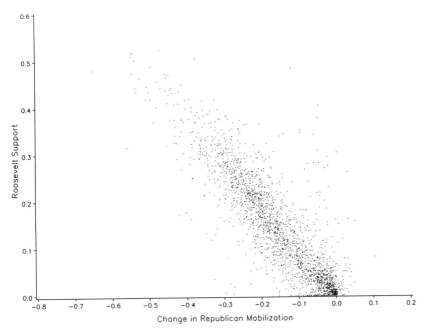

Fig. 5.1. Roosevelt's support and change in Republican mobilization as a proportion of total eligibles, 1908–12

Republican vote, thus allowing the Democratic candidate, Woodrow Wilson, to win the election. Thus, it is likely that most of the former Republicans who supported Roosevelt in 1912 returned to support the Republican nominee in 1916. An examination of some of the data help to reinforce this expectation.

Figure 5.1 is a scatterplot portraying change in Republican mobilization between 1908 and 1912 on the horizontal axis and Roosevelt's mobilized support on the vertical axis. Each dot on the figure represents a county. Note that there is a very clear relationship between a decline in Republican support during the 1908–12 period and Roosevelt mobilization in 1912. Figure 5.2 is a similar portrayal, but for the period from 1912 to 1916. Note from figure 5.2 that Republican mobilization increased dramatically in the later period in areas where Roosevelt mobilization was high. In both figures, the relationship between Roosevelt mobilization and changes in Republican mobilization appears very clear and in the expected directions.

In terms of the connection between the mobilization of new voters and Roosevelt's support, there appears to be no clear pattern. Figure 5.3 presents a scatterplot for these data with respect to change in the nonvoting population. If many new voters supported Roosevelt in 1912, the expectation would be an increase in total mobilization in areas with high levels of Roosevelt support. In figure 5.3, the horizontal axis represents change in the nonvoting popula-

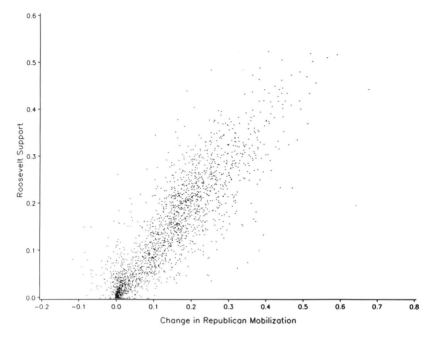

Fig. 5.2. Roosevelt's support and change in Republican mobilization as a proportion of total eligibles, 1912–16

tion. A positive value indicates that there was an increase in total mobilization in those areas. A negative value indicates a decrease in mobilization. Note that, while some counties seem to have experienced an increase in mobilization together with a high level of support for Roosevelt, no clear national pattern exists. These results, together with those shown in figures 5.1 and 5.2, suggest that most of Roosevelt's support in 1912 came from disaffected Republicans, not new voters. Nonetheless, these results merely establish our expectations with regard to the formal model that is the center of this analysis.

In fact, the results of the estimations of the dynamic system reinforce the interpretation of the scatterplots with regard to Roosevelt's support. Figure 5.4 presents a phase diagram that is comparable to those used in chapter 4 concerning the 1928–36 realignment. This phase diagram characterizes change in Republican mobilization and support for Roosevelt between 1908 and 1916. National, urban, and farm area trajectories are presented in the figure. What is so interesting about this figure is that there appears to have been very little difference in the mobilization patterns between urban and farm areas. Indeed, the national pattern of decreased Republican support between 1908 and 1912 combined with Roosevelt mobilization is a pattern that was not largely affected by the contextual setting. Moreover, the rebound in Republi-

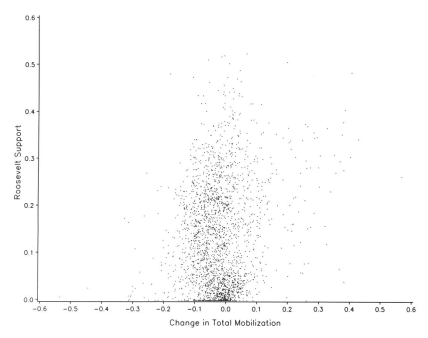

Fig. 5.3. Roosevelt's support and change in total mobilization as a proportion of total eligibles, 1908–12

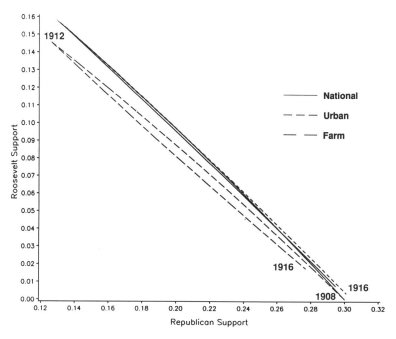

Fig. 5.4. Roosevelt-Republican trade-offs as a proportion of total eligibles, 1908–16

can strength following the 1912 election seems to have been a consistent pattern across the country. Yet perhaps the most interesting aspect of these results is that the yo-yo pattern of Republican and third-party support appears atypical of other third-party competitions, as will be seen in the next analysis.

However, before turning to the other third-party elections, it is useful to show the relatively weak relationship between the change in Democratic mobilization between 1908 and 1916 and Roosevelt's support. Figure 5.5 presents the phase diagram of these Democratic and Roosevelt mobilization trade-offs. Note that, nationally and in urban areas, there appears to have been a very slight decrease in Democratic mobilization between 1908 and 1912 that occurred simultaneously with the appearance of Roosevelt's support in 1912. There seems to have been a slightly larger relationship between Democratic mobilization loss and increased Roosevelt support in farm areas, as can be seen by the relatively larger diagonal tilt of the early farm trajectory. This indicates that Roosevelt may have attracted some previously Democratic voters living in farm areas, but the difference between farm and urban areas

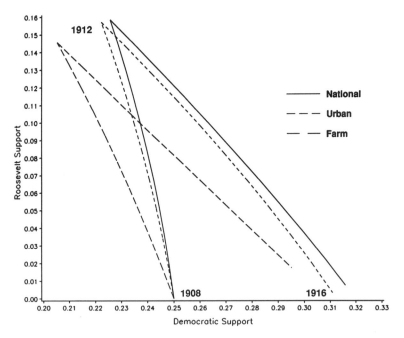

Fig. 5.5. Roosevelt-Democratic trade-offs as a proportion of total eligibles, 1908–16

does not appear to be great. These results strongly suggest that most of Roosevelt's 1912 support came at the expense of the Republican party with very little impact on the Democrats. The large increase in Democratic mobilization that occurred following the 1912 election (indicated by the diagonal tilt of the later trajectories) suggests that many of the former Democrats who supported Roosevelt in 1912 (admittedly few in total numbers) returned to the Democratic party in 1916 together with more substantial numbers of new voters as well. The value of the phase diagrams over the scatterplots is that the trajectories of the phase diagrams are computed while simultaneously controlling for all other partisan and nonvoter movements.

Cracking with a Shift: A Third Party and a Minor Realignment

A case in which third-party activity coincides with a group's shift of support from one of the major parties to another is that of John Anderson's candidacy in 1980. On the surface at least, it would seem that John Anderson threatened the Republican party as much as the Democratic party. On one hand, John Anderson was a Republican. On the other hand, he held generally moderate views that seemed closer to those of Jimmy Carter than those of Ronald Reagan. The setting of this third-party movement is not all that different from that surrounding the candidacy of Theodore Roosevelt. In both cases, a Republican with a generally progressive ideological perspective split from the choice of his party and set up an independent movement. However, the outcome in terms of the mass partisan dynamics could not have been more different.

Figure 5.6 contains a phase diagram showing the mobilization trade-offs between Anderson support and that of the Republican party for the 1976–84 period. Note the generally vertical direction of the urban and national trajectories between 1976 and 1980. This indicates that Republican mobilization was not negatively affected by the Anderson third-party movement in urban areas or nationally. However, in farm areas, Republican mobilization actually increased in areas that also experienced some Anderson support (although Anderson's overall support was lower in those areas). This adds further support to the idea that Anderson's candidacy, despite his Republican credentials, had little negative impact on the Republican party's ability to mobilize supporters. However, it is not yet clear whether Anderson's supporters tended to vote for Ronald Reagan in 1984, since the later increase in Republican mobilization may have come from new voters.

The phase diagram presented in figure 5.7 helps in interpreting the results for the Anderson-Republican mobilization trade-offs. Note that, in the national, urban, and farm area trajectories of figure 5.7, there was a dramatic decline in Democratic support that coincided with mobilization for the Ander-

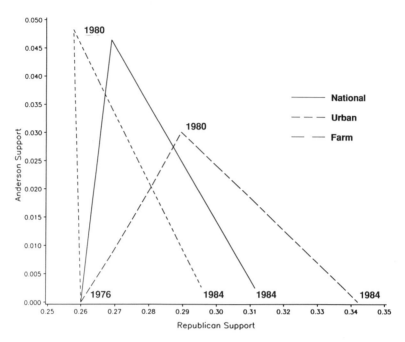

Fig. 5.6. Anderson-Republican trade-offs as a proportion of total eligibles, 1976–84

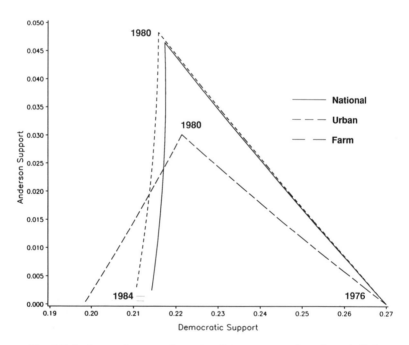

Fig. 5.7. Anderson-Democratic trade-offs as a proportion of total eligibles, 1976–84

son candidacy between 1976 and 1980. But also note that Anderson's support was lower in farm areas than in urban areas, and, after the 1980 election, farm areas experienced a further decrease in Democratic mobilization. These results, considered together with those shown in figure 5.6, strongly suggest that Anderson attracted mostly former urban, Democratic supporters in 1980. This finding corresponds with analyses of survey data for that election (e.g., Rosenstone, Behr, and Lazarus 1984, 119). In 1984, many of Anderson's supporters may have returned to the Democratic party, but not in sufficient numbers to increase overall Democratic mobilization. Indeed, in farm areas, Democratic mobilization continued to decline after 1980.

Perhaps the most interesting aspect of the Anderson candidacy is the way his movement coincided with change in the ranks of the nonvoters. Figure 5.8 contains the national urban and farm area trajectories for the Anderson and nonvoter trade-offs. First, examine the trajectory for the nation. Note that the average nonvoter activity did not change much between the entire 1976–84 period. However, the comparison of the urban and farm trajectories shows what underlies this apparent nonactivity. Between 1976 and 1980, Anderson support coincided with a decrease in the nonvoting population in farm areas (thus, there were significant numbers of new voters in those areas) and an increase in the nonvoting population in urban areas (i.e., urban areas experi-

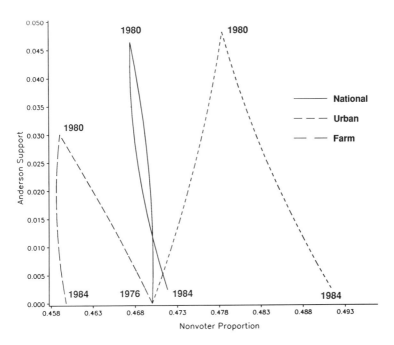

Fig. 5.8. Anderson-nonvoter trade-offs as a proportion of total eligibles, 1976–84

enced a degree of demobilization in correspondence with increases in Anderson support). Although Anderson's support in farm areas was lower than in urban areas, these data suggest that some new voters in farm areas in 1980 may have supported Anderson. The general demobilization in urban areas combined with substantial support for Anderson in these areas supports the suggestion made by Rosenstone, Behr, and Lazarus (1984) as well as others that third parties rise when there is general voter discontent with the major parties. Following the 1980 election, it appears that the new voters in the farm areas did continue to participate in the 1984 election. This is indicated by the vertical nature of the trajectory between 1980 and 1984. However, urban areas continued to experience an increased level of demobilization. Further farm area gains for the Republicans seem to have come at the expense of the Democratic party.

In summary, in 1980, Anderson seems to have gotten his support predominantly from previous Democratic supporters in urban areas of the country as well as some new voters in farm areas only. These data suggest that some 1980 farm area Democrats may have shifted their support to the Republican party in 1984. It is not yet clear whether this shift occurred together with Anderson's small new voter farm area support. Nonetheless, Anderson's candidacy does seem to have coincided longitudinally with a minor partisan shift of farm voters from the Democratic party to the Republican party. This finding corresponds with the general notion that third-party activity occurs during times of potential realignment, even though the realigning activity may be small. The analysis of the partial derivatives of the model that is presented later in this section helps to clear up the current ambiguities of how Anderson's urban and farm voters tended to vote in 1984.

The Labyrinth: Contextually Complex Mass Dynamics

Robert La Follette's third-party movement in 1924 is an interesting case in which the third party seems to have drawn voters from both of the major parties. Subsequent to the 1924 election, some of La Follette's supporters shifted back to their previous support for each of the major parties. However, other supporters may have switched major parties, and yet others may have demobilized completely. Thus, the election of 1924 can be seen as a deviating election for those voters who later returned to their former major party. Yet the election can also be characterized as a realigning election for those voters who switched from one of the major parties to the other, where La Follette's movement acted as a catalyst for that realignment. Those voters who demobilized completely seem to have been caught in the middle of the changing times. The analysis will help illustrate these complexities.

Senator La Follette, a Republican, raised issues that were not far removed from those of the earlier progressive Republican, Theodore Roosevelt.

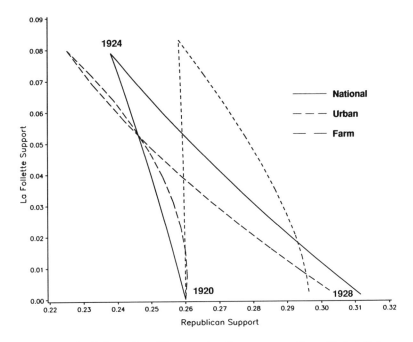

Fig. 5.9. La Follette-Republican trade-offs as a proportion of total eligibles, 1920–28

However, La Follette's stance in support of farmers ideologically reached back beyond Roosevelt to the Populist movement of the 1890s. As would be expected, and as my analysis demonstrates, much of La Follette's support came from farm areas.

Figure 5.9 presents the phase diagram of mobilization trade-offs between La Follette's support in 1924 and Republican mobilization between 1920 and 1928. Beginning with the earlier 1920–24 period, note that there was virtually no change in Republican mobilization in urban areas that occurred concomitantly with an increase in La Follette support. However, in farm areas, there was a large drop in Republican mobilization that coincided with mobilization for La Follette. This indicates that La Follette did attract some previously Republican support from farm areas. Note also that, after the 1924 election, Republican mobilization increased in both urban and farm areas, with this later farm area mobilization more than making up for the earlier losses to La Follette. In combination, these results suggest that La Follette's farm-based Republican support returned (in large part) to the Republican party in 1928, with additional Republican mobilization coming from some of the many new voters who appeared in both parties in that later election.

Figure 5.10 suggests a somewhat different picture for the Democratic

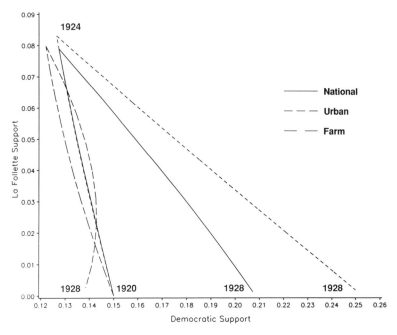

Fig. 5.10. La Follette-Democratic trade-offs as a proportion of total eligibles, 1920–28

and La Follette interaction. Figure 5.10 presents the mobilization trade-offs for La Follette support and Democratic mobilization between 1920 and 1928. Begin the inspection of this figure with the trajectory for the farm areas. Note that, in farm areas, there was a moderate decline in Democratic mobilization that coincided with La Follette's 1924 gains, suggesting some Democratic farm area support for La Follette. However, note that, after the 1924 election, the trajectory yo-yo's back toward the starting point and ends up indicating a level of Democratic mobilization that does not quite make up for all of the earlier losses. At first glance, it appears that some of these previously Democratic La Follette farm area supporters may have demobilized completely after the 1924 election.

These results for La Follette's Democratic farm area support are more understandable when viewed from the perspective of the urban voters. After the 1924 election, the greatest gains in Democratic support came from urban areas. This can be seen from the dramatic diagonal trajectory for urban areas between 1924 and 1928 in figure 5.10. Apparently Al Smith, the Democratic presidential nominee, was not as well received by farm area Democrats as he was by urban area voters (a point suggested repeatedly in the historical literature). One can hypothesize that, in large part, the problem with Al Smith in the farming areas was one of religion. Populism had its base in the Protestant and rural farming areas. Al Smith's Catholicism probably was poorly received in these areas, and it is unlikely that those Protestant rural farmers appreciated his appeal to the urban immigrant vote.

What is so interesting from the perspective of this analysis is the behavioral difference between the Republican and Democratic farm-based supporters of La Follette and, in particular, the relatively constant level of mobilization of farm-based Democrats during a period of increased national mobilization. While there has been some evidence that some of the Republican farm supporters of La Follette later switched to the Democratic party in particular areas (see, especially, McRae and Meldrum 1960), it does not appear to have been the dominant characteristic of these mass dynamics.

This relationship between La Follette's 1924 support and the relatively constant level of Democratic mobilization that occurred in farming areas in 1928 is quite dramatic from the perspective of changes in total mobilization. From table 5.1 it is clear that the total vote increased from 1924 to 1928 from 45.0 to 52.0 percent of the eligible electorate, an approximate increase of 7.0 percent. However, if one breaks this down for urban and farm areas, the urban increase during that same time period is approximately 9.0 percent, whereas in farm areas the total vote increased only 1.5 percent. On one hand, it is very likely that the Democratic party gained many farmers who supported La Follette in 1924 in selected areas of the nation (a point emphasized in my analysis of the partial derivatives of the estimated system). In general, change in Democratic mobilization between 1924 and 1928 in those areas that supported La Follette in 1924 is positive. However, these gains had a minimal impact on total Democratic mobilization because of the relatively dramatic increases in mobilization that occurred in urban areas, and the appearance of some Democratic (and probably mostly nonimmigrant Protestant) demobilization in other farming and rural areas that had not shown enthusiastic support for La Follette.

It seems that, with regard to La Follette's 1924 third-party movement, the most accurate generalization that may be extricated from this case is that third-party movements can potentially yield very complicated voter dynamics on the mass level in which all sorts of activity takes place, especially during periods characterized by overall increases in voter mobilization across all parties. It is an example of third-party dynamics characterized by large-scale voter volatility.

This analysis of La Follette's movement encourages some final comments regarding the evidence presented in chapter 4 on the 1928–36 realignment. It is clear that, by 1924, many farmers were discontented with the Republicans. La Follette's movement clearly indicates that many of these voters were looking for a partisan vehicle of escape. That is, their previously patterned electoral behavior was ready to break; they were weakly institution-alized. It seems clear that these farmers were looking for help after 1924, but neither party was willing to offer it in 1928. What happened in 1932 was their answer. It was not just the depression that forced so many farmers to support Franklin D. Roosevelt. The depression certainly had its impact. But it had its impact on many farm voters who were waiting to make a run for it for the better part of a decade. This helps explain why the 1932 part of the realign-ment was so different in character than that which happened in 1936. The 1932 Republican farm revolt was a partisan crisis that was simply waiting to happen. Roosevelt's appeal to farm supporters was a natural appeal for that setting. But the 1936 election was the election that truly broke from historical precedents, embracing millions of urban, immigrant, and worker new voters. It was that election that so completely changed the ideological character of Democratic party politics in the years ahead.

Sponges: A Major Party Absorbs the Third Party

This section presents a discussion of two examples in which a major party positioned itself to maximize the absorption of the third-party supporters. I begin with James B. Weaver's candidacy in 1892 and conclude with an analy-sis of the 1968 election and George C. Wallace.

In 1892, the People's party supported a number of issues that were not yet enthusiastically supported by either of the major parties. These issues were particularly important to farmers, who were hit by low prices for their products, high transportation costs in getting their products to the major cities, and a changing national political climate that was beginning to favor increas-ingly urban industrial interests over rural agricultural interests. The Republi-can party was well positioned to support those growing northern and eastern industrial interests. On the other hand, the Democratic party depended more heavily for its support on southern, midwestern, and generally agricultural areas. Thus, from the perspective of the times, it is understandable that the Democratic party would more easily be able to position its ideological stance to absorb a constituency that was in its own back yard, so to speak.

My analysis clearly confirms our expectations that the mass dynamics of the Populist third-party movement reflect voter activity that was substantially different for farming areas when compared with urban areas. Figure 5.11 is a phase diagram characterizing the Populist and Democratic party trade-offs from 1888 to 1896. Note that, with all of the trajectories between 1888 and 1892, there is some moderate decline in Democratic mobilization combined with substantial Populist mobilization. This suggests that Populists received only a portion of their support from former Democratic supporters. Note, however, that the trajectories for the farm areas differ dramatically from the national average and the urban trajectories between 1892 and 1896. In the later period, it seems that most of those former Democratic farmers who

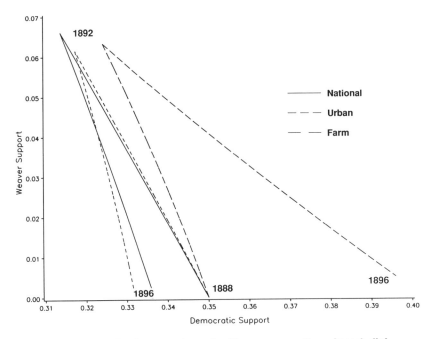

Fig. 5.11. Populist-Democratic trade-offs as a proportion of total eligibles, 1888–96

defected to the Populist party in 1892 returned to the Democratic party and joined with a large wave of farm area new voters following the joint nomination of William Jennings Bryan in 1896. However, Democratic voters in urban areas did not behave accordingly. Only a portion of the urban voters who abandoned the Democratic party in 1892 returned to the party by 1896, as can be seen by the generally yo-yo characteristic of the urban trajectory over the entire 1888–96 period.

Figure 5.12 fills in the picture for the mobilization of new voters during the 1888–96 period. Figure 5.12 shows the Populist and nonvoter mobilization trade-offs for this period. It is clear from table 5.1 that total mobilization decreased in 1892. This is reflected in figure 5.12 by the slight diagonal tilt to the right of the national trajectory between 1888 and 1892. The national trajectory is generally paralleled by the urban trajectory. However, note that the trajectory for the farm areas tilts slightly in the opposite direction (i.e., in the direction of a smaller nonvoting population—indicating a modest increase in turnout in farm areas that coincides with the Populist support of 1892). Yet the largest increase in turnout occurs in farm areas after 1892. This is indicated by the dramatic diagonal of the trajectory for these areas between 1892 and 1896.

In combination, this evidence indicates that some new voters supported

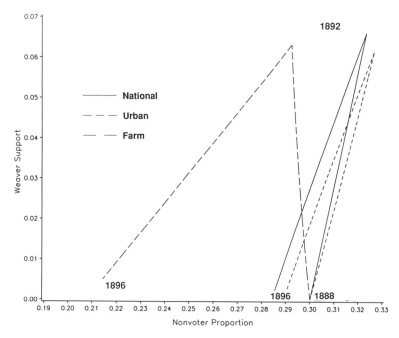

Fig. 5.12. Populist-nonvoter trade-offs as a proportion of total eligibles, 1888–96

the Populists in 1892 in farm areas. Moreover, the evidence shown in figures 5.11 and 5.12 tells us that many of these 1892 farm area Populist supporters, as well as many additional farm area new voters, supported William Jennings Bryan in 1896. In a very real sense, the People's party was absorbed by the Democratic party in 1896. However, the absorbtion was not just of those rural voters who supported the People's party in 1892. The absorbtion included many sympathetic farm voters who had not yet turned out to vote. Thus, the absorbtion had two components: (1) the previously mobilized Populists, and (2) the sympathetic but not yet mobilized farm-based Populist supporters. Given this dynamic, it is not surprising that the People's party could not again mount an effective national challenge following the 1896 election.

A second example in which one of the major parties was particularly well suited to absorb the third-party movement is the case of George Wallace's run for the presidency in 1968. The Democratic party was not in a position to attract the supporters who were so enthusiastically supportive of Wallace in 1968. In particular, President Johnson's embrace of the civil rights movement was the most obvious barrier between the party and southern, white voters. Moreover, the southern states were in the middle of a long period in which the

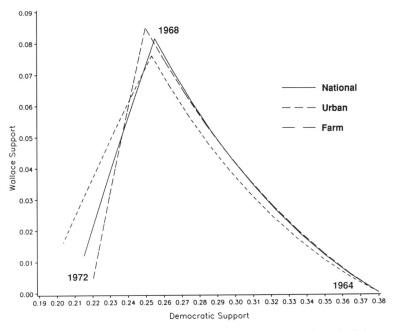

Fig. 5.13. Wallace-Democratic trade-offs as a proportion of total eligibles, 1964–72

Republican party was making strong gains in terms of presidential voting (see Asher 1988). Yet the analysis of this situation is potentially complex since Republican party mobilization increased consistently during the 1964–72 period (as seen in table 5.1).

I begin by examining the mobilization trade-offs between the Wallace movement and the Democratic party that are shown in figure 5.13. There are two basic points to be drawn from this figure. The first is that there is no appreciable difference between urban and farm areas in the effect of Wallace mobilization on Democratic demobilization during the entire 1964–72 period. This is particularly true of the early, 1964–68 period. This suggests that Wallace's movement was not the cause of the loss of support for the Democrats, since it is unlikely that his movement would not leave differential traces on the Democratic mobilization in such diverse areas. (Indeed, a visual examination of a scatterplot of Wallace support over change in Democratic mobilization shows no apparent relationship between the two.)

The situation is different with regard to Republican mobilization. Figure 5.14 is the phase diagram of the vote mobilization trade-offs between the Wallace movement and the Republican party. Note that, in the early, 1964–68 period, Republican mobilization increased substantially in farm areas despite

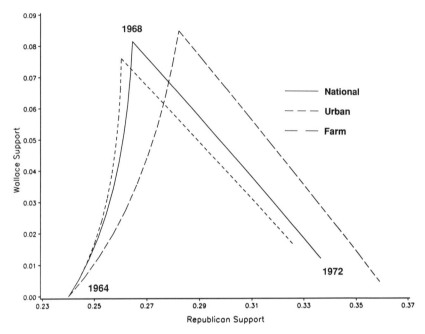

Fig. 5.14. Wallace-Republican trade-offs as a proportion of total eligibles, 1964–72

a strong showing for Wallace. This increase in Republican mobilization sur-passed that which occurred in urban areas. However, note that, after 1968, further increases in Republican mobilization tended not to differ according to social context, as can be seen by the relatively parallel nature of these urban and farm area trajectories. However, due to the consistent increases in Republican mobilization throughout the entire period, these results do not yet tell us whether Wallace's farm support hindered what would have been even greater Republican gains in these areas in 1968. In this case, I will wait to pursue this matter until I examine the partial derivatives of the entire system.

To summarize these results with regard to Wallace, at this point it can be said that Wallace's movement did not have a differential influence on Demo-cratic mobilization with respect to social context (i.e., urban and farm). This suggests that Democratic mobilization was somewhat independent of Wallace mobilization. Yet Republican mobilization was affected differentially by the Wallace movement. In particular, farm areas experienced both substantial levels of Republican mobilization as well as Wallace support. Whether the Republicans would have experienced even higher levels of mobilization in 1968 in the absence of a Wallace candidacy is not yet clear.

A Look at the Partials

The phase diagram analyses are particularly useful in depicting how partisan vote mobilization in particular areas, as defined by certain social contexts, changes in terms of the aggregate trade-offs between parties. However, there is an additional means of verifying the analyses that involves examining the parts of the system that explicitly specify change in one party as coming from change in another. While the many parts add up to a characterization of the total aggregate change for each party, the individual parts can sometimes be useful in resolving ambiguities as well as confirming results.

These parts are the partial derivatives of the system. They are computed from the original equations, equations 5.1, 5.2, and 5.3, and they help determine whether the system detects a transfer of mobilization from one party to another. For example, the equation that expresses longitudinal change for the Democratic party (eq. 5.2) is composed of inputs from the Republican party, the third party, and nonvoters. The inputs from the third party would be the partial derivative of that equation with respect to third-party support. Numerically, this is the quantity $(g + [vD])$. If the partial derivative is negative, this indicates that the Democratic party lost support to the third party in areas where there was third-party mobilization. If the partial derivative is positive, the interpretation is that the Democratic party gained support in these areas.

The partial derivatives of the equations characterizing over-time change in the Democratic and Republican parties with respect to change in the third-party movements are presented for all five third-party movements in table 5.2. The table is divided into two periods. The first is the period preceding the third-party movement, while the second is the period following the election with third-party participation. For example, period 1 for the Populists would be from 1888 to 1892, whereas period 2 would be from 1892 to 1896. The partial derivative of the equation for Democratic change with respect to third-party mobilization is labeled $\partial D / \partial L$. The corresponding partial derivative for Republican change with respect to third-party mobilization is labeled $\partial D / \partial L$, which is equal to the quantity $(y + [cR])$.

The interpretation of the partial derivatives found in the table is quite simple if one limits oneself to a discussion of the sign of each value. The magnitudes of the partials are difficult to compare across different third-party movements since their calculation is based on different values of support for the Republicans and the Democrats at the time of the third-party movements. Indeed, since the partial derivatives change at different points along each trajectory due to the changing values of party support, the partials in table 5.2 are actually averages for each period. Nonetheless, some magnitude comparisons between the Democratic and Republican parties are heuristically useful when they are limited to the case of one third party.

Additional caution must be used when examining the magnitudes of the

TABLE 5.2. Averaged Partial Derivatives of the System with Respect to Third-Party Mobilization

	Period One			Period Two		
	National	Urban	Farm	National	Urban	Farm
Populist						
$\partial D/\partial L$	−.015[a]	−.014	−.016	.069[a]	.071	.020
$\partial R/\partial L$	.003	.010	.025	.010[b]	.008	.041
Roosevelt						
$\partial D/\partial L$	−.007[a]	−.016[c]	−.018	.135[a]	.200[a]	−.112[c]
$\partial R/\partial L$	−.027[a]	−.028	−.025	.165[a]	.214[c]	.085[c]
La Follette						
$\partial D/\partial L$	.020[c]	.033[c]	.139[c]	.899[a]	.883[a]	.999[c]
$\partial R/\partial L$	−.124[a]	−.011[a]	−.988[a]	.366[a]	.236[c]	.381[b]
Wallace						
$\partial D/\partial L$	.122[a]	.122	.122	.027[a]	.028	.025
$\partial R/\partial L$	−.023[a]	−.023	−.023	.084[a]	.085	.081
Anderson						
$\partial D/\partial L$	−.002	.017[c]	−.004	.214[a]	.233[a]	.186[a]
$\partial R/\partial L$	.005[c]	−.001	.003	.003[a]	.003	−.001[b]

Note: The partials are computed from the quantities $\partial D/\partial L = g + (vD)$ and $\partial R/\partial L = y + (cR)$.
[a] Both the uniform (g and y) and social (v and c) parameters are significant at $p < .05$.
[b] The social parameters are significant at $p < .10$.
[c] The uniform parameters are significant at $p < .10$.

partials however. This is because not all of the partials are computed from parameter estimates that are statistically discernable from zero. Each partial in table 5.2 is computed using two parameter estimates (one for the social and one for the uniform components of the model). The significance of the estimates is indicated in the table. If only one estimate passes the significance test, then the partial should probably be examined with some degree of caution. Partials without an indicated level of significance are computed from parameter estimates that did not pass the test of significance. One final note on the matter of significance is that the significance tests for the partials listed under the columns labeled "national" test the parameter estimates for difference from zero. The tests for the partials listed under the columns labeled "urban" and "farm" test the parameter estimates in terms of their difference from the national-level estimates. The usefulness of this distinction will become clear as the data in the table are discussed.

Since, in this section of the analysis, I am primarily concerned with enhancing the interpretations of the evidence obtained using the phase diagrams, I can proceed chronologically in the discussion of table 5.2. Thus, I begin with the Populists, using the same section labels as those used earlier to help give structure to the discussion.

Sponges

For the Populists in period one, note that the national-level partial derivative for Democratic change with respect to Populist mobilization is negative. The urban and farm area partials are also negative and of similar magnitude. The urban and farm area partials are computed from parameter estimates that did not significantly differ from the national-level estimates. This does not mean that there was absolutely no difference in Populist mobilization from the Democrats between the urban and farm areas. It is just that this part of the model could not distinguish these differences from the data in terms of mobilization specifically from the Democrats to the Populists with a high level of statistical certainty. In this case, it suggests that the differences between urban and farm areas in terms of vote switching from the Democratic party to the People's party was not large. This conforms to the phase diagram analysis of the early period (fig. 5.11).

The negative sign for the national-level partial for the Populists confirms my earlier statement that early Democratic mobilization did suffer somewhat from the Populist movement. The positive partials for Republican change (computed using parameter estimates that do not pass the test of statistical significance) suggest that the Republicans were insulated from major vote-switching losses due to the Populist mobilization. Both the negative partials, indicating some Democratic vote switching, and the positive (and insignificant) partials, indicating the absence of Republican vote switching, are expected results given the earlier analysis, and these results correspond with historical interpretations of the Populist movement. The positive (and computed from significant parameter estimates) national-level partial for the Democratic party for the later period suggests that the Democratic party did gain (from vote switching) in areas that experienced Populist mobilization in 1892. The relatively lower national-level Republican party partial (which is also plagued with some significance problems) suggests that the Republican party did not gain as heavily from the previous Populist mobilization due to vote switching, an entirely expected result. Interestingly, what gains the Republican party did make from vote switching from the Populists appear to have been in areas with a strong Republican presence (indicated by the significance of the estimate for the social component of the partial). (The slightly larger magnitude Republican partial for farm areas was computed from parameter estimates that did not significantly differ from the national-level estimates and, thus, is of little concern here.)

The Party Cracker

The partials with regard to Theodore Roosevelt's 1912 campaign are negative for both the Republican and Democratic parties. However, the larger magnitude partials are associated with the Republican party, as expected (reinforcing the obvious, that Roosevelt pulled most of his supporters from the Republican party). The mostly positive and significant partials for the second period indicate that Roosevelt's supporters tended to switch back to the Republican party. However, the significant and positive partials for the Democratic party, both nationally and for urban areas, suggest that some of Roosevelt's supporters may have switched to support the generally progressive Democratic incumbent, Woodrow Wilson, in 1916. This suggests a realigning movement of some voters from the Republican party to the Democratic party due to ideological reasons, where Roosevelt's third-party candidacy four years earlier seems to have acted as the catalyst for the change.

The Labyrinth

The partials for La Follette's third-party movement are of particular interest since they reveal an aspect of realignment that was not clear from the phase diagrams. Note that the partials for the Republican party in period one are all negative, and that magnitude differences suggest that the Republican party lost the greatest amount of its support to La Follette in farm areas. The partials for the Democratic party in period one are all positive, indicating that La Follette had much less impact on Democratic mobilization than Republican mobilization.

The most interesting aspect of the partials for La Follette's third-party movement is seen when one compares the results for period one to the results for period two. In period two, both Republican and Democratic partials are positive and generally significant. However, the larger partials are associated with the Democratic party. This confirms results reported elsewhere (McRae and Meldrum 1960) that suggest that La Follette's candidacy did spark a minor realignment of some voters from the Republican party to the Democratic party. Moreover, in farm areas, it seems as though the realignment took place uniformly (rather than in areas where the Democratic party had previous strength). However, when the Republicans regained some of the farm area La Follette supporters, they did so mainly in areas in which they were already strong (indicated by the significance of the social component of the Republican partial). These results are particularly enlightening since there was also a lower level of mobilization for the Democratic ranks in some farm areas, which was shown in the phase diagrams. (Indeed, additional analyses not presented here suggest that a substantial number of farm area—and probably Protestant—Democrats switched to the Republican party in 1928. This occurred mostly in areas in which the Republican party already had a significant presence.) Thus, while some La Follette farm area supporters went Democratic in 1928, some other farm area voters switched from the Democratic party to the Republican party, thereby diminishing overall Democratic mobilization gains in farm areas. Moreover, the positive partials for the Republican party in period two suggest that the Republican party did manage to retrieve a good number of their "lost" La Follette supporters as well.

Sponges

George Wallace's impact on the mass electoral dynamics of the 1960s and early 1970s is less complicated than that of La Follette. For the first period, all of the Republican partials are negative, whereas all of the Democratic partials are positive. Moreover, there seems to be little difference between urban and farm areas with regard to Wallace's candidacy. The results indicate that George Wallace modestly hindered Republican mobilization more than Democratic mobilization. After the 1968 election, the large national-level positive partial for the Republican party indicates that most of Wallace's supporters embraced Nixon's 1972 reelection bid.

Cracking with a Shift

The Anderson results for period one seem more difficult to interpret than those for Wallace. When comparing the results between parties, the Anderson partials oscillate in sign and are computed with (at most) only one significant parameter estimate. It seems that the data for Anderson in period one do not lend themselves well to the model's ability to sort out a consistent pattern. The phase diagram analysis that accounts for total mobilization trade-offs between parties (showing vote mobilization shifts coming from all parts of the model, including the intercept term) is probably the most fruitful one that these data will allow for this initial period. However, the partials for the second period do show a pattern that does clear up an ambiguity in our earlier analysis. In the second period, the partials for the Democratic party are substantially larger (and positive) than those for the Republican party. This indicates that Anderson's 1980 supporters tended to shift their support to the Democratic party. Certainly, at least some of these former Anderson supporters were drawn to the Democratic party for ideological reasons. Yet, perhaps others were influenced by his endorsement of the Democratic candidate, Walter Mondale, in 1984. These results parallel those reported using large-sample survey data in the *New York Times* after the 1984 election (Nov. 8, 1984). From that report, 67 percent of the former Anderson supporters voted for Mondale in 1984, and 29 percent voted for Reagan.

Some Insights Drawn from Survey Data

Two of the third-party competitions examined here (Wallace and Anderson) took place during times for which survey data are available. The analysis presented below relies on National Election Study data collected by the University of Michigan Center for Political Studies during the 1968 and 1980 campaigns.

In my analysis of these survey data, voters are separated with regard to their vote choice, and means for selected variables are computed for each group of voters. A test is then made to determine whether the means are statistically different for the group of third-party supporters and each group of major party supporters. The variables that are chosen for the analysis are selected with an eye toward revealing traces of deinstitutionalizing electoral politics among third-party supporters.[1]

The means of nine variables for Humphrey, Nixon, and Wallace supporters as measured following the 1968 presidential campaign are presented in table 5.3. The t-statistics that are presented in the table test the difference between paired means. For example, the first entries in the table correspond to the respondents' partisan identification. The partisan identification variable is measured using the traditional seven-point partisan identification scale: (1) strong Democrat, (2) weak Democrat, (3) Independent but leaning Democratic, (4) Independent, (5) Independent but leaning Republican, (6) weak Republican, and (7) strong Republican. The mean partisanship for Humphrey supporters is 1.94, and the mean partisanship for Wallace supporters is 3.18. The t-statistic testing the difference between these two means is -7.0, which (probabilistically) is highly significant, suggesting that the means are indeed statistically different. In short, Wallace supporters were more independent (and thus less Democratic) than Humphrey supporters. The comparable means for Nixon and Wallace supporters are presented on the right side of table 5.3. Reading these numbers in a corresponding fashion, Wallace supporters were more independent (and thus less Republican) than Nixon supporters. In short, Wallace supporters tended to be much more independent than the major party supporters. This result lends evidence to the idea that third parties tend to attract voters with relatively weaker partisan bonds, at least with respect to psychological commitments to the major parties.

Comparing the means across the other variables, Wallace supporters do not seem to be much different from the major party supporters with respect to the amount of information that they have about politics, nor with respect to the interest that they have in the campaign. But Wallace supporters are different from the major party supporters in terms of their feelings of efficacy with respect to the major parties as well as with respect to the nation's political leaders. This suggests that these third-party supporters base their support, in

---

1. The analysis of survey data presented here is kept methodologically simple—T-tests for the differences between means—since simplicity is all that is needed here and simplicity is heuristically superior to complexity in the absence of a need for greater complexity. More sophisticated analyses were conducted, however, including logistic regression with regard to vote choice. None of the more sophisticated strategies yielded additional substantive insight with regard to the questions pursued.

TABLE 5.3. Differences in Means between Wallace Supporters and Major Party Supporters for Selected Variables, 1968

Variable	Humphrey-Wallace Means		t	$p > |t|$	Nixon-Wallace Means		t	$p > |t|$
Party identification	H	1.94	−7.0	.0001	N	5.00	9.9	.0001
	W	3.18			W	3.18		
Information about	H	3.14	.73	.4685	N	3.23	1.50	.1364
politics	W	3.05			W	3.05		
Interest in politics	H	3.41	−.08	.9403	N	3.45	.30	.7623
	W	3.42			W	3.42		
Feeling of party	H	3.38	4.94	.0001	N	3.44	5.27	.0001
efficacy	W	2.35			W	2.35		
Feeling of leader	H	3.57	5.46	.0001	N	3.76	6.41	.0001
efficacy	W	2.43			W	2.43		
Respondent's class	H	2.69	1.07	.2881	N	3.21	3.76	.0002
	W	2.49			W	2.49		
Respondent's years	H	48	1.79	.0744	N	56	5.53	.0001
education	W	44			W	44		
Respondent's	H	21.6	.24	.8133	N	22.9	1.81	.0729
income (scaled)	W	21.4			W	21.4		
Age of Respondent	H	46	1.08	.2833	N	48	2.14	.0340
	W	44			W	44		

Note: All *t*-tests are conducted under the assumption of unequal variances between groups.

part, on their relative lack of faith and/or trust in the leadership or partisan political establishment.

Regarding socioeconomic influences, Wallace supporters had about the same class status as Democrats, but a lower class status than that of Republicans. Their levels of education were lower (on average) than either Democratic or Republican supporters. Wallace supporters in general were about as wealthy as Democratic supporters, and perhaps a bit less well-off than Republican supporters. Note that Wallace supporters did tend to be a bit younger than the major party supporters (on average), although the differences are less statistically robust with respect to Democratic supporters. Age is a variable that is of particular interest here since the expectation is that third-party supporters tend to be those voters who have the weakest institutional ties to the major parties. One indication of such a weakness would be relatively shorter voting histories, of which age would play a major contributing role. Yet age is only one contributor to the institutionalization process and, even then, an indirect contributor. Indeed, historically, many sectors of the American electorate have been underrepresented at the polls, regardless of individual ages. Nonetheless, the evidence presented in table 5.3 does lie in the expected direction with regard to age. On average, older individuals would be expected to have longer voting histories than their younger counterparts, and

TABLE 5.4. Differences in Means between Anderson Supporters and Major Party Supporters for Selected Variables, 1980

Variable		Carter-Anderson				Reagan-Anderson		
		Means	t	$p > |t|$		Means	t	$p > |t|$
Party identification	C	2.02	−8.5	.0001	R	5.00	6.48	.0001
	A	3.69			A	3.69		
Information about	C	4.56	−.67	.5059	R	4.65	−.02	.9812
politics	A	4.65			A	4.65		
Interest in politics	C	3.54	−.15	.8809	R	3.80	1.53	.1299
	A	3.57			A	3.57		
Feeling of party	C	2.54	−1.02	.3119	R	2.85	.26	.7930
efficacy	A	2.79			A	2.79		
Feeling of leader	C	2.95	−1.75	.0833	R	3.13	−1.04	.3000
efficacy	A	3.38			A	3.38		
Respondent's class	C	2.62	−6.53	.0001	R	3.29	−3.30	.0013
	A	3.94			A	3.94		
Respondent's	C	5.41	−7.03	.0001	R	6.42	−3.29	.0013
education	A	7.20			A	7.20		
(scaled)								
Respondent's	C	13.3	−4.34	.0001	R	15.8	−1.01	.3164
income (scaled)	A	16.5			A	16.5		
Age of Respondent	C	48	5.34	.0001	R	46	4.37	.0001
	A	38			A	38		

Note: All t-tests are conducted under the assumption of unequal variances between groups.

those older individuals should deviate from supporting one of the two major parties less often as a result.

Table 5.4 presents the means and their associated difference tests for the parties involved in the 1980 election. Comparisons are made between Carter and Anderson supporters as well as Reagan and Anderson supporters. Interestingly, many of the results in this table parallel those obtained from table 5.3 with regard to the 1968 election. Anderson supporters tended to be much more independent in their partisan identification than Carter or Reagan supporters. Moreover, they did not differ much from the major party supporters with respect to their levels of information or interest about politics. Thus, third-party supporters seem to be interested and informed independent voters.

Yet one difference that does exist between Anderson and Wallace supporters is that Anderson supporters did not consistently have significantly different feelings of efficacy toward either the major parties or political leaders in comparison with major party supporters. This is a bit of a surprise since much of the literature on third-party movements argues that third parties arise at times when voters feel particularly frustrated with the abilities of the major parties to deal effectively with current issues. The data in table 5.4 suggest, however, that such an explanation may be too simplistic. Anderson's movement may have tapped a potential for support that was more closely tied to disenchantment with President Carter himself rather than leaders of parties in general. Any incumbent president would have been extraordinarily unfortunate to be running in 1980. Interest rates were very high, inflation was escalating due to the increasing cost of foreign oil, and Americans were being held hostage in Iran. Anderson's candidacy may, thus, be an example of a particular type of third-party candidacy (and probably atypical of most other third-party movements) that prospers opportunistically due to the short-term misfortunes of a sitting president rather than as a result of a more profound emergence of a crosscutting issue or ideological divide.

Regarding socioeconomic matters, Anderson's supporters tended (on average) to have a higher class status than either Democratic or Republican supporters. Moreover, Anderson supporters tended to be better educated than the major party supporters. Only Anderson and Carter supporters were differentiated by income in a significant manner, however. These class, education, and income patterns differ in comparison with those associated with Wallace's support in 1968, suggesting that the socioeconomic patterns of third-party movements may be highly variable and idiosyncratic across elections. However, with respect to age, the finding presented here again supports the idea that third parties gather support in greater proportions from individuals with shorter voting histories, and thus weaker institutionalized partisan bonds. Anderson supporters tended to be (on average) eight to ten years younger than Reagan and Carter supporters, respectively.

Remarks

It is interesting to pull generalizations from the diverse array of dynamic patterns found here among the third-party electoral politics in the United States during the last hundred years. A few observations drawn from these analyses help in this regard.

My analyses clearly suggest that third-party movements do not always split the party with which the third-party candidate was previously affiliated. This observation leads to one of the most important generalizations that arise from this analysis of third parties. That is, the partisanship of the third-party candidate has no consistent impact on the mass dynamics of third-party support. Something other than the candidate's partisanship drives these voters' movements. Roosevelt did split the Republican party, but Anderson attracted mostly Democrats, and Wallace attracted mostly Republicans. Moreover, La Follette gained support from both Republicans and Democrats.

Thus, it seems that third-party politics involve issues that often cut across previous partisan lines. In this sense, third-party politics have the potential to act as catalysts for realignment in the classic sense (as characterized by Sundquist [1983]). Sometimes a third-party candidate splits from one of the major parties because he finds himself alienated from that party's political and social priorities. As in the case of Roosevelt and La Follette, this can sometimes mean that the candidate takes some of his issue-driven soulmates from his previous party as his electoral base. But on other occasions, the candidate leaves by himself, finding that his soulmates never resided with his former party. He finds his electoral base elsewhere, some from new voters, but more likely from the ranks of the other major party.

Another important conclusion to be drawn from these analyses is that third-party politics unambiguously have the potential to lead to realigning politics. Sometimes the causal connection between the third-party candidate and the realignment of one or more groups of voters between the major parties is not clear, as in the case of farm voters between 1980 and 1984, suggesting that the third-party appearance is primarily symptomatic of more general systemic volatility. But in other cases, the third party clearly acts as a destabilizing force, taking supporters from one party and giving them back to another. In part, this was a dynamic of La Follette's movement, when some of his farm area supporters shifted from the Republican party to the Democratic party. Even some of Roosevelt's supporters seemed attracted to the Democratic progressivism of Woodrow Wilson in 1916.

A third generalization drawn from these analyses is that third-party politics can have a highly variable impact on the major parties. Thus, from a leadership perspective, the influence of a third party on major party mobilization is not easily predictable. From a practical point of view, neither major party may benefit from changing their issue stances or their ideological orientation in order to prevent defections (i.e., before the fact) to the third party. It is a gamble, but there is a very clear possibility that the third-party dynamics will not affect at least one of the major parties in any significant way. Moreover, it is not a simple matter to determine (in advance) which party may be most affected.

For example, Wallace's candidacy did not significantly affect Democratic mobilization, despite his affiliation with that party. It seems that many of Wallace's supporters had already left the Democratic party on the presidential level, and his candidacy merely diminished Republican mobilization. Also, Weaver's candidacy in 1892 similarly affected Democratic mobilization without having much of an influence on Republican mobilization. Interestingly, in both of these cases, the party that was affected by the third-party movement later positioned itself to attract the large majority of the third-party supporters. Moreover, it does not matter with which party the third-party candidate was originally affiliated. Nor is it required that the third-party candidate later switch parties in order for the masses to make the transition to the other major party.

Third-party supporters are weakly institutionalized partisans in the sense that their electoral behavior is not well patterned, having broken with the major parties and voted for a third party. These voters are potentially more tied to the issues that drove them to the third party than to their previous party of choice. Such voters can be particularly sensitive to the issue cues of the major parties once the third-party candidate is out of the picture. Thus, it may make little sense for the major parties to make ideological concessions to third-party concerns until after the partisan impact of the third party is known.

Third-party supporters seem to have their own sense of direction. The third-party candidates seem to tap this frustration in the current leadership of the parties. But the third-party candidates are not political or social institutions. Their attractiveness quickly fades. The voters are left with the same sense of what they want from the political fabric, and they search out a place where they are comfortable. In this sense, third-party politics are politics of pure potential for volatility, for the most important generalization that can be drawn from these analyses is that the potential in the mass dynamics of such politics is one of great variety. It reinforces the idea that third parties really do arise in periods of electoral deinstitutionalization, since—by definition—in a period of high institutionalization such variety in partisan dynamics would be the rare exception rather than the rule.

On an individual level, variety seems to be the rule across third-party movements in terms of the socioeconomic characteristics of such supporters. Supporters of third parties are more independent than major party supporters with regard to their partisan identification. This is important to note, since it demonstrates a correspondence between partisan identification—a psychological commitment to a party—and partisan institutionalization, its behavioral counterpart. Third-party supporters do not seem to differ dramatically from major party supporters in terms of their interest in politics or their level of information about politics. Thus, third-party supporters do not seem to be people who care and know little about the politics of their societies. In this sense, such voters compare more favorably with what scientists have come to expect from "independent leaners" rather than "pure independents" in the American electorate generally (e.g., see Asher 1988). As citizens, they are "plugged in," so to speak.

But in at least one critical way, third-party supporters do differ from major party supporters. Their level of partisan institutionalization is relatively low. Evidence for this is that these third-party voters tend to be younger (on average) than their other voting countrymen and countrywomen. Their relative youth gives evidence of shorter voting histories, implying fewer electoral experiences from which to develop deeply ingrained, patterned electoral behavior.

Throughout these analyses, it is interesting to observe the inherent stability in the electoral system overall, however. In each of the five cases examined here, the supporters of the third parties did not usually demobilize. Indeed, third-party supporters are generally quick to reaffiliate themselves with one of the major parties. Thus, third-party politics is an example of electoral volatility, defined in terms of weak partisan institutionalization and shifting partisan ties, within the context of a stable overall political system.

TABLE A5.1. Unconditioned Parameter Estimates for the People's Party

	1888–92		1892–96	
Parameter	Estimate	χ^2	Estimate	χ^2
f	0.11383	100,816	−0.02393	6,320
b	0.00512	27	−0.01806	318
m	0.18764	302,352	0.00746	611
a	−0.00048	0	0.03622	1,112
g	−0.01126	13	0.05744	379
q	0.01957	3,837	0.03965	13,046
s	0.09546	78,791	−0.01063	1,060
w	0.02744	443	0.07387	4,232
v	−0.01242	6	0.03415	523
k	−0.09071	635,535	−0.00851	7,317
j	−0.06054	311,353	0.09373	773,949
y	0.00280	1	−0.00089	0
c	0.00113	0	0.03279	403
x	0.07292	152,340	0.03150	544,183
p	0.05244	665,353	−0.11371	75,054,209
e	−0.04452	48,157	0.05504	1,937,062
u	0.02210	11,144	0.07306	3,559,982
z	−0.00251	0	0.03011	369

	Goodness of Fit	
Republican	0.134920	0.724199
Democratic	0.076421	0.020866
Populist	0.395729	0.460414
Nonvoter	0.097637	0.265785

Note: Chi-square *df* = 3.

TABLE A5.2. Conditioned Parameter Estimates for the People's Party, 1888–92

Parameter	Urban Estimate	Urban χ^2	Farm Estimate	Farm χ^2
f_1	0.002862	96.29	0.037047	121.93
b_1	0.005306	50.15	0.000121	0.00
m_1	−0.001062	31.53	0.026334	225.94
a_1	−0.000079	0.02	−0.019958	7.83
g_1	0.000492	0.01	0.000463	0.00
q_1	−0.001008	20.91	−0.026102	25.81
s_1	0.014760	7,868.39	−0.008383	26.55
w_1	−0.001792	4.38	0.003573	0.10
v_1	0.000191	0.00	−0.001642	0.00
k_1	0.000066	0.86	−0.013615	14.78
j_1	−0.004487	3,181.29	0.019554	18.23
y_1	0.002138	0.11	0.005994	0.01
c_1	0.000384	0.00	0.003481	0.00
x_1	0.001278	151.41	0.033274	105.80
p_1	−0.001487	1,555.90	−0.001421	0.09
e_1	−0.000584	14.11	−0.031173	281.23
u_1	−0.001436	206.44	−0.001779	3.35
z_1	0.000058	0.00	−0.000111	0.00

	Goodness of Fit	
Republican	0.135155	0.145336
Democratic	0.081705	0.082546
Populist	0.408529	0.398450
Nonvoter	0.099092	0.105077

Note: Chi-square $df = 3$.

TABLE A5.3. Conditioned Parameter Estimates for the People's Party, 1892–96

Parameter	Urban Estimate	Urban χ^2	Farm Estimate	Farm χ^2
f_1	−0.003161	231.22	0.016104	51.66
b_1	−0.000703	1.16	0.011855	6.93
m_1	0.000141	1.24	−0.034093	675.32
a_1	0.006862	240.65	0.002169	0.08
g_1	0.000612	0.00	−0.017468	0.09
q_1	0.000046	0.07	−0.018574	28.34
s_1	−0.001860	217.99	0.018143	151.74
w_1	0.006475	182.86	−0.010782	1.15
v_1	0.000254	0.00	0.001755	0.05
k_1	−0.002294	1,698.37	0.020552	48.65
j_1	0.000264	24.49	0.001461	0.43
y_1	−0.000689	0.01	0.010576	0.04
c_1	0.000041	0.00	−0.001477	0.02
x_1	−0.000601	313.72	−0.018328	1,467.43
p_1	0.000922	8,613.97	0.008412	0.29
e_1	0.003517	8,970.76	0.002614	64.57
u_1	−0.001134	2,384.67	−0.009638	2,623.26
z_1	0.000158	0.00	−0.003250	0.14

	Goodness of Fit	
Republican	0.724723	0.728047
Democratic	0.036695	0.047234
Populist	0.468817	0.462999
Nonvoter	0.262690	0.276519

Note: Chi-square $df = 3$.

TABLE A5.4. Unconditioned Parameter Estimates for Roosevelt

Parameter	1908–12 Estimate	1908–12 χ^2	1912–16 Estimate	1912–16 χ^2
f	0.13506	104,026	−0.00560	185
b	0.00357	11	−0.01325	89
m	0.17130	1,046,952	−0.00617	1,440
a	0.05333	3,590	0.03962	2,944
g	−0.00295	9	0.12518	17,728
q	−0.06892	59,126	0.05283	30,802
s	0.16573	1,707,666	−0.09167	312,763
w	0.10685	14,630	0.04308	1,837
v	−0.01700	33	0.03494	1,508
k	−0.11906	1,895,943	0.06545	710,118
j	−0.22240	11,090,921	0.16128	4,612,692
y	−0.02325	884	0.15837	30,145
c	−0.01823	35	0.02824	560
x	0.01781	3,682	−0.05465	514,570
p	0.15093	4,819,578	−0.17126	78,731,617
e	0.19589	352,930	−0.05233	279,503
u	−0.07490	248,553	0.12407	10,822,372
z	−0.05847	902	−0.00422	40

	Goodness of Fit	
Republican	0.827902	0.765381
Democratic	0.238694	0.565533
Roosevelt	0.796259	0.810231
Nonvoter	0.025300	0.337797

Note: Chi-square $df = 3$.

TABLE A5.5. Conditioned Parameter Estimates for Roosevelt, 1908–12

Parameter	Urban Estimate	Urban χ^2	Farm Estimate	Farm χ^2
f_1	−0.002652	104.952	−0.014080	11.862
b_1	−0.001867	4.650	−0.001662	0.016
m_1	−0.000400	38.587	−0.008457	542.839
a_1	−0.001680	21.811	−0.005952	5.637
g_1	−0.002839	20.198	−0.003539	0.662
q_1	−0.000019	0.014	0.002186	0.770
s_1	−0.000275	35.552	−0.004930	323.286
w_1	0.005269	257.893	−0.008336	11.907
v_1	−0.001286	0.250	−0.000128	0.000
k_1	−0.000034	0.772	−0.000030	0.011
j_1	−0.000002	0.004	0.000000	0.000
y_1	−0.000353	0.553	0.000530	0.025
c_1	−0.000074	0.001	0.000215	0.000
x_1	0.000000	0.000	−0.002958	1.158
p_1	−0.000002	0.003	−0.000013	0.003
e_1	−0.000016	0.007	−0.004363	1.879
u_1	−0.001003	405.689	−0.003910	181.635
z_1	−0.001992	5.358	0.003778	0.787

Goodness of Fit		
Republican	0.827625	0.828245
Democratic	0.211679	0.259730
Roosevelt	0.797094	0.797282
Nonvoter	0.002179	0.077880

Note: Chi-square $df = 3$.

TABLE A5.6.   Conditioned Parameter Estimates for Roosevelt, 1912–16

Parameter	Urban Estimate	χ^2	Farm Estimate	χ^2
f_1	−0.001754	135.7	−0.039245	511.6
b_1	−0.001328	1.7	−0.003050	0.0
m_1	−0.010408	64,719.1	0.034823	14,144.9
a_1	0.024752	21,216.5	−0.009790	39.4
g_1	0.020629	9,243.2	−0.079114	1,349.2
q_1	0.008551	6,906.1	−0.038893	1,243.2
s_1	−0.008347	35,247.3	0.021833	5,939.6
w_1	0.017042	2,523.3	−0.015918	44.5
v_1	0.003470	45.3	−0.011153	4.6
k_1	0.000011	0.4	−0.000123	0.5
j_1	0.000026	1.4	−0.000076	0.2
y_1	0.015943	3,303.7	−0.026228	144.6
c_1	0.001929	4.4	−0.001845	0.1
x_1	−0.005198	13,508.4	0.033159	4,070.9
p_1	−0.000017	3.0	0.000070	1.0
e_1	−0.004911	5,821.0	0.034192	1,956.3
u_1	0.002071	19,285.3	−0.020352	44,036.4
z_1	−0.015446	2,234.5	0.015455	76.0

	Goodness of Fit	
Republican	0.773780	0.771512
Democratic	0.604562	0.590473
Roosevelt	0.810857	0.818237
Nonvoter	0.384328	0.353385

Note: Chi-square $df = 3$.

TABLE A5.7.   Unconditioned Parameter Estimates for La Follette

Parameter	1920–24		1924–28	
	Estimate	χ^2	Estimate	χ^2
f	−0.05514	107,546	0.31848	3,659,257
b	0.00956	118	−0.02905	7,834
m	0.02464	92,001	0.19122	4,519,492
a	−0.15905	65,289	−0.16359	75,676
g	0.01875	303	0.86644	561,035
q	−0.08789	61,732	0.19683	2,950,322
s	0.01055	13,585	0.21618	46,691,366
w	0.07353	31,202	0.88579	25,343,482
v	0.00603	1	0.17835	249,918
k	−0.00045	102	−0.10812	5,090,874
j	−0.00111	485	−0.18868	92,817,432
y	−0.11203	7,855	0.28477	388,555
c	−0.04808	328	0.28147	3,207,369
x	−0.21723	795,140	0.52396	3,284,326,958
p	0.00019	28	−0.52047	116,235,290,182
e	0.31798	5,959,364	0.36584	4,325,849,567
u	0.04918	635,369	0.50808	40,898,969,889
z	−0.02839	268	0.35439	9,416,551

	Goodness of Fit	
Republican	0.032541	0.571844
Democratic	0.109185	0.732120
La Follette	0.675020	0.904524
Nonvoter	0.294989	0.672767

Note: Chi-square *df* = 3.

TABLE A5.8. Conditioned Parameter Estimates for La Follette, 1920–24

Parameter	Urban		Farm	
	Estimate	χ^2	Estimate	χ^2
f_1	0.01060	8,194.1	−0.04520	7,028.0
b_1	−0.01576	471.6	0.00758	2.0
m_1	−0.00278	2,095.2	0.01332	7,115.0
a_1	−0.01253	538.7	0.00216	1.4
g_1	0.00435	37.7	0.03858	196.7
q_1	0.03104	10,794.5	0.02903	480.9
s_1	−0.01155	29,964.6	0.03048	33,971.4
w_1	0.04655	30,635.2	−0.07337	6,839.0
v_1	0.00052	0.0	0.00948	0.3
k_1	−0.00002	0.3	−0.00030	7.8
j_1	0.00030	67.8	−0.00164	229.1
y_1	0.03475	1,782.2	−0.31018	10,161.6
c_1	0.01232	46.1	−0.12566	148.7
x_1	0.00334	251.6	−0.11394	17,516.9
p_1	−0.00001	0.1	−0.00002	0.1
e_1	−0.01441	24,746.8	0.05210	20,493.1
u_1	0.00684	21,772.7	0.00226	427.9
z_1	−0.00233	4.7	0.01133	12.6

	Goodness of Fit	
Republican	0.095539	0.117797
Democratic	0.112567	0.134863
La Follette	0.677606	0.682767
Nonvoter	0.329175	0.343545

Note: Chi-square $df = 3$.

TABLE A5.9. Conditioned Parameter Estimates for La Follette, 1924–28

Parameter	Urban Estimate	Urban χ^2	Farm Estimate	Farm χ^2
f_1	−0.02375	33,626	−0.03053	3,463
b_1	0.13413	77,269	−0.17314	5,775
m_1	0.02679	151,641	−0.01453	5,014
a_1	0.03310	9,559	−0.11069	6,300
g_1	−0.00958	80	0.17527	2,460
q_1	−0.09291	183,723	0.21317	74,304
s_1	0.01692	64,844	−0.03449	42,848
w_1	0.07715	81,563	−0.11524	12,730
v_1	0.01175	1,131	0.02572	1
k_1	−0.00034	74	0.00026	5
j_1	−0.00119	964	0.00106	84
y_1	−0.04122	1,421	−0.00417	1
c_1	−0.00805	5	0.03397	5
x_1	−0.02083	242,969	0.03184	93,051
p_1	−0.00017	7,439	−0.00010	0
e_1	0.01643	6,542	−0.02023	180
u_1	−0.00063	14,475	−0.00109	6
z_1	0.03724	27,756	0.02848	2

	Goodness of Fit	
Republican	0.618611	0.648757
Democratic	0.741271	0.763779
La Follette	0.920623	0.918666
Nonvoter	0.683911	0.663754

Note: Chi-square $df = 3$.

TABLE A5.10. Unconditioned Parameter Estimates for Wallace

Parameter	1964–68 Estimate	1964–68 χ^2	1968–72 Estimate	1968–72 χ^2
f	0.01875	10,070	0.01209	16,733
b	−0.16266	122,573	−0.01638	1,195
m	0.50536	25,583,238	0.09246	2,566,245
a	−0.55263	1,907,703	0.05196	33,628
g	0.12515	12,262	0.02423	1,486
q	0.27931	5,175,449	−0.03217	57,853
s	0.02729	81,929	0.05535	725,166
w	0.22252	293,114	0.12926	280,296
v	−0.01029	20	0.01013	249
k	−0.22684	23,992,889	−0.06839	6,463,500
j	−0.08791	5,093,471	0.07534	6,405,147
y	−0.01526	246	0.07743	12,629
c	−0.03051	165	0.02118	2,155
x	−0.27615	10,654,492	0.09611	40,849,825
p	0.05894	5,387,092	−0.08641	667,386,491
e	0.12292	1,495,209	0.08097	50,674,450
u	0.18562	10,242,015	−0.06892	78,488,731
z	−0.29956	38,604	0.06173	106,698

	Goodness of Fit	
Republican	0.405756	0.814269
Democratic	0.773690	0.124543
Wallace	0.688358	0.656445
Nonvoter	0.147456	0.188719

Note: Chi-square $df = 3$.

TABLE A5.11. Conditioned Parameter Estimates for Wallace, 1964–68

Parameter	Urban Estimate	χ^2	Farm Estimate	χ^2
f_1	−0.0000101	0.0	−0.0002748	0.7
b_1	0.0001179	0.1	−0.0001925	0.1
m_1	−0.0007358	142.3	−0.0002329	1.6
a_1	0.0000195	0.0	0.0000210	0.0
g_1	−0.0000124	0.0	−0.0000175	0.0
q_1	−0.0007667	138.7	0.0015273	84.2
s_1	0.0001322	7.6	0.0020868	200.7
w_1	−0.0000198	0.0	0.0002170	0.1
v_1	0.0000087	0.0	−0.0000096	0.0
k_1	−0.0011060	1,505.9	−0.0008443	136.6
j_1	−0.0012573	3,105.7	0.0049282	7,131.6
y_1	−0.0000463	0.0	0.0001982	0.0
c_1	0.0000041	0.0	0.0000313	0.0
x_1	−0.0004035	90.1	0.0003126	7.9
p_1	−0.0016035	11,847.1	0.0007883	412.3
e_1	−0.0002511	8.8	0.0000435	0.1
u_1	−0.0008621	741.1	0.0004124	17.8
z_1	0.0000555	0.0	−0.0000232	0.0

Goodness of Fit		
Republican	0.418940	0.423430
Democratic	0.775379	0.774930
Wallace	0.697253	0.688982
Nonvoter	0.188518	0.144131

Note: Chi-square $df = 3$.

TABLE A5.12. Conditioned Parameter Estimates for Wallace, 1968–72

Parameter	Urban Estimate	Urban χ^2	Farm Estimate	Farm χ^2
f_1	−0.0065813	4,026	−0.0007878	18
b_1	−0.0010493	10	0.0000975	0
m_1	0.0080971	50,865	0.0002207	4
a_1	0.0216145	17,832	−0.0005770	2
g_1	0.0006034	0	−0.0004190	0
q_1	−0.0016502	453	0.0018718	84
s_1	0.0015254	1,601	0.0025964	477
w_1	0.0139654	3,766	−0.0021062	20
v_1	0.0000943	0	−0.0001116	0
k_1	−0.0075178	127,487	0.0031780	4,414
j_1	−0.0048107	53,908	0.0045235	7,135
y_1	0.0002220	0	−0.0009959	0
c_1	0.0000373	0	−0.0002476	0
x_1	0.0000729	19	−0.0025732	4,363
p_1	0.0030600	483,766	−0.0052467	262,708
e_1	0.0045231	42,534	−0.0017529	1,972
u_1	−0.0010554	15,193	−0.0030040	17,615
z_1	−0.0010498	4	−0.0004816	0

	Goodness of Fit	
Republican	0.830230	0.818554
Democratic	0.129950	0.128149
Wallace	0.676414	0.664126
Nonvoter	0.179887	0.182811

Note: Chi-square $df = 3$.

125

TABLE A5.13. Unconditioned Parameter Estimates for Anderson

Parameter	1976–80 Estimate	1976–80 χ^2	1980–84 Estimate	1980–84 χ^2
f	0.05460	203,521	−0.02358	74,974
b	−0.04114	9,741	−0.04494	12,702
m	0.10268	1,821,201	0.01073	26,930
a	−0.05105	26,475	0.03349	13,918
g	−0.00096	0	0.20384	42,403
q	−0.01545	15,499	0.01946	31,363
s	−0.04782	376,281	−0.03217	248,162
w	0.04509	24,850	0.12754	343,154
v	−0.00412	2	0.04543	25,817
k	−0.08718	6,466,075	0.01051	148,731
j	0.04786	2,148,976	0.05676	4,601,090
y	0.00500	14	−0.00546	35
c	0.00181	1	0.02671	15,673
x	−0.00275	1,740	0.00811	1,294,576
p	0.04625	7,108,077	−0.07889	2,090,358,745
e	0.10155	2,747,994	−0.00855	2,529,143
u	−0.05588	1,806,545	0.07786	375,547,821
z	−0.00141	1	0.02469	18,145

	Goodness of Fit	
Republican	0.293844	0.744471
Democratic	0.568363	0.209127
Anderson	0.804656	0.807045
Nonvoter	0.363007	0.448297

Note: Chi-square $df = 3$.

TABLE A5.14. Conditioned Parameter Estimates for Anderson, 1976–80

Parameter	Urban Estimate	Urban χ^2	Farm Estimate	Farm χ^2
f_1	0.006711	1,631.8	−0.017542	7,428.7
b_1	0.002003	12.5	−0.005033	50.2
m_1	0.007999	29,095.5	0.021674	45,165.6
a_1	−0.008686	1,997.8	0.004838	150.9
g_1	0.006166	31.9	−0.000566	0.1
q_1	0.000562	29.3	0.015866	8,457.8
s_1	0.010373	56,169.3	−0.009403	10,287.2
w_1	−0.005395	303.0	−0.002074	24.0
v_1	0.000900	0.2	−0.000044	0.0
k_1	−0.005418	39,140.7	−0.003966	6,956.2
j_1	−0.007990	92,204.6	0.007428	27,252.5
y_1	−0.002246	4.3	−0.000733	0.2
c_1	−0.000048	0.0	−0.000014	0.0
x_1	0.005238	10,198.7	−0.004461	2,156.3
p_1	−0.000402	932.4	−0.005820	54,138.6
e_1	−0.000675	68.5	−0.007677	5,121.4
u_1	0.000472	404.6	0.006811	16,729.6
z_1	0.001986	4.2	−0.000025	0.0

	Goodness of Fit	
Republican	0.338344	0.325524
Democratic	0.567614	0.585854
Anderson	0.808138	0.820173
Nonvoter	0.393593	0.384668

Note: Chi-square *df* = 3.

TABLE A5.15. Conditioned Parameter Estimates for Anderson, 1980–84

Parameter	Urban Estimate	χ^2	Farm Estimate	χ^2
f_1	0.004781	627	0.006349	1,107
b_1	−0.001285	3	0.003013	20
m_1	0.012184	52,312	−0.001373	173
a_1	0.002496	100	−0.009265	450
g_1	0.006166	12	−0.008659	20
q_1	−0.000108	1	0.002710	150
s_1	0.000702	299	0.015684	16,822
w_1	0.002001	43	−0.013694	798
v_1	0.001125	34	−0.002446	7
k_1	−0.008665	67,010	−0.006461	17,432
j_1	−0.002267	9,374	−0.002014	1,318
y_1	0.000199	0	−0.000861	0
c_1	0.000154	0	−0.001961	5
x_1	0.002071	185,738	−0.000618	562
p_1	−0.001074	820,331	0.006684	1,051,905
e_1	−0.002124	102,107	0.004198	27,309
u_1	0.000494	53,207	−0.006596	227,228
z_1	−0.000958	99	−0.000921	3

	Goodness of Fit	
Republican	0.753856	0.755485
Democratic	0.180900	0.234346
Anderson	0.809482	0.819385
Nonvoter	0.397586	0.438580

Note: Chi-square $df = 3$.

CHAPTER 6

When Women Came to the Party

An extraordinary electoral phenomenon occurred in the United States in 1920. During that year, the electorate virtually doubled with the passage of the Nineteenth Amendment to the U.S. Constitution that extended the franchise to women in all of the states.[1] Yet curiously, only one political party, the Republican party, benefited from the increase in the pool of eligible voters. In 1916, the Republican presidential candidate received 8.5 million votes, whereas the incumbent Democratic candidate, Woodrow Wilson, received 9.1 million votes. (Going back as far as 1896, both parties tended to average between 6 and 9 million votes each.) Following the passage of the Nineteenth Amendment in 1920, the Republican total approximately doubled, rising to 16.1 million votes, while the Democratic total remained at 9.1 million. To be more precise with regard to the Democratic totals, between 1916 and 1920, the Democratic party increased its total presidential mobilization by less than 20,000 votes. In fact, outside the South, the Democratic vote actually decreased (see Kleppner 1987, 143). Considering that there had been a sitting Democratic president for the previous eight years who had successfully guided the country through a world war and who was a supporter of women's suffrage (Luardini and Knock 1980–81; McDonagh and Price 1985, 418), the gap in the response from women between the two parties is truly remarkable, ecological considerations or candidate differences between Cox and Harding notwithstanding.

This chapter examines the election of 1920 with respect to the differential rates of female mobilization into the two political parties. These female voters were new voters, and the 1920 election offers an ideal opportunity to investigate the mechanisms of new voter mass mobilization, particularly under circumstances of franchise extension. However, since Democratic party mobilization in 1920 showed no significant increase, the substance of this chapter deals almost entirely with the increase in mobilization for the Republican party. It is important to point out how small the change in Democratic mobilization was across the country between 1916 and 1920. Relative to Republican mobilization, there was very little change across states among the Democratic

---

1. Some states had extended the franchise to women before 1920. However, these were generally states in the West with relatively small populations. For a more detailed examination of the state by state successes of the women's suffrage movement, see McDonagh and Price 1985.

vote totals. Moreover, there was very little county-level change for the Democrats. From some perspectives, this lack in Democratic longitudinal mobilization variation is an amazing empirical fact.

The election of 1920 is often thought of as reflecting a desire among the populace for a "return to normalcy." Part of the reasoning is that most of the earlier part of the century was a Republican-dominated period, and the 1920 election returned the Republicans to power. But in terms of electoral dynamics, 1920 did not end up being a normal election, or a return to anything that might have been considered "normal" prior to that election. The electorate was *doubled* in that election, and whatever the popular desire of that time may have been, that fact by itself distinguishes the election of 1920 from other elections in a major way. Moreover, the landslide victory of the Republicans over the Democrats in 1920 was of historic proportions. Previously, elections had been much closer, as was Woodrow Wilson's reelection in 1916. Two-to-one victories were, and still are, not typical events. Indeed, that landslide helped propel the Republicans into another decade of political dominance. In short, the dynamics of the 1920 election suggest that something of much greater proportions may underlie the "return to normalcy" concept, either as an issue or as a characterization of that election.

Nonetheless, the "return to normalcy" concept does address one important aspect of the 1920 election. As an issue, it does not introduce a new line of cleavage. There is no reason to suspect that women in Democratic households would have had any reason to vote Republican. Indeed, there is every reason to suspect the opposite, that Republicans would have received the vast majority of their increased support from women in Republican households. Given the minute changes in the Democratic vote totals and the minimal level of state and county variation, it may be that a precise determination cannot ever be made of the impact of women voters on Democratic party mobilization. Nonetheless, although ecological considerations are always important, the available evidence clearly suggests that the extension of the franchise did not affect Democratic recruitment in a meaningful way. The next most obvious question is to ask where all those new female Republican voters came from in 1920.[2] Thus, this analysis proceeds with the causal assumption that the doubling of the Republican mobilization in 1920 was primarily due to the doubling of the electorate during that same year.

While little has been written about the election of 1920, some initial guidance with regard to the question of where all those new female Republican voters came from can be found in selections from the broad literature on the women's suffrage movement. A useful summary and examination of many

---

2. A rather extensive statistical analysis of the Democratic presidential vote was conducted by the author and is not reported here. In none of the analyses was there evidence that the extension of the voting franchise to women had any significant impact on changes in the patterns of Democratic support.

of the primary themes found within the literature on women's suffrage, viewed from the perspective of state referenda on the suffrage issue, can be found in recent work by McDonagh and Price (1985). (See also Kleppner 1987, 171–75). In terms of these characterizations of the suffrage literature in general, opposition to women's suffrage came from a variety of sources, such as from many sectors of the population that opposed prohibition, German-Americans, southern Europeans, many Catholics, and people living in urban areas (due to opposition from the political machines). Support for women's suffrage came from rural areas, people favoring prohibition, native-born non-southern Protestants, the better educated, and the younger generation. In general, opposition is usually seen as a consequence of a desire to preserve existing interests (as in the sale of liquor) or traditional conservative ways of life (as with Catholics and German immigrants). On the other hand, support is generally seen as an attempt to enlist the electoral assistance of women (in a coalitional sense) with regard to particular causes (e.g., prohibition and restrictions on child labor) as well as an attempt to protect nonimmigrant interests as opposed to the interests of recent immigrants.

When one moves from a study of the suffrage movement to studying voting patterns following the passage of the Nineteenth Amendment, the transition encounters some parallels as well as some inconsistencies. In a seminal study by Merriam and Gosnell (1924), nonvoting was examined in a Chicago mayoral election in 1923. Using extensive survey data from which to draw their conclusions, these researchers report (among many things) that women tended not to vote or to register as often as men. Given the lack of extended voting histories among women at the time, this is, to some extent, an expected result (see also Kleppner 1982, 62). They find that indifference to politics and general inertia tended more strongly to influence the nonvoting behavior of women than men. This was particularly true for white females of foreign parentage living in poor neighborhoods. Such voters also tended to be timid about the election procedures, lacking strong educational backgrounds and fearing ridicule at not knowing how to fill out the ballot. There also were still a large number of antisuffragists who felt, for a variety of reasons, that voting was not an appropriate activity for women.[3]

Some particularly interesting findings of Merriam and Gosnell regard nonimmigrant whites. The overall turnout for the 1923 mayoral election was not as high as it was for the 1920 presidential election. However, the greatest decrease in voting and registration was found within the most prosperous neighborhoods among individuals of nonimmigrant parentage. Merriam and Gosnell suggest that the lack of dramatic interest in the local campaign more easily affected that group of voters. Additionally, the younger generation tended to vote in smaller numbers than those somewhat older, despite the

---

3. For a dramatic portrayal of the reasons women were against female suffrage, see Flexner 1975; Goodwin 1913; and Lamar (n.d.).

younger group's general support for women's suffrage. Perhaps the most critical of Merriam and Gosnell's findings about the nonimmigrant female population is that women's political clubs held a particularly important role in arousing interest in voting among women who lived in prosperous neighborhoods. In contrast, in working-class neighborhoods, the lack of such women's groups left the mobilization efforts to party organizations that were generally less successful in mobilizing the female population.

An Examination of Some Basic Questions

I begin my analysis by focusing on some of the most basic questions that have been raised in some of the electoral literature relevant to the 1920 election. A useful tool with which to begin is a map of the United States. The type of map employed here is called a *surface map*, the first of which is presented in figure 6.1. With a surface map, each state has a value given to it with regard to some variable. In figure 6.1, the variable is the total change in new votes going to the Republican party between 1916 and 1920. The surface of that state is then "lifted," with the center being the highest point. This allows for an easy comparison between the various regions of the United States with regard to the variable.

From figure 6.1 it is clear that, in 1920, the Republican party gained the vast majority of its new votes from the northern states east of the Mississippi River. This reflects the larger population densities found in that region and is an expected result, given that we are looking at changes in total votes and not proportions of the eligible population. However, the magnitude of these gains for the Republican party emphasizes the geographical structure of Republican strength at that time, which in a very real sense dates back to the Civil War.

The picture changes quite dramatically when the focus of the question of the geographical strength of the Republican party shifts away from the change in total votes to the change in Republican support from within the pool of eligible voters. Figure 6.2 is a surface map in which the surface variable is Republican change as measured as a proportion of the total adult population. Note, from figure 6.2, that the Republican party did manage to gain an equally large share of the pool of total eligibles in much of the Midwest as well as in the Northeast. Their gains in the Far West and in the South were relatively small.

It is perhaps not surprising that the Republicans did so poorly in the South relative to the Northeast and the Midwest, given the nature of Democratic dominance in the South, again dating back to the Civil War. Yet the question of Republican gains in the South begs a different type of question. Since Republican strength in the South was so low to begin with, one would not expect the Republicans to make substantial inroads into the pool of southern eligibles simply through the enfranchisement of women. Indeed, many southerners feared women's suffrage because it offered a change in the status

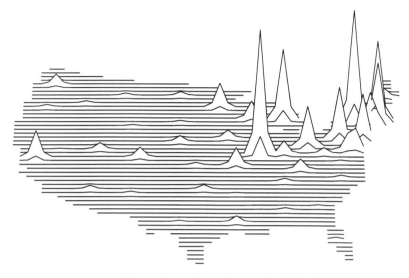

Fig. 6.1. Republican change in total votes by states, 1916–20

quo that could potentially affect white political dominance in much of the South. The fear was that southern black women might try to vote in greater proportion than southern white women. This is a point that was raised quite openly in the South during the campaigns preceding the passage of the Nineteenth Amendment, despite the prevalence of Jim Crow laws throughout the South. For example, Mrs. Walter D. Lamar, writing for the Georgia Association Opposed to Woman Suffrage, states, "Southern states that do not have a large negro population must stand together against the proposed Susan B. Anthony amendment, giving the franchise to all, and counties which have a preponderance of whites must keep the faith in behalf of those that have a large black majority" (Lamar n.d.).

Thus, we should pose the question of Republican strength in the South differently than in terms of their support from the pool of eligibles. The question should be how active was the female response to the extension of the franchise given the existing level of Republican support. One might think that the besieged Republican minority in the South might respond very favorably to any possibility to increase their strength. For example, Republican women may have felt that their vote was particularly needed. It may be that Republican husbands were especially encouraging with regard to the participation of their wives, wanting all the help they could get in a most difficult situation. It may also be that southern Republicans, just by virtue of their Republicanism, were quite used to defying the social and political norms of their communities. In this context, Republican women might likely have thought of voting as a continuation of their own previous behavior in which local social

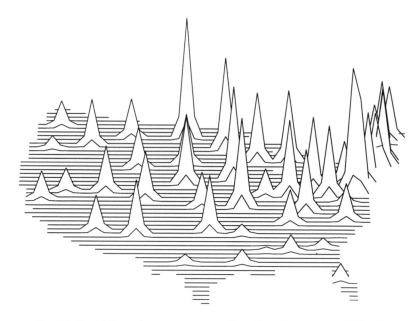

Fig. 6.2. Republican change as a proportion of adults by states, 1916–20

and political norms were ignored and even defied. These ideas do indeed gain support from an interpretation of the surface map presented here as figure 6.3.

The surface variable in figure 6.3 is Republican change measured as a proportion of existing Republican support in 1916. From this figure it is clear that Republican support in the South increased quite dramatically relative to the remainder of the nation. The evidence suggests that southern Republican women were very eager to participate in national elections, once given the franchise. The evidence also suggests that there might be a different type of dynamic characteristic to vote mobilization from the ranks of certain types of locally isolated minorities.

It is useful to pursue the question of the influence of initial Republican strength in 1916 a step further. One might assume that the Republican party would more successfully mobilize women in areas in which it already had the greatest strength. This would result, in part, from the greater levels of organizational activity for the party in such areas, thus enabling more frequent contact between party workers and eligible voters. Moreover, since much of the suffrage literature has suggested that support for extending the franchise to women was more strongly based in rural than urban areas, it might likely be assumed that the greatest increase in Republican change would come from rural areas with high levels of initial Republican support.

These ideas are introduced by way of an examination of results presented in figure 6.4. Figure 6.4 is a three-dimensional scatterplot. One of the floor axes is the level of farm density in each state (measured in acreage, standard-

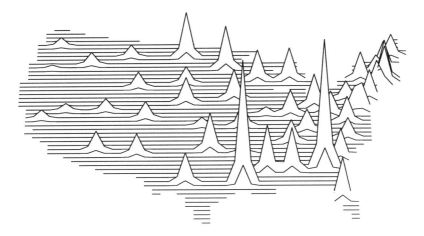

Fig. 6.3. Republican change as a proportion of 1916 Republican mobilization by states, 1916–20

ized with a mean of zero and a standard deviation of one). The other floor axis is the initial Republican strength in 1916, measured as a proportion of eligibles as defined by 1920 standards (i.e., both men and women) to permit a comparison with subsequent levels of mobilization. The vertical (height) axis is the level of Republican change between 1916 and 1920, again measured as a proportion of eligible voters. Each point drawn in figure 6.4 represents a state. Thus, all of these data represent averages for all counties within each state. The "balloons" represent nonsouthern states, whereas the "pyramids" represent southern states. The different graphical representations for the nonsouthern and southern states are used to more easily differentiate the national, compared with the regional, variations intrinsic to these data. States in which women were awarded the franchise before 1916 (generally low population, western states) have been removed from this analysis since it is assumed that change in Republican strength between 1916 and 1920 in those states would be due to factors other than the extension of the franchise elsewhere.[4]

The data presented in figure 6.4 do suggest that the Republican party did, indeed, gain somewhat more support in farm or rural areas in 1920 than in areas that were less rural, and thus more urban, in character. Moreover, note that the greatest Republican gains came from those states in which Republican strength was already at its highest level. As per our prior expectations, these initial results suggest that Republican change between 1916 and 1920 was a phenomenon somewhat enhanced by a rural environment as well as by the

---

4. The states in which the franchise had been extended to women before 1916 are Wyoming, Idaho, Colorado, Utah, Washington, California, Oregon, Kansas, Arizona, Illinois, Nevada, and Montana (see McDonagh and Price 1985, 417).

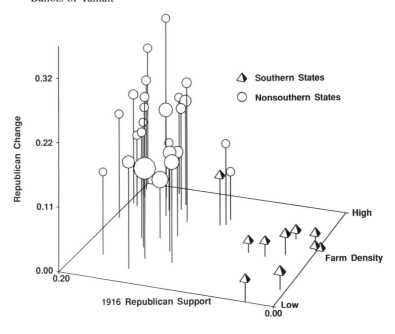

Fig. 6.4. Initial strength and Republican change as a proportion of total eligibles, with farm density, 1916–20. Symbol size represents population size.

existence oℓ previously established Republican partisan strengths and, consequently, the existence of active local party and social organizations that would participate in mobilization activities directed toward new women voters.

The Interactions

The data shown in figure 6.4 suggest that there is some characteristic of areas with higher levels of Republican mobilization in 1916 that triggers a relatively more active mobilization of women voters in 1920. The existence of a stronger Republican organizational presence, including the presence of Republican women's organizations, in such areas has been suggested as one causal contributor to this phenomenon. This interpretation is consistent with some of the observations made by Merriam and Gosnell (1924). However, one likely contributing reason for such an effect, one that is consistent with the concepts of electoral mobilization that are discussed throughout this volume, is that the degree of partisan change depends, in part, on the existing level of Democratic support in each area. Republican women may have gone to the polls when they felt the party's greater need in competitive elections. Also, it would be logical for Republican party organizations to make a more determined effort to enlist the support of new women voters if the local political environment is competitive. Since encouraging women to vote broke some of the norms of the society at that time, it is likely that those norms would be less fiercely resisted when political survival was more clearly at risk. In situations with no previous real threat from the political opposition, the existing social norms would likely decay more slowly. This expectation finds interpretive correspondence with empirical findings that have been reported repeatedly in a related body of sociological and electoral literature (see, especially, Beck 1974; T. Brown 1988; Gans 1962).

To capture formally the potential for partisan mobilization activity as a phenomenon dependent on the level of political competition, change in Republican mobilized support between 1916 and 1920 can be written as a function of both previous Republican strength as well as the joint level of partisan activity. This latter concept can be operationalized as the multiplicative interaction between the levels of previous Republican and Democratic mobilized support. All this can be captured in the expression,

$$\text{Republican Change}_{1920 - 1916} = aR_t + bR_tD_t. \tag{6.1}$$

In equation 6.1, a and b are parameters of the model, R_t represents the proportion of the adult population (i.e., the eligibles) that supported the Republican party in 1916, and D_t is the comparable quantity with regard to the Democratic party. Parameters a and b act to structure the characterization of change in Republican party support between 1916 and 1920 (i.e., the left hand side of eq. 6.1) as a function of initial Republican strength (a) and the competitive interaction between the Republican and the Democratic partisan populations (b).

As with interaction terms introduced in other chapters of this volume, this interactive expression, bR_tD_t, is symmetric. That is, the expression has its greatest impact in equation 6.1 (thus, in describing change in Republican support) when both R_t and D_t are high. This condition would be characteristic of a competitive political environment between both parties and is a desired trait of the model, given the electoral expectations described here.

The Estimation and Interpretation

Equation 6.1 is estimated below with ordinary least squares regression using county-level data for all of the United States. Iterative solutions to differential equations of the type employed in previous chapters are not required for this model since the model is written as a difference equation spanning only two elections. (An alternative, continuous-time specification is examined later in this chapter.)

The results of the estimation of equation 6.1 are presented in table 6.1. The data include all counties in the United States in which the voting franchise was not awarded to women before 1916 (there were over 2,200 such coun-

TABLE 6.1.   Parameter Estimates for a Model of Republican Change, 1916–20

Variable	Parameter Estimate	SE	$p > \lvert t \rvert$	Standardized Estimate
Republican	0.29	0.050	0.0001	0.54
Democratic	−0.04	0.050	0.4072	−0.08
Rep × Dem	1.09	0.310	0.0005	0.31
Nonimmigrant	−0.08	0.005	0.0001	−0.61
African-American	−0.13	0.010	0.0001	−0.33
Workers	−0.04	0.009	0.0001	−0.09
Urban	−0.00	0.000	0.0001	−0.07
Farm Density	0.01	0.001	0.0001	0.13
North	0.16	0.008	0.0001	—
South	0.12	0.008	0.0001	—

Note: $R^2 = .9261$; adjusted $R^2 = .9257$; $N = 2{,}260$.

ties). A number of additional control variables are included in the model as well. They are initial Democratic support in 1916 (Democratic), the proportion of the adult population that was nonimmigrant and of nonimmigrant parents (Nonimmigrant), the proportion of the adult population that was African-American (African-American), the proportion of the adult population that was wage earners (Workers), a population density measure to account for levels of urbanization (Urban), a farm density measure based on the proportion of each county's land that was utilized for farming (Farm Density), as well as two regional intercept dummy variables (one for the southern states and one for the nonsouthern states, South and North respectively).[5] The data were weighted by population while conducting the estimation.[6]

The estimated model fits these data quite well. Moreover, the estimates themselves are not plagued by major significance problems, with the exception of the control for initial Democratic strength that is included here only to

---

5. A number of other control specifications were attempted with these data. None of the other specifications, regardless of functional complexity, appeared to offer any additional explanatory power or to affect any of the other parameter estimates.

6. When using proportional data, a generalized least squares strategy is often pursued to avoid problems with heteroskedasticity among the residuals. This is typically accomplished by weighting each observation by $NP(1-P)$, where N is the population of each aggregation and P is the proportion supporting a political party. This procedure is followed due to the binomial origins of the proportional measure (see Brown 1982, 288; Hanushek and Jackson 1977, 193). In the current analysis, however, the dependent variable is written as a difference between Republican proportional totals in 1916 and 1920, and proportional change is distributed normally. Nonetheless, guided by the philosophical principle that it is better to be safe than certain, a test was conducted on the dependent variable used here and the estimated equation's residuals to ensure that the structure of these data corresponded to that of a normal distribution. The test was positive ($p < 0.01$).

ensure an unbiased estimate for the partisan interaction term.[7] The estimates for the regional intercepts have values that correspond to expectations, the South having the much lower level of base change. Farm areas are positively associated with greater change for the Republican party between 1916 and 1920, whereas urban areas do not show a clear association with increased Republican support. Indeed, the magnitude of the urban influence is quite small. Levels of African-American and worker populations are also negatively associated with greater change in Republican mobilization. Note, however, that the sign of the estimate for the nonimmigrant population is negative. This is an unexpected result and requires some explanation. But it is important to note that all of the other results pertaining to our control variables match prior expectations, especially in light of observations made in the extant voting and suffrage literatures pertaining to that time.

To understand the significance of the unexpected sign for the estimate for the Nonimmigrant control variable, it is useful to address the general nativist issue as it has been raised in the literature on the women's suffrage movement. The women's suffrage movement is often viewed, in part, as a nativist movement opposed to the influence of recent immigrants on American society. Kleppner describes a complicated logic that characterizes this view in terms of the salient political issues of that time. "Male exclusionists noticed that native-stock women were disfranchised while foreign-born males exercised the right to vote. And they presumed that most of the newly franchised women would use their ballots to support such native Protestant causes as immigration restriction, the abolition of alien suffrage, and prohibition" (Kleppner 1987, 171–72).

Note that Kleppner's point (and the one being addressed here) is not whether distinctions should be made about turnout in 1920 between certain types of immigrant groups. Some researchers have suggested that northern Europeans tended to support the concept of suffrage more often than southern Europeans or Germans (see McDonagh and Price 1985; Merriam and Gosnell 1924). The question addressed here focuses on whether there was a particularly strong nativist response to voting in 1920, given the anti-immigrant tone of certain aspects of the suffrage movement. Presently, no substantial evidence (one way or the other) has been reported in the relevant voting literature

---

7. The potential problem of multicollinearity was thoroughly examined in the process of conducting the estimations presented in table 6.1. Multicollinearity was not found to be a problem in the current specification, despite the presence of an interactive term in the model. Instrumental variable techniques, ridge regression, and a variety of other tests were examined in the evaluation of multicollinearity. None of the instrumental variables used caused major or significant changes in the original parameter estimates. With regard to the ridge estimations, very small levels of bias rapidly led to stable estimates that were very close to the original estimates (statistically and in real terms). The other tests similarly suggested little or no multicollinearity problems with the estimates presented here.

regarding whether nonimmigrants voted in greater proportions than immigrants. Indeed, Merriam and Gosnell noted relatively large decreases in turnout and registration among prosperous nonimmigrant populations in the 1923 Chicago mayoral election (Merriam and Gosnell 1924, 251). It is useful to be reminded that supporting suffrage in general is one thing, but actually turning out to vote is a separate question altogether.

The interesting point made by the negative sign for the estimate for the Nonimmigrant variable is that this offers no evidence at all that nonimmigrants voted in any higher proportions than immigrants in 1920. Indeed, a straightforward interpretation of the negative direction of the estimate suggests the opposite, that immigrants voted in higher proportions than nonimmigrants. It should be noted that this result was tested with a large number of alternative ordinary least squares model specifications. Neither simple, nonlinear variable constructions nor exotic, functional specifications could change the direction or significance of this result. The result reflects a very definable pattern within these data. Moreover, the result does not disappear if all southern counties are removed from the analysis. In short, this is a very curious result that begs for explanation. An explanation of this result is pursued directly in the next section of this chapter.

The analysis of the interactive influences on change in Republican party support is not easily discerned from the numbers in table 6.1. These results are much more easily explained and interpreted using the model predictions that are presented in table 6.2. Table 6.2 shows the predicted change in Republican party mobilization between 1916 and 1920 under four different partisan conditions in 1916. These are (1) where both Republican and Democratic mobilization is initially low (i.e., in 1916), (2) where Republican mobilization is high but Democratic mobilization is low (i.e., only nonvoters and Republicans are present), (3) where Republican mobilization is low but Democratic mobilization is high, and (4) where there is both high Republican and Democratic mobilization. The fourth condition reflects a highly competitive political environment. All of the numbers in Table 6.2 are measured as proportions of total adults (i.e., 1920 eligibles).

From table 6.2, note that in areas of low Republican base mobilization, change in Republican turnout improves only slightly in the absence of a strong Democratic opposition. In areas of high Republican base mobilization, change in Republican mobilization is much greater regardless of the initial Democratic strength. However, the greatest increase in Republican mobilization comes from areas where there is both a strong Republican and Democratic presence in 1916, that is, in areas of greatest political competition.

These results confirm our theoretical expectation with regard to the earlier discussion of new voter recruitment under conditions of partisan competition. One strong incentive to the recruitment of women into the ranks of Republican supporters in 1920 was the existence of a more threatening Democratic opposition. Thus, women voted in higher numbers and, perhaps, sup-

TABLE 6.2. Predicted Republican Change, 1916–20

Republican Base, 1916	Democratic Base, 1916	
	Low (0)	High (0.4)
Low (0)	0.16	0.14
High (0.4)	0.28	0.44

port from women was more actively solicited when the political climate suggested that their support was critically important to the Republican party's electoral survival.

One should not dismiss this result as "common sense" or "obvious." To say that women were recruited with the emphasis placed on where they were needed adds something to the interpretation of the electoral realization of the suffrage movement. Women of that period can be viewed, at least in one sense, as representative of other groups that had historically been denied access to the political process. The development of their institutionalization to the voting process, and probably to a political party as well, has its genesis in incremental fits and starts, heavily conditioned by factors relevant to the existing structure of political power, especially the existence of some organizations that actively sought their participation.

From this perspective, it is not clear whether or how much the extension of the franchise in 1920 alerted women to some internal sensibility that they must immediately run to the polls. Rather, it seems that their electoral participation was dependent, to some extent, on organizations, both women's voting groups and a male-controlled political establishment. The general rule to draw from this is that new voters respond favorably to organized efforts at recruitment. This was as true for the Democratic party's organization of new urbanites and workers in 1932 as it was in 1920 for the Republicans. Indeed, nothing shows this new voter dependence on recruitment organizations more clearly than the apparently complete lack of mobilization among women for the Democratic party in 1920.

The Question of the Nonimmigrants

My interpretive conclusions seem reinforced when we address the empirical puzzle of the electoral participation of nonimmigrants. There is a plausible explanation for this result that seems particularly helpful here.[8] It may be that this result is a consequence of the interaction between immigrants and nonimmigrants. That is, it may be that nonimmigrants voted in much greater num-

---

8. Thanks must be expressed to Karen O'Connor, who offered helpful suggestions regarding the nativist response to immigrant voting.

bers in areas where there were many immigrants. From a family perspective, one idea is that many husbands might have been more encouraging of their wives' participation if they felt particularly strong feelings of indignation toward the electoral participation of local immigrants. Thus, with such a scenario, it is not that immigrants voted in larger numbers than nonimmigrants, but that nonimmigrants voted in larger numbers when they lived near immigrants.

This interpretation of the nonimmigrant empirical oddity presented earlier is especially plausible from a view of the suffrage movement as partially a nativist response to an increasingly immigrant social environment. This view is evident in much of the extant literature on the suffrage movement. Crudely stated, local social norms may have been more supportive of the electoral participation of local nonimmigrant women if, in fact, there was nothing to stop the "foreigners down the street" from voting. If such a psychological phenomenon did occur on the level of the masses, then there should be a trace of it in the electoral dynamics, and, as the subsequent analysis demonstrates, there is.

The model presented as equation 6.2 to characterize the change in Republican mobilization between 1916 and 1920 is a simple, continuous-time logistic structure with a single growth parameter. After introducing this simple model, it is enhanced by making that growth parameter a function of the level of the immigrant population in each county.

$$dR/dt = gR(1 - R - D_{1920})$$ (6.2)

In equation 6.2, R is the proportion of the eligibles supporting the Republican party, D_{1920} is the proportion of the eligibles supporting the Democratic party in 1920, and g is the growth parameter of the model. This model is similar to the logistic growth model presented in chapter 3. The quantity $(1 - R - D_{1920})$ represents the potential electorate that is available for Republican mobilization, and this quantity acts to limit the growth of R (Republican mobilization) as it approaches the limit. The estimation of equation 6.2 in the absence of a Democratic counterpart model is a reasonable approach, given the virtually complete absence of significant change in Democratic mobilization between 1916 and 1920.

The theory that nonimmigrant women voted in greater numbers in the presence of immigrants can be operationalized by writing the growth parameter, g, in equation 6.2 as a function of the level of immigrants in the local area. However, there are two expectations here. The first is that the immigrants themselves are not expected to have voted in unusually great numbers in 1920. Thus, Republican mobilization should be lower in areas that have increasingly large immigrant populations. However, at some point (call it a *tipping point*) the dynamic changes. Republican mobilization should increase in areas with large immigrant populations due to the nativist response to those populations described above. Thus, we are expecting both a decrease and an increase in Republican mobilization, all conditional upon the size of the local immigrant population. A continuous-time model is used because we are expecting this up and down dynamic to influence the longitudinal pattern of partisan growth.

Following this logic, the growth parameter, g, of equation 6.2 is written as a quadratic function of the level of local immigrant populations. Parameter g is now

$$g = f + b(Foreign) + m(Foreign^2). \tag{6.3}$$

The entire model can now be expressed as equation 6.4:

$$dR/dt = (f + b[Foreign] + m[Foreign^2]) \times R(1 - R - D_{1920}) + a. \tag{6.4}$$

Parameter a also has been added to the model (at the end) as an intercept. This is similar to all of the other continuous-time specifications presented in this volume, and its inclusion here is a practical aspect of all attempts to fit nearly all models to a body of data.

One last caveat. Immigrants in that time period tended to settle in urban areas. Thus, if the nativist up and down dynamic actually occurred, it should be more evident in urban areas than in rural areas, due to the higher density of immigrants in the urban areas. For this reason, we wish to condition the model (eq. 6.4) with respect to social environment, in this case urbanization and farm density. The same measures for the conditioning variables, urbanization and farm density, are used here as have been used in previous chapters. This requires that we write each of the parameters in equation 6.4 as linear functions of the conditioning variables. The previously used form, that is, $f = f_0 + f_1X$, is useful here, where X represents the value of the conditioning variable.

The data that are used to estimate equation 6.4 are for all counties in all nonsouthern states in which the extension of the voting franchise to women occurred in 1920. There are approximately 1,500 such counties. The South is excluded from the analysis to focus on those areas (mostly in the populous Northeast and Midwest) in which significant Republican gains were made.

The results of the estimations of equation 6.4 are presented in tables 6.3–6.5. The same type of iterative estimation techniques that were discussed in previous chapters have been used to determine the estimates presented in these tables. Readers interested in the details of the estimation procedure should refer to the Appendix.

Note that the unconditioned and conditioned models fit these county-level data very well. Moreover, the parameter estimates are typically not plagued with significance problems, with the exception of the conditioned estimates for intercept a. It is difficult to interpret the parameter estimates

TABLE 6.3. Unconditioned Parameter Estimates
for the Republican Party, 1916–20

Parameter	Estimate	χ^2
f	1.15381	2,699,005
b	−0.09195	60,783
m	0.01873	11,393
a	0.01648	56,818

Note: Goodness of fit = 0.8994; $p < .01$ for all parameter estimates; chi-square df = 1,444.

directly, however. It is not that it could not be done; it is just that most readers would prefer not to do it. For this reason, two easily interpreted trajectory surfaces have been prepared that allow for an immediate evaluation of the theory of the nativist electoral reaction to the presence of local immigrant populations. These surfaces are presented as figures 6.5 and 6.6.

It is best to begin the interpretation with figure 6.5. Figure 6.5 represents a trajectory hypersurface for equation 6.4 under a characteristically farm-oriented social environment. Time (between 1916 and 1920) and proportion of immigrants in the population are represented on the "floor" of the figure. Republican mobilization, measured as a proportion of the total eligibles, is represented on the vertical axis.

Note that Republican mobilization is increasing over time in all areas (i.e., in areas with both high and low levels of immigrants in the population). However, note that Republican mobilization rises higher in 1920 in areas with fewer immigrants than in areas with greater numbers of immigrants. This is expected, since we are assuming that immigrants tended to vote in lower numbers than nonimmigrants in general. Moreover, there tended to be fewer immigrants in farm areas than in urban areas, and the evidence shown in figure 6.5 suggests that there was no increased nativist mobilization response to the presence of rural immigrant populations.

Yet recall that our expectations regarding the nativist "up and down"

TABLE 6.4. Farm Density–Conditioned
Parameter Estimates for the Republican Party,
1916–20

Parameter	Estimate	χ^2
f_1	0.116241	100,731
b_1	−0.069046	122,942
m_1	0.010771	32,327
a_1	0.000051	1

Note: Goodness of fit = 0.9055; $p < .01$ for all parameter estimates except a_1; chi-square df = 1,444.

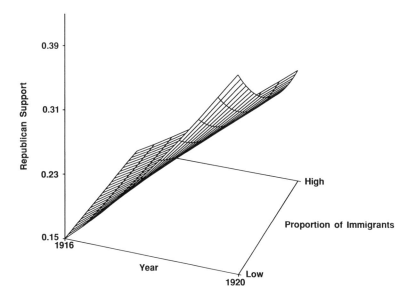

Fig. 6.5. Republican growth by social environment, 1916–20, farm trajectory surface

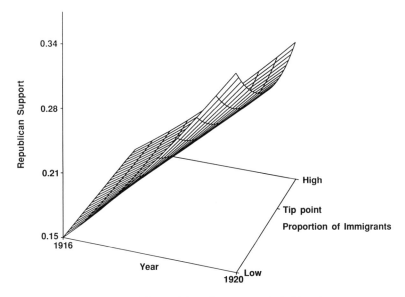

Fig. 6.6. Republican growth by social environment, 1916–20, urban trajectory surface

**TABLE 6.5.   Urban-Conditioned Parameter
Estimates for the Republican Party, 1916–20**

Parameter	Estimate	χ^2
f_1	−0.0061366	7,560
b_1	−0.0056185	75,776
m_1	0.0021481	53,541
a_1	−0.0000197	9

Note: Goodness of fit = 0.9008; p = .01 for all parameter estimates except a_1; chi-square df = 1,444.

mobilization reaction to the presence of immigrants in their local environment are greater in urban environments. Figure 6.6 presents the trajectory hypersurface for urban environments. In figure 6.6, the aggregate evidence of a nativist reaction to the level of the local immigrant populations is evident. Republican gains between 1916 and 1920 are greatest in areas with the fewest immigrants. As the number of immigrants increases in the local environment, the magnitude of the Republican gains tends to decrease, a pattern followed by the trajectory surface for farm environments. However, in urban areas with larger immigrant populations (i.e., where the proportion of immigrants in the population is high), Republican gains reverse their decline and begin to increase.

It is this turnaround in Republican mobilization in urban areas with large numbers of immigrants that is interpreted here as the evidence of the nativist reaction to the presence of immigrants in the local environment. Apparently, low numbers of immigrants in urban areas did not produce a nativist reaction. However, immigrant densities beyond a tipping threshold created an entirely different electoral dynamic.

Discussion

Given the aggregate evidence presented here, one must reach out for a psychological motivation underlying these mass dynamics. Since we lack survey information for this time period, any psychological interpretation must be recognized as a guess, however well guided by an understanding of the period's political history. But such a guess is better than no interpretation at all, and alternative viewpoints are encouraged.

The current interpretation of these results parallels that offered with respect to the data indicating that Republican mobilization was greater in areas in which competition with the Democratic party was most intense. The Republican party establishment encouraged the electoral participation of women in 1920 with greater emphasis in those areas with the greatest partisan need for survival. Moreover, men of that time (reflecting the previous and general social norms) were more supportive of women participating in areas in which indignation was strongly felt with respect to immigrant voting.

This interpretation of the dynamics of Republican mobilization again points to an understanding of the electoral institutionalizing process for groups of new voters. When new voters enter an electorate in large numbers due to a change in some structural feature of the voting process, they are particularly susceptible to the recruitment efforts of the current political establishment. In such situations, new voters turn out in larger numbers when the existing political establishment actively encourages them to turn out. The "existing political establishment" can also include active organizations of new voters such as women's social groups or the church organizations of southern African-Americans (as was the case during the civil rights campaigns of the 1960s). But the dependence of new voters on some type of organized recruitment seems clear.

This is an important result in terms of identifying a critical element in electoral volatility due to new voters. It also parallels the results in chapter 4 for new urban voters during the 1932 and 1936 elections. They were mobilized in large numbers only when they were actively recruited. In terms of the 1920 election, the extension of the franchise is only partially the granting of the right to vote. It is just as much the granting of the right to be recruited, and the impact of new voters can be greatest when someone organizes an effort to go out and get them.

This analysis does not solve one important puzzle. What in the world were the Democrats doing in 1920? In hindsight, they certainly had a motivation, especially in competitive areas, were they to act on it. A quantitative analysis will not help much in answering this question, because the current analysis suggests that new voters are dependent, to a large degree, on the recruitment efforts of the political establishment. Thus, we need to ask why the Democratic political establishment did not make a major effort to recruit women in 1920. To answer this, a nonquantitative historical analysis is more likely to bear fruit. One needs to identify the elites of the day in many areas of the country, and to assess their motives and strategies in that crucial election.

CHAPTER 7

Stability and Complexity in the Congressional Mobilization Cycle

Perhaps nothing in American electoral politics is more constantly in a state of large-scale change than congressional vote mobilization. Congressional vote mobilization in the United States is fundamentally structured by the timing of presidential elections. This chapter offers a new approach to the study of this congressional mobilization cycle, both in terms of the types of questions raised as well as methodology. In general, the focus is on important and previously overlooked characteristics of the structure of the congressional mobilization cycle from the 1950s to the mid-1980s that contribute to aggregate electoral volatility in that cycle. Of particular interest is the electorate's ability to institutionalize large, short-term disturbances—"shocks" that are consequences of the presidential elections—into the mobilization cycle.

To study electoral institutionalization from the perspective of the congressional mobilization cycle can at first seem problematic and warrants some explanation. The problem is that presidential elections appear constantly to destabilize congressional mobilization. Every four years, the excitement of the presidential contest brings many voters to the polls. Two years later, many of those voters do not participate in the off-year congressional elections, thus reducing turnout. But many voters do vote in the off-year elections as well, and the high levels of seat retention among congressional incumbents across many elections suggest that electoral institutionalization is high on the congressional level, despite the magnitude of the mobilization shifts every two years. From this perspective, it seems very reasonable to investigate the process of electoral institutionalization as a mass phenomenon on the congressional level and, in particular, to inquire into the dynamics of this process as it operates to absorb the recurrent mobilization disturbances.

The extant electoral literature contains a wide variety of approaches to the study of congressional voting. Because of this, locating the intellectual contribution of a piece as different as the current analysis can benefit from some guidance.

The approaches found in the extant literature employ a diverse array of theoretical perspectives, both on the individual and the aggregate levels. Heuristically, two recent works serve as excellent examples of the variety of approaches typical of this literature. In terms of commonalities, both investigations explore congressional voting during approximately the same time period as the analysis presented in this chapter. Marra and Ostrom (1989) present an aggregate-level model that explains change in House seats as a function of the public's approval of the president's job performance, dramatic events, partisan identification, and the number of marginal seats at risk in any given election. Marra and Ostrom's research is an excellent example of an attempt to blend a number of theoretical approaches into the specification of one model. Jacobson (1989) also uses aggregate data to explore congressional voting. Jacobson's approach is to focus on the ability of talented and strategically thinking politicians to run for election when the chances of success for their party are relatively high (with respect to time). The research investigates the influences of the political elite as a mediating factor on the referendum characteristics of congressional elections.

Some of the variables, both dependent and independent, that Jacobson uses are conceptually related to those used by Marra and Ostrom, such as change in House seats on the dependent side and presidential approval on the independent side. Moreover, the questions raised by each reflect an intellectual correspondence regarding topical debates in the literature. However, the two examples of research also reflect valid but different theoretical perspectives in their approaches to these questions. Thus, we have a situation of related questions, alternate model specifications, and (most important) different expectations with regard to each respective set of results.

This point of contrasting theoretical perspectives is important to make here because my analysis presents a view of congressional voting from another, different theoretical perspective, a perspective tied to the concept of electoral institutionalization. Some of the variables used here are similar to those used in research drawn from entirely different points of view. But the model specification explored here is very different from the specifications found elsewhere, and the expectations of my current analysis are also very different. It is *not* that the specifications and expectations found elsewhere are incorrect, for they are not. They are just directed at different questions. The intellectual contribution of this chapter is my approach to raising and answering new questions about mass congressional mobilization, more so than challenging current answers to older questions. If the contribution is significant to our understanding of the phenomena, subsequent investigations are likely not only to refine the answers, but to further develop the questions, connecting them more closely to evolving topical debates.

The Basic Theoretical Structure

All presidential competitions are not the same in their ability to "shock" the normal rhythms of the congressional mobilization cycle. Some presidential competitions are unusual in the magnitude of their impact on congressional turnout. Moreover, there are long-term mobilization trends that are not clearly tied, in a causal sense, to particular presidential competitions (Ferejohn and Calvert 1984; Kawato 1987). Thus, there are two components to the mobilization cycle that are critical to the current analysis. The first component identifies a "base" of mobilized voter support for each of the two major parties. This base is unique for each party and is independent of the four-year cyclical surges in mobilization associated with the presidential calendar. It is very close to the level of support given to each party during off-year elections. However, changes in off-year support are often viewed as a consequence of aspects of previous on-year competitions. Thus, *base mobilization* refers to the level of mobilized voter support that would be given to each party in a mythical world with only off-year elections. Changes in this base reflect fundamental, long-term changes in a party's electoral support.

The second component of the mobilization cycle that is critical to my analysis is the ability of certain types of presidential competitions to disturb the underlying base of congressional support. Disturbances can vary in magnitude and duration. Moreover, greater magnitude disturbances may have greater longitudinal impacts as well. This is an argument made explicitly by Przeworski (1975) and Sprague (1981) in reference to voting in situations of highly institutionalized electoral politics. In this sense, the "memory" of an electoral system is the length of time in which a particular event is felt in the base support of the political competitions that follow.

To the extent that the base of partisan congressional support and its over-time response to electoral disturbances are conditioned by salient political issues and events, the dynamic structure of the congressional mobilization cycle should reflect the localized social reactions to the politics of the day. This analysis characterizes the structure of the mobilization cycle as dependent on particular social environments. For example, due to the civil rights movement of the 1960s, the mobilization cycle should be different for African-Americans in the southern states during this time than, say, whites. Thus, there must be an identification of the national components of the overall cycle. But variations in that cycle should appear as conditional on relevant social environments. The purpose of this identification is not to systematically outline all meaningful variations in the cycle for all large groups in the United States. Rather, the strategy is to show that variations in the cycle do indeed occur and to offer insight into the causal relationships underlying the structure of such variations.

My analysis begins with a description of the primary influences on the congressional mobilization cycle as they have been identified in much of the extant electoral literature. This section assists in identifying the theoretical considerations motivating the construction of a formal model of the cycle. The model is evaluated with respect to an unusually complete collection of county-level data for all of the United States during the period from 1950 through 1984. The results are then examined to reveal anomalous structural characteristics of the underlying dynamics. Variations in the dynamic characteristics of the cycle that correspond with different social environments are examined heuristically to identify critical aspects of divergence from the national structure.

Borrowing from Some Current Theories

The extant electoral literature related to congressional mobilization ranges across an amazingly wide range of topics. A conceptual organization of a comprehensive collection of such material is beyond the scope of this analysis. However, some crude guidelines can help to represent some of the major themes of the literature that, in turn, will assist in placing the subsequent modeling effort within that larger body.

In very (and perhaps unfairly) general terms, the vote mobilization literature with particular relevance to the present analysis can be grouped according to three approaches. They are identified here as (1) surge and decline, (2) political economy, and (3) party organizational activities. With regard to the so-called surge and decline phenomenon, authors such as Campbell (1960), Key (1964, 567–71), and Stokes and Miller (1962, 531–34) focus on the role of presidential elections in increasing voter interest in political campaigns, consequently increasing vote mobilization for the lower level nonpresidential elections. The more successful a party's presidential candidate, the greater the mobilization of voters for that party's congressional candidates, relative to the other party. While some research has indicated that this effect may have diminished (Ferejohn and Calvert 1984), the influence of presidential contests on the congressional vote nonetheless persists. More recently, however, much of the debate has focused on a particular aspect of the surge and decline phenomenon. That is, the president's party consistently loses support in off-year elections, relative to the other party. While much research has focused on this phenomenon with regard to U.S. congressional elections, the pattern has also been evident in gubernatorial and state legislative races as well (Campbell 1986; Chubb 1988; Patterson and Caldeira 1983).

To explain this phenomenon, some have argued that midterm elections are adjustments to the outcomes of preceding presidential elections (Hinckley 1967; also see Franklin 1971). Some researchers see the off-year process as one that is structured by the mobilization of different types of votes. Voters are classified according to whether they are "core" (i.e., strong partisan) or "peripheral" (i.e., weak partisan) voters (Glaser 1962a and 1962b). The research, as is perhaps typical of much voting research, has spawned its own debate, and there are claims both supporting and contesting such distinctions of voter types (e.g., Arseneau and Wolfinger 1973; Campbell 1987; DeNardo 1980; Petrocik 1981b). Another body of research has developed a set of alternative hypotheses that characterize the off-year elections as referenda on the president's popularity and his handling of the economy (Cover 1986; Fiorina 1977; Kernell 1977; Kramer 1971; Piereson 1975; Tufte 1975). Abramowitz, Cover, and Norpoth (1986) have gone a step farther, finding that the outcomes of midterm elections vary differentially, dependent on whether the election is the first or second such election for the president's party.

The second major area of the congressional electoral literature that is relevant to this study is actually a subfield of the very broad area of political research loosely labeled "political economy." The focus of much of this research has been to identify aggregate and individual patterns of voting that correspond (in predicted directions) to fluctuations in the economy. Some research has tried to identify the strong emotional characteristics associated with such economic fluctuations (Conover and Feldman 1986). Fiorina (1977) has developed a model explaining how voters "retrospectively" use their opinions of the president's performance on a variety of issues, including economic issues. And many of the current debates have concentrated on determining whether voters respond to their own personal economic situations (the so-called pocketbook theory of voting) or to perceived national economic fortunes (i.e., "sociotropic voting," see Kinder and Kiewiet 1981; Kramer 1971; Lewis-Beck 1985; Markus 1988; also see Chappell and Keech 1985).

The final broad approach to the mobilization literature that is of special interest here is that of party mobilization. Gosnell (1927) was one of the first to explore this interesting aspect of voting behavior, noting that campaign voter-contact activity really did make a difference in turning out the vote. In the modern era of electoral competitions in a context of weak party organizations, few researchers qualitatively distinguish between party- and candidate-sponsored mobilization activities. While debate does exist, one finding in the literature is that political activity on the part of candidates and the party elite (using a variety of means) is of significant importance in mobilizing congressional votes (e.g., Beck 1974; Jacobson 1987b; Mann and Wolfinger 1980). Moreover, this is a general finding, extending to noncongressional elections as well (e.g., Patterson and Caldeira 1983). In this analysis, mobilization activities on the part of the political elite are seen to enhance the process of institutionalization by reinforcing the bonds of contact between the candidate or party organizations and voters.

It is useful to pause and summarize the specific points that will be directly employed in my modeling effort. First, and most obviously, there is an on-year/off-year cycle to congressional mobilization that is directly tied to the timing of presidential elections. Second, congressional mobilization for a particular party in an on-year is in proportion with the success of the party's presidential nominee. Third, in off-year elections, the president's party almost always loses some congressional support relative to the other party. Fourth, the performance of the economy can affect the success of the president's party in congressional elections. Finally, candidate and party activities maintain and enhance local levels of electoral mobilization. Considered individually, these basically descriptive points are neither controversial nor novel. However, my work connects these points in the construction and interpretation of a dynamically specified formal model of the mobilization process. The model is then used to reveal some nonobvious stability characteristics of this process.

The Dynamic Structure of Congressional Mobilization

Among the primary aims of the modeling effort described here is the segregation of the base level of congressional mobilization for each party from the effect of the presidential contests (i.e., the on-year surge) while simultaneously controlling for the impact of change in the national economy. The time frame for this analysis, the years from 1950 to 1984, spans thirty-four years and eighteen congressional elections. The model of the congressional mobilization process developed below is a time-dependent system of interconnected difference equations that are evaluated with respect to aggregate partisan strengths for the entire time period. Within the system are states that correspond to the base level of mobilization for each party.

Throughout this analysis, mobilization is conceptualized and measured as the proportion of eligible adults who cast their ballots for a political party in an election. The use of the mobilization measure, instead of an alternative vote-share measure, is consistent with practices followed by Przeworski (1975), Przeworski and Sprague (1986), Brown (1987), and others in related research on political mobilization.

In this study, congressional mobilization for a political party is initially characterized as a function with three components. The first is the base level of mobilization for that party. This is the most complicated of the three primary components of the model, and it receives expanded treatment below. The second component is the effect of the presidential election in swelling the ranks of mobilized partisan supporters. Finally, the influence of the national economy on the congressional elections is included as a separate effect. Using CD_t to represent the level of congressional mobilization for the Democratic party at time t, this quantity can be functionally expressed as in equation 7.1,

$$CD_t = DBASE_t + g(PD_t) + b(PRESIDENCY_t)(ECONOMY_t). \quad (7.1)$$

Here, $DBASE_t$ represents the base level of Democratic congressional mobilization at time t. PD_t is the mobilized proportion of the electorate (i.e., eligibles) voting for the Democratic presidential candidate, and g is a parameter reflecting the proportional impact of presidential mobilization on congressional mobilization. This characterization of the relationship between presidential and congressional mobilization is entirely consistent with evidence reported in the related electoral literature, and merely states that increases in congressional mobilization are proportional to the level of partisan mobilization in the presidential contest. Note that for off-year elections, $PD_t = 0$.

The last term in equation 7.1 is an interaction term between two variables that capture the partisan control of the presidency together with per capita change in the gross national product, all at time t. The *PRESIDENCY* term is a directional control variable that is scaled 1 if there is a Democrat in the White House at time t and -1 if there is a Republican president (a design used similarly by Chubb 1988). The variable labeled *ECONOMY* represents the per capita change in GNP at time t. The economic measure (per capita change in GNP) has been transformed to have a mean of zero and a standard deviation of one, enhancing the intuitive interpretation of a measure of good and bad national economic fortunes that is relative across time. The combined interaction term acts as a control variable, the effect of which is captured by parameter b.

The base of congressional mobilization for a party ($DBASE_t$ in eq. 7.1), as viewed here, is linked to two factors. The first is that a party's base level of mobilization in any particular election is dynamically tied to its base level of mobilization during the two previous elections. This is due to the on-year/off-year character of the mobilization process. If an electoral shock is added to the system during any one election, its subsequent influence will necessarily reverberate through two critically different types of partisan competitions. Thus, the base of a party's congressional mobilization should follow a second-order time-dependent process.

The second factor to consider in characterizing a party's base level of mobilization is the level of support that must be discounted from an on-year's level of total mobilization to arrive at a predicted value for the next election's off-year base. Recall that the concept of a base level of mobilization is comparable to the level of mobilization that would occur in a world of only off-year elections. Thus, in order to construct a model capturing the movement of the base mobilization process, a way must be found to translate on-year mobilization outcomes to approximate what would likely have occurred had each election been a continuous sequence of off-year elections.

There are two relevant parts to the problem. Primarily, the increased level of mobilization that a party experienced in the previous on-year election at time $t - 1$ (relative to the election before that at time $t - 2$) must be removed from the mobilization expectations for the current off-year congressional election at time t. However, another adjustment is required. One result in the congressional electoral literature about which there is little (if any) controversy is that the president's party suffers in the off-year elections (although the debate continues about the cause of this phenomenon). If base mobilization is written as a second-order time-dependent process, then the expectation for a current off-year result must take into account the effect of presidential incumbency on the congressional election.

The mobilization concepts described here can be combined with equation 7.1 (restated below as eq. 7.4) to represent the entire dynamic system of congressional mobilization as a system of equations (beginning with notation for the Democratic party).

$$X_{D(t-1)} = CD_{t-1} - (PD_{t-1}[g + j(DINC_t) - k(RINC_t)]); \qquad (7.2)$$

$$DBASE_t = m[X_{D(t-1)}] + a[X_{D(t-2)}] + f; \qquad (7.3)$$

$$CD_t = DBASE_t + g(PD_t) \\ + b(PRESIDENCY_t)(ECONOMY_t). \qquad (7.4)$$

Equation 7.2 models congressional mobilization after it has been adjusted for the presidential surge effect as well as the effect of presidential incumbency. All this is defined as the state of the system $X_{D(t-1)}$. This is then used as an input into equation 7.3. When time $t - 1$ is an off-year election, then the level of presidential mobilization, PD_{t-1}, is zero and $X_{D(t-1)}$ is simply the level of congressional mobilization, CD_{t-1}. If the election at time $t - 1$ is an on-year election, then $X_{D(t-1)}$ is adjusted to eliminate the increase in mobilization that is due to the presidential election. Thus, the quantity $g(PD_{t-1})$ is subtracted from CD_{t-1} to account for that year's presidentially related mobilization surge. Note that parameter g also appears in equation 7.4. This maintains the formal consistency of the overall system and is also discussed more fully below.

The amount of mobilization loss in off-year elections also depends on which party occupies the White House in the current off-year. This is the "president's party takes a beating in the off-year election" phenomenon. For example, without controlling for presidential incumbency, if the current election at time t is an off-year election with a Democratic incumbent, then the model in equation 7.3 would tend to overpredict the current level of Democratic base mobilization ($DBASE_t$). This is because the current off-year level should be lower by an amount proportional to the previous election's level of presidential mobilization for the Democratic party. The reverse would be true if the incumbent president is a Republican. Thus, we require additional inputs to the system that are proportional to the level of presidential mobilization at time $t - 1$ to control for the effect of presidential incumbency.

In equation 7.2, variable $DINC$ is coded as a 1 if the president is a Democrat during an off-year election at time t, and as a 0 if the president is a Republican. In a compatible fashion, the variable $RINC$ is coded as a 1 if a Republican is president in an off-year at time t and 0 otherwise. Parameters j and k measure the change from the previous on-year level of presidential mobilization that would occur due to the effect of presidential incumbency in the current off-year election. Thus, if there is a Democratic president during the current off-year election, then the amount of congressional mobilization dropped from the Democratic party totals from the previous election will be an amount equal to $j(DINC_t)(PD_{t-1})$. Similarly, if there is a Republican in the White House, the input from the previous election must be increased by an amount proportional to the previous level of presidential support, as structured by parameter k.

Note that equation 7.3 is a second-order, linear difference equation with constant coefficients. The theory of such equations is complete (Goldberg 1958). Equation 7.3 characterizes base congressional mobilization for the Democratic party as a second-order time-dependent process. Parameters m and a structure the flow of the second-order process. Parameter f is a constant input that represents a fixed minimal level of what might be called "constant mobilization" that is independent of previous levels of mobilization. In an analogous sense, parameter f has a dynamic parallel to the intercept of a static linear model. Equations 7.2 and 7.3 are described further using graph algebra in the appendix to this chapter.

In terms of the overall system, equation 7.3 produces a predicted level of base mobilization (intuitively conceptualized as a simulated continuous sequence of predicted off-year election totals) for each election year that is then substituted into equation 7.4. Equation 7.4 estimates total congressional mobilization by linearly combining the estimated base mobilization with the estimated impact of the presidential contests (in on-years) and recent economic performance on the congressional elections.

The Republican party counterpart to this system for the Democratic party is identical in form to equations 7.2 through 7.4 and is presented here as equations 7.5 through 7.7.

$$X_{R(t-1)} = CR_{t-1} - (PR_{t-1}[w - j(DINC_t) + k(RINC_t)]);\qquad(7.5)$$

$$RBASE_t = q[X_{R(t-1)}] + s[X_{R(t-2)}] + v;\qquad(7.6)$$

$$CR_t = RBASE_t + w(PR_t) + d(PRESIDENCY_t)(ECONOMY_t).\qquad(7.7)$$

In equations 7.5 and 7.6, $X_{R(t-1)}$ is the state of the system for the Republican party that is the mirror image of $X_{D(t-1)}$ for the Democratic party. The base level of congressional mobilization for the Republican party at time t is $RBASE_t$, and CR_t is that party's total level of mobilization. Note that parameter w occurs in both equations 7.5 and 7.7. Also, parameters j and k occur in equation 7.5 and equation 7.2, although with opposite signs in each equation. Throughout the model, the sharing of particular parameters maintains the accounting compatibility of the entire system and enhances the substantive interpretations of the interdependent character of the structure.

The entire formal system is a time-dependent structure of six equations. The system is symmetrical with respect to political parties, and it is entirely general in its ability to capture complex structural over-time congressional mobilization change. Models of this type have been explored for social scientific use by Coleman (1964 and 1981), Huckfeldt, Kohfeld, and Likens (1982), Luenberger (1979), Przeworski and Sprague (1986), Sprague (1981), Rapoport (1983), Simon (1957), Tuma and Hanna (1984), as well as others. Such models are also commonly encountered in the literature on population biology, in which population change within an interdependent ecosystem is best modeled from the perspective of generational transitions and seasonal fluctuations (May 1974; Nisbet and Gurney 1982). The mathematical theory of such equations is complete (Goldberg 1958), as is the theory and practice of the graphic analysis of such systems (Kocak 1989; Mesterton-Gibbons 1989).

One final modification is made to the structure before evaluating the system with respect to a body of data. As the system stands, it is capable of characterizing the on-year/off-year congressional mobilization cycle for the entire United States. However, here we are interested in how the entire system may vary in response to different social environments. For example, in the southern states during the 1960s and 1970s, African-Americans began to vote in larger numbers. We are interested in whether or not their response to the congressional mobilization cycle would be similar to that of the rest of the nation. If newly mobilized voters tend to vote more predominantly in on-year elections, compared with off-year elections, then the on-year/off-year swings should be larger in predominantly southern African-American areas. Furthermore, if weakly institutionalized voters are more volatile as a group in their longitudinal behavioral reactions to electoral disturbances, then we would like to know if the system is more stable in some environments than in others. To answer these and other questions related to system responses to differences in social environments, each of these parameters are written as a linear function of a conditioning social variable as in the analyses in previous chapters.

Estimating the System

The data used in this analysis to evaluate the model of congressional mobilization are aggregate county-level electoral totals combined with county-level census information. These data are for all counties in the United States (approximately 3,000) for the eighteen congressional elections from 1950 through 1984.[1] Using this unusually complete set of data, partisan support for each party is computed as a proportion of the total set of eligible voters as determined by age. In all of the computations reported in this analysis, all county-level observations are weighted by population. Details of the estimation procedure are contained in the Appendix.

In the analysis that follows, the system is evaluated with respect to six conditioning variables. These variables are (1) urbanization (a density measure is used), (2) farm activity measured as the proportion of total county acreage under cultivation, (3) a conditioning variable for counties in nonsouthern states (coded 1 for nonsouthern counties, zero otherwise), (4) a

---

1. All of the data utilized in this analysis were made available by the Inter-University Consortium for Political and Social Research. The data for more recent elections (i.e., since the 1950s) are distributed in a much more readily usable form than those corresponding to earlier elections.

conditioning variable for southern states (coded 1 for counties in the southern states, zero otherwise), (5) the proportion of white residents, broken down by southern and nonsouthern regions, and (6) the proportion of African-American residents, again broken down by southern and nonsouthern regions.

The system is evaluated with respect to each of these conditioning variables while simultaneously controlling for all partisan movements identified in the model. Crucially, when estimating the system with respect to the conditioning variables for whites and African-Americans, the conditioned estimates are evaluated twice—once for the pre-1964 period and again for the post-1964 period. This is done to enable a comparison between the system during these two very different periods in American electoral history. Each of the conditioning variables, except the southern and nonsouthern dummies, are transformed to have a mean of zero and a standard deviation of one. This technically assists in the comparison of the relative effects of the different conditioning social environments on the overall system.

The conditioning variables are not chosen to represent a complete collection of all of the relevant social environments that might structure the congressional mobilization cycle. They are chosen to serve as heuristic tools that should show differences between major sectors of U.S. society. For example, there have been rural and urban divisions in U.S. politics that have been repeatedly reported in the electoral literature, particularly the realignment literature (Chubb 1978; Ladd and Hadley 1978; Lubell 1965; Petrocik 1981a; Sundquist 1983). It would be very interesting to see if these historical alignment differences are in any way mirrored by differences in other, more regularly cyclical electoral movements. A comparison between the North and South conditioning variables will help us understand if regions with substantially different social and developmental histories respond differently to similar electoral forces.

The conditioning variables for white and African-American areas in the South allow for a particular test of ideas that are inspired by discussions of southern race mobilization dating back to V. O. Key (1949), but recently enlivened by Black and Black (1987), Carmines and Stimson (1989), Huckfeldt and Kohfeld (1989), and Stanley (1987). Historically, whites in the South have been particularly strident in their opposition to the expression of African-American civil and political rights. In the 1960s and 1970s, politics in the South began to radically change as southern African-Americans began to vote in large numbers. Two related questions are of great interest to us here with regard to this change in voting patterns. First, what is the effect on the stability of the base level of congressional mobilization when large numbers of new voters (i.e., African-Americans) begin to participate in the electoral system? For example, are there wild swings in mobilization as these new voters participate in one election but abandon their participatory role in another? Specifically, how long does it take these new voters to become institutionalized, participating in a self-regulating and smooth functioning mobilization cycle?

The second question relating to these race-oriented conditioning variables regards the electoral activity of the whites. Specifically, what is their parallel behavioral response with regard to the congressional mobilization cycle during a time of increased African-American participation? Since, in the South, whites had been regularly participating in electoral politics for a longer time than African-Americans, a comparison between the time-dependent stability characteristics of the base levels of mobilization for white and African-American areas should yield substantial insight into whether the length of time of participation yields institutionalized benefits in terms of stability to the overall system. (This idea is also linked to ideas on racial mixing that have been suggested by Schelling [1978].)

Some readers may wonder if any comparison using southern pre-1964 African-American mobilization makes sense, given the restrictions on the African-American franchise at the time (the Jim Crow laws). However, despite these restrictions, many African-Americans in southern states did manage to vote, although in smaller numbers than whites. Indeed, Black and Black (1987, 137) have reported that African-American voter registration in the Deep South in 1956 was 21 percent. (It was 29 percent in the peripheral South.) Thus, there is sufficient variation in African-American voting in the South to discern the longitudinal dynamics in these data, and to make comparisons between this and other voter groups.

As with the analyses presented in previous chapters, the present analysis uses aggregate-level data to estimate mobilization processes involved in the congressional electoral cycle. Elsewhere, survey and aggregate data have been productively used countless times—sometimes separately, sometimes in combination—to investigate matters relating to congressional elections. My analysis is aimed at complementing these existing studies by employing an unusual treatment of aggregate data. The survey data that are available for this time period are not adequate for the present investigation. Panel data, which this analysis would require due to the need to recreate numerous longitudinal histories, are available for only limited periods. Moreover, the sample sizes of surveys for certain subgroups in the population are extremely small. The aggregate measures offer a unique opportunity to examine the congressional mobilization cycle using the relatively small, county-level units. These measures also allow contextual interpretations that refer to social environments that experience differences in voter turnout.

Results

The parameter estimates for the entire system, including the conditioned estimates, are presented in tables 7.1–7.3.[2] Table 7.1 shows the estimates for

---

2. The estimation requirements, as well as the software used in these analyses, are discussed in the Appendix.

TABLE 7.1. **Unconditioned Congressional Mobilization Parameter Estimates, 1950–84**

Parameter	Estimate	χ^2	Parameter Content
m	0.40773	857,927,573	Democratic Base Parameter
a	0.37938	726,007,070	Democratic Base Parameter
f	0.05047	302,498,398	Democratic Base Parameter
b	0.00311	469	Dem. Economic Press/Incumbency Interaction
g	0.23549	10,419,946	Dem. Press/Congressional Surge Effect
j	0.10928	5,319,837	Dem. Press/Incumbency Off-Year Effect
q	0.55073	1,511,797,044	Republican Base Parameter
s	0.32154	539,320,393	Republican Base Parameter
v	0.02023	52,129,362	Republican Base Parameter
d	−0.01352	9,529	Rep. Economic Press/Incumbency Interaction
w	0.22807	6,832,486	Rep. Press/Congressional Surge Effect
k	0.02810	941,556	Rep. Press/Incumbency Off-Year Effect

Notes: Chi-square $df = 1$. Republican goodness of fit = 0.670; Democratic goodness of fit = 0.611.

the unconditioned parameters and a brief description of each parameter's function in the model; the estimates associated with mobilization for the Democratic party are above those for the Republican party.[3] The fits of the model to the data are also included in the table. The chi-square statistics test the significance of each parameter's impact on the predicted values of the model. These statistics are explained more thoroughly in the Appendix. Tables 7.2 and 7.3 show the estimates for the conditioned parameters.

The most interesting information to extract from the estimation of the model can be obtained from a tabular and graphic analysis. Before doing this, however, note that the model fits these data fairly well. Given the historical, contextual, and geographical scope of the data involved (approximately 3,000 counties and more than 30 elections), this is an important observation. Moreover, all of the unconditioned estimates have the correct sign. All of the estimates are positive with the exception of parameter d, which controls for the effect of the economy on Republican congressional mobilization. This parameter should have the opposite sign as parameter b (its Democratic counterpart) due to the scaling of the presidential incumbency component of the economic interaction variable.

---

3. All of the results presented in this study were thoroughly examined for potentially problematic statistical properties. Two of the primary areas of focus were potential serial correlation and heteroskedasticity problems. These checks required an examination of residuals at each of the yearly cross-sections as well as among pooled residuals. The checks on serial correlation additionally required an analysis of individual county residuals across elections as well as an analysis of the yearly means. A variety of other tests were also performed. In general, the model seems to capture virtually all of the systemic dynamic movement in these data. None of the checks revealed any indication of problems.

TABLE 7.2. Conditioned Congressional Mobilization Parameter Estimates, 1950–84

Parameter	Urban		Farm Density		Northern		Southern		Southern White		Southern African-American	
	Estimate	χ^2	Estimate	χ^2	Estimate	χ^2	Estimate	χ^2	Estimate	χ^2	Estimate	χ^2
m_1	0.00163225	30,964	−0.007612	188,662	0.014616	873,716	−0.053516	157,463	0.041399	95,503	−0.041148	104,062
a_1	0.00123652	18,074	−0.005102	83,963	−0.007835	244,501	0.021833	25,981	−0.015004	12,095	0.012461	9,215
f_1	−0.00080542	186,359	0.002200	325,162	0.000481	20,333	−0.003070	21,763	−0.000509	620	0.000813	1,739
b_1	−0.00052674	33	−0.003048	255	0.000987	35	0.020130	383	−0.012580	154	0.012270	162
g_1	−0.00025198	25	0.006051	3,621	−0.011933	20,555	0.149080	53,210	−0.092152	25,463	0.090073	27,227
j_1	0.00026327	58	−0.003191	2,595	0.010494	40,165	0.019833	1,437	−0.006178	113	0.006540	140
q_1	−0.00054380	1,294	−0.011583	279,214	−0.001097	5,437	−0.001696	39	0.004340	121	−0.004348	140
s_1	−0.00098240	4,991	0.002210	11,125	−0.008717	364,941	−0.011572	1,505	0.009988	440	−0.009816	491
v_1	−0.00055356	94,795	0.004076	1,207,347	0.001970	365,411	−0.004432	48,731	0.003070	24,235	−0.003008	25,580
d_1	−0.00027972	10	0.003546	374	−0.004890	921	0.019037	368	−0.012093	153	0.012214	173
w_1	0.00047055	29	0.005134	1,017	−0.003681	1,584	0.024037	763	0.007611	60	−0.006299	46
k_1	0.00081659	1,350	0.001344	1,181	−0.001635	2,623	−0.013704	1,621	0.006482	283	−0.006625	326
					Goodness of Fit							
Republican	0.672		0.672		0.671		0.673		0.672		0.672	
Democratic	0.612		0.612		0.612		0.620		0.616		0.617	

TABLE 7.3. Congressional Mobilization Parameter Estimates, Conditioned by Region and Ethnicity

| | Southern White | | | | Southern African-American | | | |
| | 1950–64 | | 1964–84 | | 1950–64 | | 1964–84 | |
Parameter	Estimate	χ^2	Estimate	χ^2	Estimate	χ^2	Estimate	χ^2
m_1	0.09008	41,138.7	0.014609	7,098.1	−0.088002	43,692.4	−0.013400	6,593.8
a_1	0.01031	608.9	0.007441	1,772.2	−0.011954	912.9	−0.009135	2,956.1
f_1	−0.00163	1,040.1	−0.004287	19,633.1	0.001915	1,576.2	0.004348	22,229.7
b_1	−0.01894	1,012.2	−0.008130	0.1	0.018586	1,069.0	0.007367	0.1
g_1	−0.15607	19,073.2	−0.051523	5,177.2	0.152516	19,932.8	0.048284	4,995.5
j_1	0.00153	0.4	−0.008727	127.1	−0.000802	0.1	0.008072	120.8
q_1	0.00302	0.2	0.016938	1,897.1	−0.002781	0.3	−0.016525	2,054.7
s_1	0.00526	0.0	0.020820	2,114.2	−0.005933	0.0	−0.019381	2,117.7
v_1	0.00828	27,781.5	−0.001618	3,123.8	−0.008124	29,328.8	0.001472	2,847.9
d_1	−0.03169	2,929.6	−0.010486	0.2	0.031752	3,225.5	0.010412	0.2
w_1	0.00685	18.1	0.007588	66.8	−0.005896	15.1	−0.006713	57.4
k_1	0.01010	36.7	−0.002356	20.7	−0.010013	40.4	0.001577	10.3
			Goodness of Fit					
Republican	0.732		0.617		0.732		0.617	
Democratic	0.672		0.609		0.672		0.609	

(*continued*)

TABLE 7.3—*Continued*

Parameter	Northern White 1950–64 Estimate	χ^2	Northern White 1964–84 Estimate	χ^2	Northern African-American 1950–64 Estimate	χ^2	Northern African-American 1964–84 Estimate	χ^2
m_1	0.069175	45,014.2	0.007674	2,733	-0.060038	36,053	-0.008952	4,400
a_1	0.006523	326.6	-0.020674	19,495	0.025861	5,149	0.031197	52,347
f_1	-0.011994	34,448.4	0.001257	1,812	0.001273	433	-0.003904	20,018
b_1	-0.024802	1,060.6	-0.003111	0	0.027772	1,482	0.005875	0
g_1	-0.026479	457.4	-0.017162	681	0.032659	1,078	0.024281	1,670
j_1	-0.018979	519.9	0.033644	6,611	0.021593	653	-0.036124	8,204
q_1	-0.024519	26,087.0	-0.048105	306,243	0.030070	39,446	0.045990	301,701
s_1	0.009018	4,018.0	-0.009955	12,822	0.002194	235	0.022677	72,198
v_1	0.015949	62,377.0	0.022381	637,966	-0.022048	133,027	-0.024422	870,052
d_1	-0.060613	6,486.6	-0.014150	0	0.061318	7,408	0.012864	0
w_1	-0.024739	1,087.2	0.001697	20	0.032838	2,213	0.007427	418
k_1	-0.013879	1,119.0	0.018749	5,070	0.015048	1,283	-0.014500	3,244
				Goodness of Fit				
Republican	0.735		0.622		0.737		0.622	
Democratic	0.659		0.608		0.660		0.609	

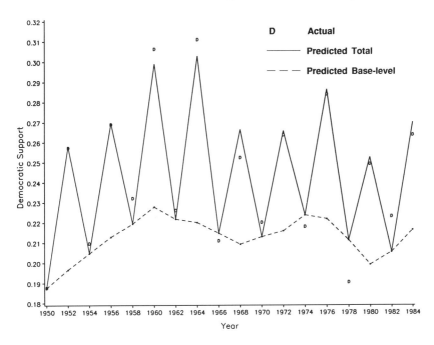

Fig. 7.1. National Democratic congressional mobilization as a proportion of total eligibles, 1950–84

A Check on the Behavior of the System

A graphic representation of the model can provide a comprehensive view of the behavior of the overall system. This serves as a useful check to insure that the system (as estimated) is behaving as expected. A representation of the unconditioned system for national data is shown in figures 7.1 and 7.2. Figure 7.1 displays both the system's predicted means and the actual means of congressional mobilization for the Democratic party during the entire period of study. The letter *D* scattered on the figure represents the national means of actual mobilization for the party over time. The continuous line represents the level of congressional mobilization for the Democratic party as predicted by the entire system. The dashed line represents the base level of Democratic congressional mobilization during the same time period. Figure 7.2 displays mobilization information for the Republican party and has a parallel structure to that of figure 7.1.

Some useful insights regarding long-term partisan trends can be gleaned from a comparison of the Democratic and Republican national representations in figures 7.1 and 7.2. In figure 7.1, note that the Democratic base level of mobilization has remained generally stable over time, gaining during the

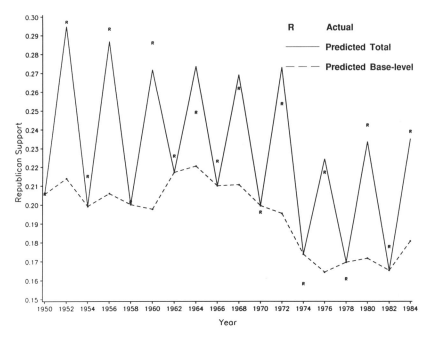

Fig. 7.2. National Republican congressional mobilization as a proportion of total eligibles, 1950–84

1950s and varying stochastically afterward. However, the Republican base level of mobilization, as is seen in figure 7.2, has dropped precipitously since the mid-1960s, seemingly bottoming out in the mid-1970s. On-year mobilization for both parties has generally followed the base-level trends. Comparing on-year congressional mobilization between parties, except for large surges in 1960 and 1964, the Democrats have remained remarkably stable in both predicted and actual terms, even after 1970, when the franchise was extended to citizens 18 years old. Yet Republican on-year mobilization has experienced a rather steady decline since the 1950s, and a rather large drop following Nixon's 1972 reelection as president (a reflection of a lower base).

Thus, Democratic mobilization has not followed the same pattern of decline as Republican mobilization during this time. This pattern is an initial result of the model, and it is particularly interesting, since the decline in total mobilization that has been noted elsewhere (e.g., Jacobson 1987, 98) is not shown to be consistent across both parties here. The decline in total mobilization is a consequence of a decline in base-level Republican mobilization.

In general, figures 7.1 and 7.2 show representations of the model that demonstrate strong consistency between the data and the system's behavior. There are no oddities in the system's dynamics, and the overall trends followed by the model correspond with the more easily observed characteristics of congressional mobilization during the relevant time period. Finally, in the course of these analyses, one extra check was made on the behavior of the overall system. The system was projected to the elections in 1986 and 1988. For both parties, the predicted mobilization rates were very close to those that actually occurred.

The Presidential Surge

One of the most fundamental aspects of congressional mobilization is its sharp increase during years with presidential competitions. There is no reason to assume, however, that the increase is similar across all social environments. Indeed, the aggregate level of electoral institutionalization should be a critical mediating factor in such a presidential surge. More highly institutionalized voters should be more immune to the presidential calendar. They should feel the pull to the ballot box due to their habitual support for their party. Their bonding to their party is also a bonding to the act of voting, and when elections occur, they should go to the polls with greater regularity than their weakly institutionalized counterparts.

At this point, we need to return to our definition of electoral institutionalization. Electoral institutionalization is patterned voting behavior. This includes both the act of voting as well as voting for a particular party. However, one may ask why voting in a congressional election only when there is also a presidential election is not also patterned behavior. In one sense it is. It is behavior that can be repeated. However, there is another aspect to on-year-only congressional voting, and that aspect rests with the reasons behind voting only once every four years.

Those who are the least resistant to the structure of the electoral calendar are also those who have the greatest potential for electoral volatility in general: the weakly institutionalized voters. Here is where the great potential for regime instability also arises. It is the weak point of all electoral systems: voters with weak electoral bonds surging to the polls, pushed by a generated fear or drawn by a charismatic attraction. These voters differ from the every-two-year voters in terms of what it takes to get them to the polls. Moreover, not every presidential election will have the necessary excitement to mobilize all such potential voters. Their mobilization is more keenly tied to the vagaries of each political contest. It is with these voters that the presidential surge should be the greatest.

I now add something to my definition of electoral institutionalization. The strength of a voter's electoral institutionalization is revealed, in part, by his or her resistance to the on/off structure of the electoral calender. Highly institutionalized voters are not so susceptible to the vagaries of particular contests; they will tend to show up at the polls both with greater regularity and with greater frequency. More weakly institutionalized voters are more susceptible to the presidential surge in congressional voting. Greater effort and more excitement are required to get them to the polls, and such things are usually more available during the elections that include presidential contests.

Parameters g and w measure the impact of the presidential election in swelling the mobilized ranks of the congressional vote for both parties. I begin the evaluation of the impact of this presidential surge by examining the estimated values of these parameters (as shown in tables 7.1–7.3). Note that the unconditioned estimates for both parameters are similar in magnitude (table 7.1). In each case, congressional mobilization is increased by slightly less than 25 percent of the total mobilization for each presidential candidate in a given election, relative to the base level of mobilization. While there seems to be a slight Democratic advantage in this regard, the advantage appears to be quite small.

To show how the conditioning variables can restructure the mobilization system, look at the conditioned estimates for the northern and southern states (table 7.2). These estimates are not broken down by pre- and post-1964 periods. Since the northern and southern conditioning variables were scaled as either 1 or 0, depending on geographical location, the conditioned estimates for parameters g and w can simply be added to the unconditioned estimates to determine the complete regional conditioned effect.

Note that in the northern states, both the Democratic and the Republican surge in congressional mobilization is slightly less than that indicated by the unconditioned estimates (which can be interpreted as the national average effect). This can be seen from the negative direction of the conditioned estimates for g and w in the northern states. However, in the southern states, the impact of presidential mobilization on congressional mobilization is in the opposite direction and of a much greater magnitude. Indeed, for the Democratic party, congressional mobilization is enhanced approximately 15 percent over the unconditioned national average due to the mobilization surge tied to the presidential contest. Interestingly, the Republican party gains remarkably less than the Democratic party from the presidential surge in the South. This can be seen from the relatively small value of the southern conditioned estimate for parameter w. These results reflect the dual nature of politics in the South, accurately mirroring the fact that southern Republican support on the presidential level does not fully extend to the more local electoral battles. Southerners may surge to the polls to support Republican presidential candidates, but that surge is only partially transferred to Republican congressional candidates.

A better way (easier and more productive) to examine the presidential surge effects on congressional mobilization in different conditioning social environments is to simultaneously compare the combined conditioned estimates for parameters g and w. These combined estimates are presented in table 7.4. The entries in table 7.4 are computed using the form $g_0 + g_1X$ (using g as an example and where X is the conditioning variable) to correspond to conditioning environments that are complete (i.e., totally urban,

TABLE 7.4. Presidential Surge Effects on Congressional Mobilization in On-Year Elections

Conditioning Area	Democratic Party $(g_0 + g_1X)$	Republican Party $(w_0 + w_1X)$
National	.235	.228
Urban	.238	.233
Farm	.260	.249
North (all years)	.224	.224
South (all years)	.385	.252
Southern white (all years)	.176	.233
Southern African–American (all years)	.641	.200
Southern white (pre-1964)	.142	.232
Southern white (post-1964)	.205	.233
Southern African–American (pre-1964)	.846	.204
Southern African–American (post-1964)	.429	.201
Nonsouthern white (pre-1964)	.217	.211
Nonsouthern white (post-1964)	.223	.229
Nonsouthern African–American (pre-1964)	.291	.284
Nonsouthern African–American (post-1964)	.277	.241

farm, southern African-American, etc.). Thus, the estimates represent the magnitude of the on-year congressional mobilization surge that is due to the mobilization response to the presidential contest within homogeneous conditioning environments. Moreover, many of the estimates are broken down by pre-1964 and post-1964 periods.

The entries in table 7.4 labeled National are the unconditioned estimates for parameters g and w as they are displayed in table 7.1. Most of the conditioned environments shown in table 7.4 exhibit an approximate on-year increase in congressional mobilization of about 20 percent to 25 percent of presidential mobilization with the general exception of the southern conditioning environments. Note that, for the Democratic party, the on-year congressional mobilization in the South overall is more affected by the level of presidential mobilization than outside the South (38 percent of presidential mobilization in the South, compared with 22 percent outside the South). However, in southern white areas (all years) the reverse is true. In these areas only 17.5 percent of presidential mobilization is transferred as an increase in congressional mobilization. Moreover, in southern African-American areas, 64 percent of presidential mobilization is transferred directly to an increase in congressional mobilization. This is an important result, and it is what we were expecting to find given our theoretical assumptions. Southern African-Americans have shorter voting histories, on the aggregate level, than white southerners. Thus, their level of electoral institutionalization should be lower, and the influence of the presidential surge in mobilization should be greater. This is, in fact, what we find.

The greater lesson is found when we break down southern voting by electoral period. Beginning with the Democratic party, note that the pre-1964 presidential surge in southern white congressional mobilization is the smallest of any group listed in the table. In such areas, congressional mobilization increases only 14 percent of the presidential mobilization. However, the post-1964 presidential surge increases to 20 percent.

These numbers are substantively very significant. There are few examples of a group that has been as thoroughly institutionalized into their support for an American political party than southern white voters before 1964. Communities of these voters had been voting for the Democratic party virtually exclusively since the end of the Civil War. Thus, this is precisely the group that should be least affected by the surge in congressional mobilization that is caused by presidential competitions, and this is exactly what is shown by the data for this group in table 7.4. Crucially, the influence of presidential elections increases after 1964 to more closely parallel the national effect. Following the national Democratic party's involvement with the civil rights campaign of the 1960s, the breakdown of white southerners' institutionalization to that party was probably inevitable. With the decline in Democratic institutionalization, the increased influence of the presidential elections on congressional mobilization was equally inevitable.

The data in table 7.4 for southern African-American voters strongly supports the hypothesis that a lower level of partisan institutionalization corresponds with a higher magnitude of presidential surge effects. In the pre-1964 period, the congressional mobilization surge in on-year elections is almost 85 percent of presidential mobilization. While it is true that the African-American vote during that period was severely restricted, such voters did exist in relatively small numbers. Their institutionalization was undoubtedly very low—which is probably an understatement. Yet among those who did manage to vote, the presidential elections were virtual lightning rods. After 1964, and after the effective extension of the franchise to the remainder of the southern African-American electorate, voting became a more routine experience for these voters. Electoral institutionalization necessarily increased among African-Americans and the Democratic party, and the influence of the presidential elections on congressional mobilization decreased. While the presidential surge effect is still relatively high in the post-1964 period, the effect is nonetheless half its earlier magnitude, a very significant decrease by any standard. This is as expected, since the influence of institutionalization on congressional mobilization is by definition a gradual and incremental process.

The influence of presidential competitions on congressional elections outside the South is much less dramatic than in the southern states. Nonsurprisingly, the effect for whites outside the South hover around the national averages for both parties in both the pre-1964 and the post-1964 periods. This is a very important result, since this group acts as a control group with regard to comparisons with southern voters, both white and African-American. Since there was no dramatic change in the frequency or character of voting among northern white voters between the early and late periods, there should not be a large change in the presidential surge effect. That there is, in fact, no large change helps to confirm our interpretation with regard to southern voters.

The presidential surge effects for African-Americans outside the South are a bit higher than for whites, especially in the pre-1964 period. Nonetheless, the change for the post-1964 period is in the direction of a decreased surge effect, and the actual numbers are not too different from the national averages. All of this corresponds to an African-American population outside the South that is collectively experiencing a modest increase in partisan institutionalization. It is very significant that this increase is much less dramatic than the comparable increase in institutionalization among African-Americans in the southern states. This suggests that the process of electoral institutionalization may be nonlinear in its longitudinal dynamic, although its precise specification is not yet determined. One likely specification would be a logistic process with a rapid initial growth rate, in which most of the change happens early on, with future increments occurring with decreasing magnitudes.

All of these results strongly confirm our expectations about the influence of presidential competitions on the surge in congressional mobilization and varying levels of partisan institutionalization. They also correspond closely with other results regarding the memory of the system dynamics. The total potential for volatility in the electoral system is critically dependent on the equilibria of base-level mobilization as well, a topic that we turn to first.

An Analysis of Base-Level Mobilization Equilibria

There is always longitudinal variation in congressional mobilization. Elections come and go. Mobilization surges and declines are as regular as the tides. Charismatic candidates rivet the crowds, and dull candidates put them to sleep. Parties organize the masses, and parties fail to organize the masses. All sorts of things happen, and mobilization changes: it always changes. But what is there in the middle of this change that pulls all movement back, returning aggregate mobilization in the direction of some center of gravity, some anchoring point? What stops fast mobilization growth from exploding, smashing the system boundaries? What ultimately acts as a center of perspective from which all change is relative? The answer to all of these questions is the same: the system's equilibrium level of base mobilization.

The equilibrium for partisan base mobilization simply refers to the level of mobilization that is ultimately supportable by the system. It may be that mobilization in one year is relatively high. But if the trend is downward over time, knowing its equilibrium level tells us toward what level it is ultimately heading. If mobilization is already near its equilibrium, then it is likely to stay near that level as long as the equilibrium level is stable. In the language of dynamics, such an equilibrium is called a "stable attractor."

In the system under analysis, the equilibria for Republican and Democratic base-level mobilization are calculated from equations 7.3 and 7.6. At equilibrium, and in the absence of short-term disturbances, the system tends to remain where it is; there is no deterministic movement in any of the states, and the level of base mobilization is equal across all time periods. Setting all states equal and solving for the Democratic and Republican equilibria (see Goldberg 1958), we have

$$D^* = f/(1 - m - a), \tag{7.8}$$

and

$$R^* = v/(1 - q - s). \tag{7.9}$$

In equations 7.8 and 7.9, D^* and R^* are the congressional base mobilization equilibria for the Democrats and the Republicans, respectively. The equilibria for the system in conditioning environments is similarly obtained by substituting the complete conditioned estimates.

Table 7.5 lists the estimated equilibria for both the Democratic and Republican parties under national (i.e., unconditioned) and conditioned environments. Note that, nationally, the Democratic party has an approximate 8 percent long-term advantage in mobilization over the Republican party. Given the dominance of the Democratic party in the House of Representatives, this is no surprise. Moreover, this generally corresponds with observations made elsewhere using aggregate measures (see Sprague 1981) as well as observations based on discernible recent trends evident in available survey information (e.g., Ladd 1982). The national result also serves as a baseline from which to evaluate the equilibria for the conditioned environments.

We can begin the discussion of the equilibria in conditioning environments by comparing Democratic and Republican urban equilibria. In urban areas, the Democratic advantage over the Republican party is greater than it is for the entire nation. The problem for the Republican party is that its urban equilibrium is quite low. Some of this disadvantage is certainly due to high concentrations of African-Americans in the urban areas, as is shown in other conditioned values. But regardless of cause, this result by itself suggests that overall short-term gains by the Republican party in urban areas are not likely to last. The "pull" is down, and "down" is 14 percent below Democratic mobilization.

TABLE 7.5. Equilibrium Values for Democratic and Republican Base Mobilization

Conditioning Area	Democratic	Republican
National	0.237	0.158
Urban	0.240	0.103
Farm	0.214	0.235
North (all years)	0.243	0.158
South (all years)	0.188	0.113
Southern white (pre-1964)	0.324	0.205
Southern white (post-1964)	0.240	0.183
Southern African-American (pre-1964)	0.000	0.000
Southern African–American (post-1964)	0.224	0.000
Nonsouthern white (pre-1964)	0.263	0.227
Nonsouthern white (post-1964)	0.231	0.213
Nonsouthern African-American (pre-1964)	0.194	0.000
Nonsouthern African-American (post-1964)	0.250	0.000

This urban dilemma for the Republican party is only partly offset by an advantage that they hold over the Democrats in farm areas. In farm areas, the Republicans have a clear but narrow long-term advantage. Additionally, both parties have higher levels of equilibrium base mobilization in nonsouthern states, compared with the southern regions (not broken down by time periods). The Democratic party enjoys a substantial long-run competitive advantage relative to the Republican party in both of these areas as well.

The comparison between Democratic and Republican base equilibria in southern white and southern African-American areas deserves special attention. An important observation noted in the relevant electoral literature (and previously mentioned) is that the Republican party is attracting an increasing number of white southerners (Asher 1988, 342). This movement is said to coincide with the increase in Democratic mobilization among African-Americans. The observation is important due to the magnitude of the alignment, and since it alludes to an electoral future with a more competitive, and perhaps racially polarized and highly institutionalized, two-party system on the local level in the southern states. Thus, it is of interest to ask, "To what end is this movement heading?"

Given the estimated structure of the base mobilization system for both parties, broken down by pre-1964 and post-1964 periods, the information in table 7.5 suggests that the Republican party is not yet positioned to receive a stable long-term advantage over the Democrats on the congressional level in its support among white voters. Indeed, the Republican equilibria for southern whites have changed very little between the early and late periods. (The magnitude of the later equilibrium is, in fact, lower than that of the earlier period, although the difference is not statistically discernable. The magnitude of the later period is substantially higher if one limits the analysis to the peripheral southern states, something not done here.) This finding for southern white voters corresponds with suggestions made by Asher (1988, 342) that are based on recent observations using survey data.

The problem for the Republican party is probably one of generational change. This is a point made eloquently by Black and Black (1987). At the congressional level, southern white voters are still rather firmly institutionalized supporters of the Democratic party. As younger white voters replace those who are older, however, this will undoubtedly change. Short-term gains by the Republicans on the local level will then begin to overcome short-term losses, and the gains will, in fact, reflect a long-term increase in the base equilibrium level of support.

The tremendous mobilization gap between the equilibria for the parties for southern African-American voters suggests that the Democratic party is not threatened with a precipitous and long-term decline in southern support in the near future from that sector of the population. While there was no gap in the pre-1964 period (the equilibria were both zero), this was due to the extremely weak presence of the Republican party in local elections at that time in combination with the restriction of the franchise for many African-Americans. On the other hand, both of those conditions have changed in the post-1964 period, yet only the Democratic party's equilibrium due to these voters has changed (to roughly equal the national average). From a practical point of view with respect to the Republican party, the long-term consequences of such a polarization of a major segment of the population is really quite a risky electoral strategy, especially given little longitudinal change in the equilibria for white voters in the Deep South. From such a Republican point of view, one can only hope that things are better outside the South.

But they are not. The results of my analysis strongly suggest that the equilibria for African-Americans and the Republican party outside the South have not changed between the pre-1964 and post-1964 periods. Moreover, both equilibria are zero. The post-1964 equilibrium for this group of voters and the Democratic party has increased from the earlier period. Among nonsouthern whites, however, the equilibria have decreased for both parties over time. This undoubtedly reflects an increase in independence among these voters that has been thoroughly and repeatedly documented in the relevant electoral literature. Nonetheless, the good news for the Republican party is that the Republican-Democratic partisan difference between the nonsouthern equilibria for whites is reduced, and, thus, the long-term prospects for the Republican party among such voters is improved.

In summary, the equilibria presented in table 7.5 are particularly interesting in terms of the long-run interpretations associated with them. Yet this information is very incomplete in the absence of an evaluation of the electoral system's memory. Equilibria tell us the direction that the system is heading. But they do not tell us how long it will take to get there, given perturbations away from these equilibria. This is known through an evaluation of the system's memory.

The connection between system equilibria and system memory is critical to the overall behavior of a democracy. While equilibria are assumed to be constant for long periods of time, they nonetheless can and do change eventually. The ability of a party to change them is dependent on how long electoral events can be "remembered" by the system's electoral dynamics. If the impact of major events quickly diminishes in time, then the prospects for a long-term change in the equilibria are less certain, perhaps slim. If, on the other hand, the impact of major events "rattles around" in the system's dynamics for a longer period of time, the potential for a party to capitalize on that impact in future elections is more promising.

The Memory of the System

There is an important connection between institutionalization and the memory of an electoral system. When something big happens in an election, like a critical landslide win creating a significant shift in the electoral balance, that disturbance to the former state of affairs can have a long-term impact on the nation's politics, or it can be gone with the wind in the next few elections. How long the disturbance lasts determines the historical significance of the election. Indeed, in realignment theory, this is the factor that decides between whether an election is a realigning election or merely a deviating election. All of this, in turn, depends on the level of institutionalization in an electorate.

In brief, strong ties to equilibrium imply strong institutionalization. That is, people have well-established patterns of behavior, and these patterns are not easily broken; thus the equilibrium is strong. On the other hand, when these patterns are broken due to a major political event, highly institutionalized voters will "remember" this event for a long time, implying that the disturbance will influence many future elections. Thus, in the aggregate, long social memories correspond with strong ties to equilibrium in the electoral system in the sense that it is difficult to shift these voters away from their equilibrium. These strong ties to equilibrium result from strong institutionalization. But strong ties to equilibrium do not imply quick returns to equilibrium. Since highly institutionalized voters repeat previous behavior (by definition), their return to an equilibrium can be relatively slow once a sufficiently large event has moved them away from it. Thus, highly institutionalized voters are both difficult to destabilize and slow to readjust. That is, it takes a major effort to change their behavior, but once that is done, it takes a long time for them to return to their former behavior.

Short social memories quickly purge electoral disturbances from the system. This is characteristic of systems with large numbers of weakly institutionalized voters. Weak institutionalization among voters is directly connected to weak ties to equilibrium, since the voting patterns of such voters are less deeply ingrained. They are more easily influenced by the original disturbance and less committed to their previous electoral behavior. Thus the system's ties to equilibrium are not strong. However, since such voters do not have well-established patterns of behavior, they are more likely to "forget" the disturbance in future elections, and their aggregate behavior will quickly bounce back toward equilibrium. Thus, ironically, the weaker the tie to equilibrium, the quicker will be the return to the system's former balance. Again, the strength of the tie to equilibrium is defined in terms of the ease with which voters can be moved from that equilibrium, not in terms of the rapidity of the return to equilibrium.

To test these ideas, it is helpful to remind ourselves of the historical setting of our data. When Lyndon B. Johnson won his landslide victory over Barry Goldwater in 1964, the politics of the United States was critically altered. The Republican party began to act as a voice for a more homogeneous group of conservative Americans, particularly white Americans. The Democratic party began to dramatically increase its political association with African-Americans. Many southern African-Americans, formerly denied the right to vote, experienced the genesis of their own electoral institutionalization. Many southern white Americans did not like what they saw, and their disenchantment with the Democratic party increased correspondingly. Thus, 1964 was a date around which many Americans, especially those in the southern states, experienced a change in political institutionalization. As with the earlier discussions of presidential surge effects and equilibria values, 1964 divides the data in a fashion that allows for a critical test of some of the assumptions that I have made about the institutionalizing process.

One of the primary focuses of these analyses is the hypothesis that highly institutionalized aggregate electoral behavior minimizes electoral volatility. Such highly institutionalized electorates should be resistant to severe disturbances to the electoral system, since existing voting patterns are deeply entrenched. Electorates with very low levels of institutionalization should be more vulnerable to electoral volatility since, by way of example, large groups of voters may rapidly change the direction of their partisan preferences, thus destabilizing a previous partisan balance.

In the analyses that follow, I examine the length of time (measured in numbers of sequential elections) required for an electoral disturbance to decay within a system of congressional mobilization. Substantively, this would be similar to asking how long Johnson's victory in 1964 or Roosevelt's victories in 1932 and 1936 would affect subsequent Democratic congressional politics. Yet, in addition to the speed at which a disturbance is lost from the system, we are also interested in the qualitative manner in which the effect of the disturbance decays. While decay can be gradual and monotonic (i.e., slowly dwindling away), it can also be dramatically changing and oscillatory, with the levels of volatility depending on particular social environments. The substantive implications for the overall stability of the electoral system of these different decay patterns can be quite profound and are explained more thoroughly below.

Two of the factors of the institutionalization process, the speed of decay of an electoral disturbance and the qualitative character of the decay, are critically linked. Basically, there are two types of volatility. The first is the ability of an electoral event to destabilize an existing partisan balance. This was directly addressed in the section on the presidential surge effect. Weakly institutionalized voters have greater potential for this type of volatility since their ties to equilibrium are weak. The second type of volatility is the rapidity of change after the initial disturbance, and this depends on the qualitative nature of the system's memory. It is this type of volatility to which we now turn.

Stated as a hypothesis, the higher the level of electoral institutionalization, the longer the memory of a particular disturbance should remain in the system. Substantively, this says that highly institutionalized voters should be long to remember, and thus repeat, their previous voting behavior, remembering that the initial disturbance is now part of that behavior. Thus, it is more difficult to change the behavior of highly institutionalized voters. But once their behavior is changed, the change should be relatively persistent. Weakly institutionalized voters should experience change more easily (i.e., be more volatile in their behavior), and they should deviate from their previous behavior more quickly. This should be true both in terms of their initial response to the disturbance as well as their responses in subsequent elections.

Extending this to the electoral system's qualitative response following the initial disturbance generally, I can now clearly state my second hypothesis. Thus, the corollary to the memory hypothesis is the volatility hypothesis: higher levels of electoral institutionalization should also be associated with lower levels of volatility subsequent to the initial disturbance. The rapid return to the former system's balance (i.e., equilibrium) for weakly institutionalized voters should increase the volatility of the response in the short run. Moreover, this volatility can include both the response's magnitude and direction.

Utilizing the estimated system of base congressional mobilization under various social conditions, it is possible to test the institutionalization hypotheses mentioned above. To conduct the tests, a type of figure called a *memory plot* is constructed to evaluate the time required by the system under different social environments to absorb disturbances in the mobilization system. (The general utility of memory plots is thoroughly explored in Cortez, Przeworski, and Sprague 1974.) A memory plot is constructed using the equations for base-level mobilization (eqs. 7.3 and 7.6). The system is emptied by setting the state variables (i.e., previous congressional mobilization) to zero. A unit input (i.e., the number *1*) is then inserted into the system for the first time period only. The system is then projected over a number of iterations to see how long it takes for the input to decay. Each iteration represents a simulated election.

The comparison that is made using the estimated results of the conditioned system lends itself readily to a test of both of the institutionalization hypotheses (we can call them the "memory" and "volatility" hypotheses). This is a four-fold comparison: between the memory of the system for southern and nonsouthern areas, and within each area between white voters and African-American voters.

The southern states offer the greatest potential for revealing results. White southerners have been participating in the electoral system relatively longer than African-American southerners. African-American southerners only began to vote in large numbers in the 1960s and 1970s. This difference in the length of previous voting participation along racial lines offers a particularly rich empirical setting for isolating the systemic effects of long-term repeated partisan experiences as an institutionalizing force.

We begin with a memory plot for the Democratic party in the southern states. Figure 7.3 is a memory plot for areas with populations that are virtually 100 percent African-American. There are three trajectories presented in the figure. One trajectory is labeled National and is included in all memory plots for the purposes of comparison. It is computed using the unconditioned parameter estimates. The other two trajectories are labeled Pre-1964 and Post-1964, respectively. The pre-1964 trajectory is the memory of Democratic base mobilization as estimated for the period from 1950 to 1964. The post-1964 trajectory is conceptually identical, but for the period from 1964 to 1984.

In figure 7.3, note that the initial one-unit input decays in the system for all three trajectories as the number of elections increases (i.e., following the input in the first election). This input is sometimes called a one-unit "disturbance" to the system. Its decay is the central characteristic of all memory plots. But also notice that there is a line running horizontally across the plot and intersecting the vertical axis at 0.5. This line represents the half-life point for the decay of the initial unit input. The length of time, measured in elections, needed for the trajectory to decay past this point is called the half-life of the system. In terms of its interpretation, the longer a disturbance remains in the system, the longer is its half-life, and the longer are its effects felt in future elections. To use a substantive example, one might expect the half-life of Roosevelt's reelection impact on congressional mobilization in 1936 to be substantially longer than, say, that of Truman in 1948. Note that in figure 7.3, one trajectory intersects the half-life mark more than once. In situations such as this, our attention focuses on the first instance in which a trajectory passes the half-life mark.

Note that, with all trajectories in figure 7.3, the level of mobilization in the third election is higher than that in the second election. This is a result of

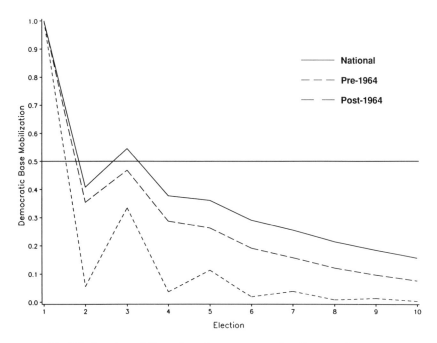

Fig. 7.3. Southern African-American memory plot, Democratic party

an oscillatory (and thus potentially destabilizing) component in the mobilization dynamics for these areas. At first glance it appears that base mobilization decreases in the second election only to increase in the third, all due to one initial shock or disturbance. This is an expected, although not always intuitive, characteristic of the system, both substantively and mathematically.

In real-world data, oscillatory components can be of much lesser magnitude—sometimes barely, if at all, noticeable—easily hidden by stochastic, short-term forces and long-term monotonic trends. However, in this analysis we must force the oscillatory characteristic of the system to be more noticeable in order to study it. The magnitude of the oscillations in figure 7.3 is an artifact of the extreme nature of the initial disturbance, here used to severely stress the mathematical structure of the system and, in so doing, reveal some of its underlying characteristics. Such exaggerated and large-magnitude oscillations, here employed heuristically, are not representative of actual oscillations as observed in these particular data.

Note that, in all of the trajectories in figure 7.3, the volatile oscillatory behavior that appears immediately after the input of the initial disturbance is hardly noticeable after the input is sufficiently decayed. In fact, the oscillatory behavior is still present even at low levels of disturbance. It is just masked by the general trend of decay, giving the appearance of a system transformed to a state of monotonic, gradual decay.

To begin the substantive interpretation of figure 7.3, note that both the pre-1964 and post-1964 trajectories remain below the national (i.e., uncondi- tioned) trajectory. This reflects the quicker decay of the initial input in pre- dominantly African-American southern social environments (and thus the shorter length of each social environment's system memory). Similarly, both the early and late trajectories cross the half-life line before the national trajec- tory. This suggests that African-American communities in the southern states in both time periods experienced lower levels of institutionalization with regard to the Democratic party than was reflected by the overall national population. (Recall that the higher the level of institutionalization, the longer the system memory.) This is as expected since African-Americans in the southern states have only recently begun to participate in the electoral system in large numbers. Note, however, that the pre-1964 system memory is much lower than that for the post-1964 period. This is an important result in the sense that it is critically anticipated, namely, that electoral institutionalization for the Democratic party has increased for African-Americans following their more regular participation in local and national elections after the civil rights campaigns of the 1960s. Thus, with regard to African-Americans in the southern states, the memory hypothesis is confirmed.

Recall that the corollary to the memory hypothesis is the volatility hy- pothesis. That is, societies with dramatically lower levels of system memory are more susceptible to greater levels of systemic volatility. The results shown in figure 7.3 suggest that this is, indeed, the case. The trajectory with the greatest level of instability (shown by the larger magnitude oscillatory swings) is that for the pre-1964 period, a period in which African-American participa- tion in the electoral system was severely restricted, in large part due to the enforcement of a variety of Jim Crow laws. The greater volatility is reflective of the differences in the length and character of the group's voting history. The difference in the level and length of volatile electoral instability is due to variations in the degree of institutionalization, which is linked to numerous, repeated, and reinforcing electoral experiences.

In general, short-term instability is greater for those groups of voters who have relatively short histories of voting, and who are thus not immunized against the destabilizing influences of large electoral disturbances. As elec- toral institutionalization increases, disturbances that do enter the system last longer, but the magnitude of consequent short-term volatile oscillatory change diminishes. This result also supports theoretical expectations about political immunization that have been suggested by McPhee and Ferguson (1962).

These interpretations are strengthened by a comparison of figure 7.3 with a memory plot for areas in the southern states with virtually 100 percent white populations. Such a memory plot is presented here as figure 7.4. In figure 7.4, note that all three trajectories remain close together, relative to the trajectories in figure 7.3. Moreover, note that none of the trajectories exhibit the magni- tude of chaotic oscillation characteristic of pre-1964 African-American com-

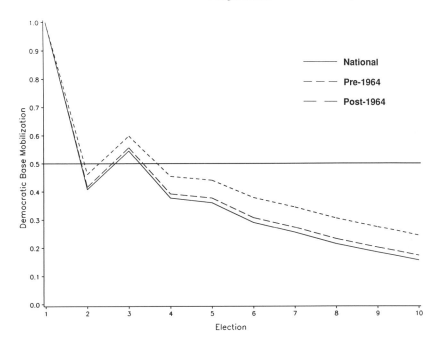

Fig. 7.4. Southern white memory plot, Democratic party

munities, as presented in figure 7.3. Since whites have been active participants in the electoral system for a much longer and continuous time than
African-Americans, it is not expected that levels of institutionalization should
differ dramatically for whites between the pre- and post-1964 periods.

Yet the southern white congressional vote is not entirely what it used to
be with respect to the Democratic party. Before 1964, there was very little
viable opposition to the Democratic party. Individual psychological bonding
to the party was very deeply based, and the change in this bonding—
described in detail by Black and Black (1987)—has been substantial in recent
years. The national Democratic party's stand on civil rights undoubtedly has
acted gradually to weaken the ties between many southern white voters and
their local party organizations, especially in the peripheral South. This is what
is reflected in the decline in system memory (and thus institutionalization)
between the early and late periods in figure 7.4. Nonetheless, the change on
the local level has been very gradual, and thus the level of institutionalization
has moved only modestly to more closely parallel the level of institutionalization found for the Democratic party nationally.

Additional light is shed on these arguments with a brief examination of
some longitudinal voting data for southern counties that are predominantly
African-American and southern counties that are predominantly white. Figure
7.5 presents off-year Democratic congressional mobilization between 1950

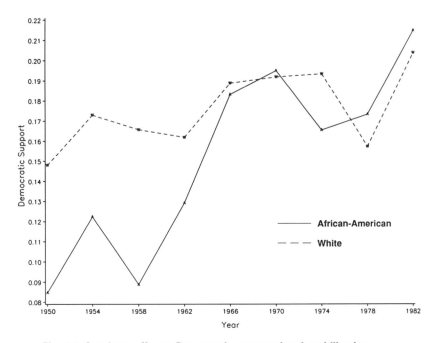

Fig. 7.5. Southern off-year Democratic congressional mobilization as a proportion of total eligibles, 1950–84, selected counties

and 1982 for both white and African-American counties. These data are intuitively comparable with base-level mobilization for both groups with the exception that on-year base mobilization is omitted.

Note from figure 7.5 that off-year mobilization in African-American counties rose dramatically in 1966 as a consequence of the Voting Rights Act of 1965. But also note that African-American mobilization volatility before 1966 and after 1966 is generally greater than for the white counties. Indeed, white counties seem to have relatively stable levels of off-year mobilization except for 1978. This interesting drop for white counties in 1978 is a consequence of the lack of white support for President Carter's policies (again, see Black and Black 1987). Carter's popularity in the southern states was clearly dependent, in part, on strong support among African-Americans. Recall that Asher has noted that Carter actually lost a majority of the white support in the South in 1976 (Asher 1988, 33).

While figure 7.5 presents mobilization averages for the white and African-American areas, a separate analysis (not shown here) using selected counties from both areas reveals remarkable mobilization differences between the areas, with African-American areas uniformly displaying the greater levels of off-year variation. This higher level of mobilization volatility is precisely what is detected in the analysis of Democratic base mobilization discussed earlier and presented as a characteristic of the system memory in figure 7.3.

At this point it is worthwhile emphasizing an interpretive caution about the memory plots. Institutionalization and system memory are not synonymous with the aggregate level of support for a party. A party can have a very low level of support from a group of voters, but the bonding of those voters to that party can be very strong, especially if they have supported that party for many years. Thus, electoral institutionalization can be high while aggregate support is low. On the other hand, the reverse is also true. Aggregate support can be very high while institutionalization is low. This, in fact, would be typical in the non-American context of many new and successful political parties, particularly in new democracies. Thus, do not confuse system memory with aggregate level of support. System memory characterizes the qualitative response of the electoral system to short-term disturbances, whereas the aggregate level of support measures a party's success in mobilizing voters.

Table 7.6 summarizes the memory results of many plots similar to those presented in figures 7.3 and 7.4. The purpose of the table is not just to summarize, however. Its other purpose is to point to areas in which further detailed analysis would be most productive.

The entries in table 7.6 indicate whether or not system memory increased or decreased between a particular group and a political party between the pre-1964 and post-1964 periods. The two groups represented in the table are whites and African-Americans. These groups are also subdivided by region. To demonstrate how the table corresponds to the memory plots presented in figures 7.3 and 7.4, note that the table indicates that system memory increased between the early and late periods for African-Americans and the Democratic party while simultaneously decreasing for white Americans. These are conclusions drawn from figures 7.3 and 7.4. Table 7.6 focuses on system memory, however, and does not give an indication of relative changes in system volatility.

In the southern states, system memory has changed with an inverse dynamic for the Republican party and the Democratic party. The increase in regular support for the Republican party in the post-1964 period among white

TABLE 7.6.   Changes in System Memory between Pre-1964 and Post-1964 Periods

	Republican	Democratic
Southern African–American	Decrease	Increase
Southern white	Increase	Decrease
Nonsouthern African–American	Increase	Increase
Nonsouthern white	Decrease	Decrease

southerners has led to an increased system memory. On the other hand, there has been a decrease in system memory with regard to African-Americans and the Republican party. This basically reflects the very low levels of institutionalization that African-Americans have toward the Republican party. There is currently no strong bonding to that party, nor has there been among these voters in the southern states in recent decades. Given that Republicans have only recently become competitive in much of the South, the situation with African-Americans probably reflects an almost complete absence of institutionalization, implying that short-term disturbances (favorable or unfavorable) to their support for that party quickly disappear.

These results are not particularly good news for the Republican party's near-future prospects in the South. Following the 1988 presidential campaign, leading Republican officials publicly voiced their concern about the low levels of African-American support for local Republican candidates, particularly at the gubernatorial, senatorial, and congressional levels. Their thoughts at the time seemed to suggest that, if Republican candidates could only gain 10 to 20 percent of the African-American vote, the party could seriously challenge the remaining Democratic dominance in the Deep South. However, these results suggest that system memory for African-Americans and the Republican party is quite low. Thus, a brief campaign for African-American support is likely to have little long-lasting influence. Short memory implies that any gains will be quickly lost in future elections. On the other hand, system memory for southern white voters and the Republican party is relatively high. If the Republican party actively seeks African-American support, there may be a consequent drop in their white support (assuming some continuity in voting along racial lines in the South). But with longer system memory for whites in the South, such a loss may be very hard to recover.

Thus, the Republicans seem to be in a situation in which the active courting of southern African-American voters may gain them little in the long run despite short-term gains among such voters, and the party may lose long-term support among white voters. According to these analyses, one Republican (and somewhat Machiavellian) strategy for the future would be to continue to appeal to young white voters, waiting for generational change and the day when their dominance in total white vote will cancel their need for African-American support.

One of the more interesting features of table 7.6 concerns voters outside the South. Note that in nonsouthern states, system memory for white voters has decreased for both the Republican and Democratic parties between the early and late periods. This clearly reflects the recent national weakening of partisan bonds and the increase in levels of independence that have been reported repeatedly in the electoral literature. However, system memory has increased among African-American voters in the nonsouthern states. This is no surprise with regard to the Democratic party, since this parallels the increase in system memory found among African-Americans in the South. But

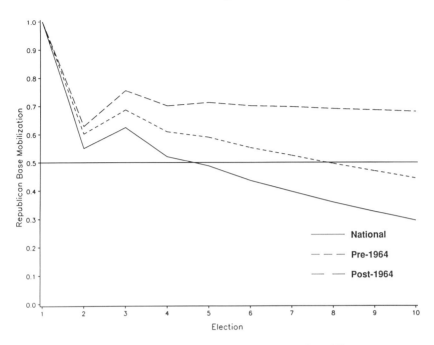

Fig. 7.6. Nonsouthern African-American memory plot, Republican party

the increase in system memory among African-Americans outside the South
with regard to the Republican party is truly an interesting finding, and it
deserves more detailed comment.

The memory plot for African-American communities in the nonsouthern
states is presented in figure 7.6. Note that the system memory for such areas
and the Republican party is higher for both early and late periods than the
national average. Indeed, the half-life of the national average for the Republican party is approximately five elections. However, the pre-1964 half-life for
African-American system memory with regard to the Republican party is
approximately eight elections, and the post-1964 half-life has not yet been
achieved, even after ten elections. Indeed, this post-1964 system memory for
African-Americans reflects the longest half-life examined in these analyses.

Why should this be so? Remember that system memory does not have
any necessary correspondence with the overall aggregate level of support for a
party. Moreover, recall that high levels of electoral institutionalization do
correspond to higher levels of aggregate system memory. While electoral
institutionalization is usually described in terms of patterned behavior between voters and a party in a positive sense (i.e., voters liking a party and
habitually voting for it), it can also refer to negative voting behavior that is
institutionalized. That is, a group of voters can react to an electoral disturbance regarding one party for a very long time by constantly voting for it or

constantly voting against it. System memory simply refers to the repetition of the behavior over many elections following the initial disturbance. In a setting of highly institutionalized electoral politics, system memory both for and against parties can be very long.

The data in figure 7.6 suggest that nonsouthern African-Americans were profoundly affected by the politics of the post-1964 period. African-Americans are one of the most ideologically homogeneous (and liberal) large groups in the United States (see Nie, Verba, and Petrocik 1979). Moreover, communities of such voters outside the South have much longer voting histories than their counterparts in the South. Thus, this situation contains two potent ingredients of institutionalization: clearly held social and political views combined with numerous electoral experiences. The extremely long system memory for African-Americans with respect to the Republican party in the post-1964 period reflects how deeply this group of voters was affected by the ideological polarization of the 1960s, 1970s, and 1980s.

This can be either good or bad news for the Republican party, depending on one's point of view. If the Republican party is interested in gaining African-American support in the nonsouthern states, then it is good news if the party can do something dramatic to attract African-Americans to the party in large numbers. The long system memory suggests that it may be worthwhile for the party in the long run. However, this is bad news for the party if the Republicans want to maintain the status quo on issues that relate strongly to African-American communities, for it is not likely that meager efforts will influence such a highly institutionalized group of voters. Moreover, anything short of a major effort to attract such institutionalized voters is not likely to have any significant effect.

The results discussed in this chapter suggest that anything less than a full commitment by the Republican party would have little impact in attracting many African-American voters. Even then, a full commitment in only one election might not have much influence either. It is logical to ask if Republican officials outside the South would ever find it in their best political interest to make such a commitment, given the magnitude and duration of that which would be required and the consequent response of their current white supporters to that commitment. From a practical point of view, it might serve long-term Republican interests if the party simply made a concerted effort not to further antagonize northern African-American voters for a long period of time. This would allow for a gradual decay of the negative institutionalization against the party, opening the possibility in the future of a more balanced electoral appeal across all races.

The Influence of the Economy

A substantial body of literature has developed in recent years that is devoted to the study of the influence of the national economy on congressional mobiliza-

TABLE 7.7. Average Change in Congressional Mobilization between Best and Worst Economic Conditions

Conditioning Area	Democratic	Republican
National	0.00236	0.01028
Urban	0.00196	0.01049
Farm	0.00005	0.00758
North (all years)	0.00311	0.01399
South (all years)	0.01766	−0.00419
Southern white (pre-1964)	−0.01203	0.03436
Southern white (post-1964)	−0.00382	0.01824
Southern African–American (pre-1964)	0.01649	−0.01386
Southern African-American (post-1964)	0.00796	0.00236
Nonsouthern white (pre-1964)	−0.01649	0.05634
Nonsouthern white (post-1964)	0.00000	0.02103
Nonsouthern African-American (pre-1964)	0.02347	−0.03633
Nonsouthern African-American (post-1964)	0.00683	0.00050

tion. Currently, the literature is not well decided on the matter, and results both for and against—variously using aggregate and/or survey data—continue to appear in the major journals. Thus, my analysis of the effects of the economy on congressional mobilization will add to this debate, probably bringing new information to bear and raising new questions rather than fundamentally resolving old conflicts. Nonetheless, this type of contribution is very important in the context of research that still seeks answers to many of its basic questions.

The model examined in this chapter is a system of equations with a highly specified structural form that controls for a large number of influences on the congressional mobilization cycle. Given this formal specification, the first question that we ask is whether or not changes in the performance of the economy affect congressional mobilization as it is characterized by this system. The second question we ask is whether or not the economic influence varies across different social contexts.

Table 7.7 presents the average change in congressional mobilization for each party that is due to changes in the economic conditions of the nation. The economic variable included in the model is the per capita change in the nation's gross national product for each year.[4] The direction of the influence of the economy in the model is controlled with regard to which party occupies

---

4. Other economically related variables (such as change in disposable income and unemployment rates) were tried in these analyses as well. The results presented here do not substantially differ when compared with the results using other measures.

the White House. The data in table 7.7 are computed by subtracting the average predicted congressional mobilization under the best of economic conditions from the average predicted congressional mobilization under the worst of economic conditions. This is repeated for each of the conditioning social environments. Interpretively, the larger the number, the larger the influence of economic conditions on congressional mobilization. Smaller (and in some instances, negative) numbers suggest little or no effect on congressional mobilization.

Let us begin the interpretation of table 7.7 by examining the national (i.e., unconditioned) differences. First, note that the Republican difference is substantially larger than the Democratic difference. Basically, this means that the difference between the best of economic times and the worst of economic times on Republican congressional mobilization results in approximately a 1.0 percent increase in that party's support. On the Democratic side, the increase is approximately 0.2 percent. It is interesting, although the reason is not immediately apparent, that the effect of the economy on Republican mobilization is five times greater than that for the Democrats.

These national figures do not suggest that the performance of the economy influences congressional mobilization to a large degree. In this respect, these results correspond with the recent longitudinal analysis by Marra and Ostrom (1989). However, other studies, such as Jacobson's (1989) analysis of House elections, have found that economic conditions do (conditionally) matter. Jacobson, for instance, finds that national economic fortunes influence change in the partisan distribution of House seats, depending on the abilities of candidates to locally exploit these economic conditions for political advantage. Yet table 7.7 does contain evidence that links these different findings. The key to understanding the link is not to assume that national economic fortunes should affect congressional mobilization equally across all social environments, for they do not.

The analysis of the conditioning variables in table 7.7 helps to unravel the dilemma. Note that changes in congressional mobilization in urban and farm areas that are due to changes in the economy are not of large magnitude, although Republican mobilization is again more sensitive to this influence than Democratic mobilization. Yet major differences do appear with respect to region and race. In both the pre-1964 and post-1964 periods, changes in the economy strongly affect Republican congressional mobilization in white communities. These changes in mobilization range from 2 percent to more than 5 percent, levels that could easily affect the outcome of numerous congressional elections. This has a direct implication for the interpretation of Jacobson's results with regard to the distribution of House seats. Changes in national economic performance may not affect national congressional mobilization in a major way, but it certainly can influence congressional mobilization among particular subgroups of the population. This, in turn, can tip the partisan scales in particular districts, depending on their competitiveness and social composition.

But for the Democratic party, white voters in both the North and the South during both the pre-1964 and post-1964 periods seem to be all but ignoring changes in the economy (based on their aggregate levels of mobilization). The group that is affected most by changes in the economy is the pre-1964 nonsouthern African-American community. Southern and non-southern African-American mobilization for the Democratic party does not seem to be strongly influenced by changes in the economy in the post-1964 period. Moreover, African-American voters, across time periods and regions, do not manifest an association on the aggregate level between Republican support and economic change.

To summarize these results, the association between national economic performance and congressional mobilization seems to be a white phenomenon with respect to the Republicans, and an African- American phenomenon with respect to the Democrats. While the association is diminishing across all groups over time, it remains a potent force affecting Republican mobilization in particular. Changes in the partisan seat distribution in the House of Representatives are a consequence of this influence on Republican mobilization, having little to do with Democratic mobilization. The Democrats do not benefit as much as the Republicans suffer when the economy is not performing well and a Republican occupies the White House. The "up-side" of this for the Republican party is that their consistently voiced concern for the growth of the national economy is well placed. Their congressional prospects substantially improve as a consequence of nationally strong economic growth.

These results support the claim that the economy affects the congressional mobilization cycle. However, the influence of the economy is not consistent across parties, social contexts, or time. The influence varies, depending upon the nature of the times and the relationship between the parties and the communities that support them. This returns our attention to the conditionality of politics, in general, and the dependence of mass movements on the particular social chemistries indigenous to localized milieus.

Remarks

In investigating a model of the congressional mobilization process, my analysis has focused on the structural properties of that process, both nationally and within varying social environments. The dynamic characteristics of the on-year/off-year cycle of congressional mobilization can be critically determined by an area's local social milieu. Much of this difference in partisan mobilization has been viewed, here, as a consequence of variations in levels of electoral institutionalization among voters. However, the conditionality of the congressional mobilization cycle with respect to variations in social environments extends even to economic influences on the cycle.

In terms of the on-year component of the mobilization cycle, the impact of the presidential election on the magnitude of the congressional vote is more critical in areas where voters have had relatively short aggregate voting histories and, consequently, lower levels of electoral institutionalization. Thus, for example, in areas of the South where there are large African-American populations, the influence of the presidential surge on Democratic congressional mobilization is larger, relative to the national average gain. Extrapolating elsewhere, other groups that have historically experienced lower levels of voter turnout, such as Christian evangelicals and Hispanics, could potentially be similarly affected. The surge in their congressional mobilization for on-year elections should be larger than the national average.

However, fluctuations in mobilization due to relatively large presidential surge effects for groups with lower levels of institutionalization are combined in an overall dynamic characterized by great potential for instability in the underlying electoral system. In short, lower levels of institutionalization yield greater short-term volatility in base-level mobilization. Thus, population subgroups with relatively short and less consistent voting histories can be more easily affected by sudden electoral disturbances.

Charismatic leaders, for example, might have a particularly strong impact on such voters. Such disturbances decay quickly among weakly institutionalized voters, as their systemically defined group memory is relatively short. However, this shorter memory can cause rapid and oscillatory change in future election mobilizations. To generalize, one lesson to be drawn from this is that, if an electoral system can withstand the "waves of the uninstitutionalized" in the short run, the system itself can likely survive. On the other hand, any electoral system that tries to float for long on a large sea of uninstitutionalized voters risks an eventual storm that may capsize the system.

Higher aggregate levels of institutionalization yield less short-term volatility but a greater potential for long-term structural change to the mobilization dynamic when a disturbance does penetrate the system boundaries. That is, among highly institutionalized population subgroups, electoral disturbances decay more slowly, enhancing the possibility of finding the residue of such disturbances in elections far in the future.

APPENDIX TO CHAPTER 7

Following this chapter's portrayal of the process and inputs of congressional base mobilization, the overall dynamic structure can be graphed as in figure A7.1 (in this case, heuristically employing notation representing the Democratic party). The graph in figure A7.1 follows the rules of graph algebra as they are used in systems theory. This form of representation is common in engineering, has been elegantly described from a social scientific perspective by Cortez, Przeworski, and Sprague (1974), and has found useful application in the analysis of political phenomena by Duvall and Freeman (1983), Przeworski (1975), and others.

Note that the term $DBASE_t$, representing the base level of congressional

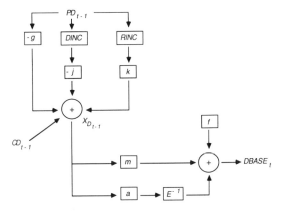

Fig. A7.1. Congressional base-level mobilization, Democratic party parameters

mobilization for the Democratic party during the current year (at time t), is located at the right of figure A7.1. Reading figure A7.1 from left to right (for the moment ignoring the inputs coming from PD_{t-1}), congressional mobilization for two previous elections is linearly combined in the construction of the base level of mobilization for the current election. Parameters m and a are variable proportions of transformation that structure the flow of the second-order process. The linear operator, E^{-1}, functions as a time delay operator and acts to extend the process to the time period $t-2$. Parameter f is a constant input that represents a fixed minimal level of what might be called "constant mobilization" that is independent of fluctuations in the overall system. This is the level of mobilization that would occur in a situation of zero social memory, a condition in which previous levels of mobilization would have no impact on current levels of mobilization. As mentioned in the chapter, parameter f is dynamically analogous to the intercept of a static linear model. The inputs in the upper left of the figure coming from PD_{t-1} act to adjust the base level of congressional mobilization for the effect of the presidential surge in mobilization as well as the influence of presidential incumbency.

CHAPTER 8

The Meaning of Volatility

Perhaps it is because electoral upheaval occurs so infrequently in the lives of American citizens that its connection to the events of more ordinary politics can seem so unsure. Yet the basic ingredients of a volatile election are always present in virtually all elections, American or not, albeit in varying degrees. In every election there are new voters, reflecting generational change if nothing else. Moreover, it is likely that there has never been a multiparty election in any large polity in the history of our planet in which there were not at least a few partisan switchers. Voters are always being institutionalized, both to their parties of choice and to the electoral system itself. And change is always present, even if it is minor.

The elections that offer the greatest degree of change are the ones that stand out the most to us, often affecting our view of our society in dramatic ways. Volatile elections often remain prominent features of our memories as citizens. We can both hate and love what they bring us, as if the elections are living messengers with a persona. They can both divide a nation or reveal its sense of unity. In part, their difference is their ability to do so much, or at least to bring to our attention that our society has changed greatly. Their persistence in our memory suggests that this difference is fundamental, involving new ingredients and structural uniqueness. But is it really so?

The answer to this question depends on one's view of electoral eco-systems. That is, it depends on whether one is looking at electoral change from within a particular system or from an external perspective. Moreover, a distinction must be made between volatility that occurs within stable system boundaries and volatility that occurs within a context of unstable system boundaries.

The general idea is comparable to waves in an aquarium. If the walls of the aquarium are stable, and the ecosystem within is relatively robust, then even relatively large waves on the surface act only to rearrange the internal scenery, not threaten the survival of the entire ecosystem. However, if the system itself is poorly constructed, if the walls are weak or the ecological balance is precarious, then large waves on the surface can lead to the extinction of species and perhaps the consequent destruction of the overall system. The relevance of the concept of system boundaries to the analyses presented in this book is best approached through a recharacterization of the ingredients of volatile electoral change.

New Voters, Switchers, and Electoral Instability

One primary concern of this book has been the mass behavior of new voters when they enter the electorate in large numbers. New voters can destabilize a previous balance in an electoral system, but they need not always do so. In 1920, millions of new voters, mostly women, entered the electoral system of the United States, and few observers at the time noted any resultant increase in the level of political instability. Indeed, the fact that the 1920 election has only now become a major focus of scholarly inquiry is indicative of the initial perception of relative stability in the electoral politics that followed the extension of the franchise to women. From that earlier historical perspective, the new female voters simply acted to reestablish the period's "normal" dominance by the Republican party that existed before Woodrow Wilson's election in 1912.

What separates the new voters of 1920 from those of, say, 1936, is that the 1920 new voters were voters without a critical national cause. Women went to the polls in 1920 because they were recruited by the Republicans when allowed, finally, to vote. Certainly they were concerned with the issues of the day. But those issues were not the issues of the depression, and the nation was not facing an internal or external crisis that could have fractured the existing political alignments.

The new voters of 1936 created a special type of political movement, and it is useful to examine it from a comparative perspective. In an article that appeared in a 1987 issue of the *American Sociological Review*, I discuss the relative role of new voters and switchers in aiding the rise of the Nazi party during the Weimar Republic. One of my basic conclusions about the Nazis is that new voters and switchers aided the Nazi electoral gains at different times. In the 1928 election, the Nazis received only a minuscule level of support (1.3 percent of the eligible electorate). However, in 1930, the Nazis received support from more than 10.0 percent of the eligible electorate, most of which came from the ranks of new voters. In July of 1932, Nazi support again increased, this time to more than 20.0 percent of the eligible electorate. However, in that election, new voters played a lessor role while switchers from other parties dominated the mass dynamics. Thus, the pattern with the Nazis was an influx of new voters followed by a wave of switching.

The pattern of new voters followed by switchers is exactly opposite that which occurred with the Democratic party between 1928 and 1936. As shown in the analyses presented in chapter 4, the 1932 election was dominated by switchers from the Republican party to the Democratic party. However, additional Democratic gains in 1936 were made up predominantly from the ranks of new voters.

What connects the two cases of the Democrats and the Nazis? Throughout the Weimar period, the Nazis offered a radical rhetoric. It was after the 1928 election that the NSDAP (the Nazi party) made the strategic decision to shift their campaigning from the urban areas to the countryside, where the Nazi leadership saw the potential for mobilizing many new voters. Thus, in 1930, the radical rhetoric of the Nazi party struck a responsive chord with many alienated and politically forgotten rural voters (mostly Protestant peasants). The new electoral balance that this created acted to further destabilize the weakly institutionalized ties of many supporters of recently established parties, causing a wave of switching in July, 1932.

In the case of the Democratic party during the 1930s, the depression was the primary force behind the wave of switching that occurred in 1932. Recall that Franklin Roosevelt's rhetoric during that election emphasized farm issues, and it was hardly radical relative to the standards established in previous elections. However, after the 1932 election, Roosevelt's rhetoric became much more radical, relative to the standards of previous electoral politics in the United States. The Nazi rhetoric during the Weimar period and the Democratic rhetoric after 1932 are, of course, not comparable by themselves. However, relative to the established norms of that time for their respective societies, they were each radical.

It is my conclusion that new voters can be attracted, in part, to radicalized rhetoric, with the term *radical* being used in the relative sense in comparison with previous political norms. The Weimar example demonstrates that new voters can be attracted to new political parties as well. Thus, we have the realization that the activity of completely noninstitutionalized voters has great potential for electoral volatility on the electoral system boundaries.

Switchers, on the other hand, seem to be more easily attracted by established political parties, following some crisis that acts to destabilize their previous partisan ties. This dynamic is opposite that suggested by Lipset, in which new voters are seen as most easily attracted to established political parties (1981, 150). My analysis suggests that new voters can be highly volatile, and that they are most easily roused in large numbers by movements with the greatest potential for radical political action. Switchers, on the other hand, need a reason to switch in large numbers, and the reason is likely not to be based on rhetoric, but in the fabric of a national crisis.

Yet the experiences of 1920 in the United States and 1930 in the Weimar Republic hint at something else about the behavioral characteristics of new voters. Apparently, new voters' involvement in an election is greatly dependent upon the mobilization activity of political parties. The almost complete lack of female mobilization for the Democratic party in 1920 is evidence of this dependence. That women in 1920 were recruited into the Republican party differentially with respect to local competitiveness with the Democratic party as well as with respect to nonimmigrant responses to an increasingly immigrant milieu, is further evidence of new voter responsiveness to the purposeful mobilization activities of groups and parties. In short, new voters begin to participate in the electoral system when someone goes out to get them. This appears to be the primary mechanism of large-scale, new voter mobilization. It is of interest to note that this discussion confirms one of the earliest empirical results in the literature on vote mobilization (Gosnell 1927).

The Nazis' rhetoric did not change significantly between 1928 and 1930. But the Nazis made the choice to move their campaign activities to the rural countryside in an attempt to mobilize new voters after 1928, and it worked. In the United States, the full strength of the depression was not enough to mobilize many new voters for the Democratic party in 1932. However, the Democratic party made a major effort to mobilize new voters in urban areas in 1936 with great results.

There are other prominent examples of new voter dependence on the mobilization activities of parties and groups. In the southern United States, African-Americans were brought to the polls in large numbers after the abolition of the Jim Crow laws, in large part due to the mobilization activities of the African-American churches. Many of the early civil rights leaders rose from the ranks of these very political church communities. Similarly, white fundamentalist Protestants were mobilized to vote in such large numbers in the 1988 presidential campaign due in part to the activities of Pat Robertson's grass roots organizations.

India, the world's largest democracy, presents a spectacular example of new voter dependence on external mobilization activity. While women have been able to vote since 1921 in India, their actual participation has depended largely on the needs of the male-dominated political establishment. Indeed, as one commentator claimed, the control is so thorough that "the women's fronts of various political parties function at the behest of male mentors" (*New York Times*, International Edition, 20 November 1989, sec. 1, 3). Similarly, members of the untouchable caste still participate in the political system only sporadically, nearly always dependent on the mobilization activities of particular local leaders.

All this is not to say that partisan mobilization activity is an absolute requirement for the recruitment of new voters. It is, of course, possible for new participants into any political arena to "catch the spirit" in a rapid and contagious fashion from a variety of sources. Recent evidence of such general political mobilization in nonelectoral settings are the mass prodemocracy demonstrations in various communist countries. Nonetheless, the findings in my analyses suggest that, in continuously operating democratic systems, new voter mobilization is greatly enhanced by activities specifically aimed at mobilizing the previously nonparticipating masses.

The discussion in chapter 5 about third parties adds yet another aspect to the generalizations about new voters and switchers. Apparently there is a sort of threshold requirement for large-scale, new voter movements that acts to limit the role of new voters in third-party activity in the United States. With regard to the Nazis of Weimar and the Democratic party of the 1930s, new voters had their greatest impact on their respective electoral systems when a radical rhetoric combined with mobilization activities was directed toward a large, nonmobilized sector of the electorate. However, in third parties in the United States, new voters play a relatively minor role except in particular social and political contexts, as discussed in chapter 5. Rather, third parties seem especially capable of attracting disenchanted supporters of the other major parties. Third parties can also act as catalysts for subsequent realignment activity. But third parties rarely carry a radicalized rhetoric combined with a large-scale grass roots mobilization effort into the electoral scenery in the United States under conditions of a national crisis. Perhaps this is what the Republican party did just before the Civil War. But such conditions are not common, and, thus, extreme electoral volatility precipitated by third parties and waves of new voters is also not common.

Nonetheless, the discussion of the congressional mobilization cycle in chapter 7 does suggest that voters with relatively short voting histories have greater potential for electoral volatility. In this case, the volatility can be viewed as subsequent switching between parties, but it is most likely to reveal itself through whether or not such voters consistently vote at all. Highly institutionalized voters tend to be those with long voting histories. They tend to be more consistent in their partisan choices as well as their recurrent mobilization. Yet if something comes along that destabilizes voters who previously had high levels of electoral institutionalization, the longitudinal trace of such a disturbance in the electoral system may be very long lasting.

Two Types of Volatility

We return to the idea of two types of volatility, defined not by the character of the initial destabilizing activity, but by the character of the social and political environment in which the activity takes place. In the case of the Weimar Republic, the boundaries of the electoral system were weak from the beginning. The state was established as a consequence of Germany's defeat in World War I. Observers at the time often suggest that the government was not well established in terms of public support. Indeed, many of the ideological, centrist parties were new to the national scene, and thus their supporters, by definition, tended to have weakly institutionalized partisan ties. Thus, internal instability caused the system to collapse.

In the case of the United States, however, the system boundaries are relatively robust. Except for the period preceding the Civil War, the system itself can be characterized as one with large numbers of highly institutionalized voters. The institutionalization acts in two ways. The electorate is institutionalized to its participation in the system; thus, their allegiance to the basic political infrastructure is strong. But the electorate also experiences high levels of partisan institutionalization as well. Thus, the United States experiences long periods with a stable electoral balance. In the literature about elections, these periods are often referred to as the major party systems of the United States, of which historically there have been five (see Eldersveld 1982,

33–35). When a crisis acts to destabilize the internal political scenery, voter commitment to the basic political system acts to maintain longitudinal political stability within the society. Thus, a new political balance has time to form within the context of an otherwise stable structural environment.

Yet the political environment in the United States may be inherently more stable in the long term than that which was found in the Weimar Republic for another reason. The reason is tied to the number of major (or at least electorally significant) parties in the respective political systems. This is connected to the logic behind characterizing conditions of rapidly changing mass electoral politics in terms of a system of differential or difference equations, as has been done in this volume. If the logic is defensible, then one should recognize that the mathematical stability of such systems is dependent, in part, on the number of equations (the number of parties) contained in each system.

This is a mathematical result that has been thoroughly explored by Robert May (1974) in connection with systems of equations that characterize change in biological ecosystems. Mathematical stability means the ability of all species (or in this case, parties) to continue to coexist without the eventual extinction of some species, leading to the deterioration of the overall biological (or political) environment. This is a consequence of the permissible ranges for the parameter values that lead to stability in the overall system. The more complex the ecosystem (i.e., the greater the number of equations characterizing the system), the more narrow is the range of permissible values for the parameters for the system to remain longitudinally stable. Of course, this argument assumes the relative constancy of other intervening factors.

In the case of Weimar, there were eight major political parties in 1928 when the NSDAP made its initial impression on the electoral scenery. By July of 1932, three of these parties were, for all practical purposes, eliminated. Indeed, all three of the parties had been newly formed during the Weimar years and, thus, were dependent on a weakly institutionalized electoral base. In the biological analogy, these parties are comparable to three species whose existence in the ecosystem is precariously balanced. In this sense, a weakly institutionalized electorate is a fragile political ecosystem, and relatively low levels of electoral volatility hold a greater potential for party extinction. Mathematically, this situation is compounded when the number of parties is large.

The Equilibrium Dance

From one perspective, an equilibrium is a political system's internal point of balance. Moreover, we now have a partial inventory of the primary factors that govern the movements of the electoral ecology when the system moves away from or back to that point of balance. There are two main categories of characteristics that govern the dynamics; their organization is determined by the level of institutionalization (weak or strong) among groups of voters.

Communities of voters that are weakly institutionalized with regard to their partisan behaviors have four common characteristics governing their aggregate dynamics. First, their aggregate memory is short with regard to the endurance of electoral disturbances within their system of voting. They can be shaken, but the destabilizing event is not likely to have a lasting impact relative to that which would occur with highly institutionalized voters. Second, communities of weakly institutionalized voters experience relatively high levels of partisan volatility. This is true both for the ease with which a political event can change their previous behavior and in the potential for volatility that exists after the event.

The final two characteristics of these aggregate dynamics connect both of the first two characteristics with the concept of system equilibrium. Weak institutionalization correlates with weak resistance to displacement from equilibrium. This characterizes the high susceptibility of such voters to dramatic changes in their voting behaviors due to destabilizing influences. This refers to their susceptibility to the initial disturbance, not the rate at which the influence of the disturbance is subsequently discarded during the return to equilibrium. Finally, since the voting behavior of weakly institutionalized voters is not highly patterned, such voters can quickly abandon recent behaviors. Thus, in the aggregate, such voters experience a rapid return to their equilibrium, quickly discarding (i.e., not institutionalizing) the destabilizing influence.

In combination, these last two characteristics imply that weakly institutionalized voters have great destabilizing potential for the electoral system: they are quick to leave equilibrium, yet quick to return. The destabilizing influence of such a partisan mobilization "shuffle" on the overall balance of the political ecology can be quite large, since longitudinally defined balance requires, if nothing else, regularity in patterned behavior. This, in turn, requires either resistance to destabilizing influences or, at least, persistence following the initial change from a previous balance.

The characteristics that govern the dynamics of voters with high levels of institutionalization are opposite those of the weakly institutionalized. First, their aggregate system memory is relatively long. Thus, when electoral events do destabilize the patterned behavior of the highly institutionalized, the longitudinal trace of this destabilization may continue long into future elections. Second, their aggregate potential for volatility is relatively low. This is true of both their susceptibility to the initial destabilizing influence as well as to their subsequent response. Third, such highly institutionalized voters display strong resistance to displacement from a system equilibrium. It takes a major event to shake these voters away from their previously patterned behavior. Finally, communities of highly institutionalized voters return to their previous

TABLE 8.1.   Characteristics of Aggregate Partisan Dynamics

Weak Institutionalization	Strong Institutionalization
Short memory	Long memory
High volatility	Low volatility
Weak resistance to displacement from equilibrium	Strong resistance to displacement from equilibrium
Rapid return to equilibrium	Slow return to equilibrium

equilibrium state of systemic balance following a destabilizing electoral event only slowly. They are good at repeating past behavior, and the initial disturbance becomes part of their past behavior. Such voters take relatively long to "forget" that disturbing event in the aggregate.

These characteristics of aggregate partisan dynamics are summarized in table 8.1. It is of particular interest to note that many of the empirical findings reported in table 8.1 closely correspond to theoretical expectations suggested by Robert Huckfeldt (1983) for social processes very similar to those investigated here.

These are forces that cause the dynamics of a political ecology to dance around an equilibrium under times of stress. But are the equilibria really stable for long periods of time? Are they fixed, and are the partisan trajectories the only things that reveal systemic dynamic movement? The results discussed in chapter 7 suggest that political equilibria can remain relatively fixed for substantial periods of time. However, there is no guarantee that this will always be the case. Moreover, it may be that future voting research will find occasion to model the dynamics of "floating equilibria" in the same way that I have explored the dynamics of aggregate partisan trajectories. Recall that the equilibria change when the parameter values are no longer constant. And that, in turn, depends on the changing politics of the period.

It is useful to remind ourselves that biologists used to think that ecosystems contained fixed equilibria. That view is now being challenged, and many biologists argue that the real constant in nature is eternal turmoil (see *New York Times*, national edition, 31 July 1990, B5). This is mentioned here not as a dire warning for future political research, but as a note of caution when addressing different types of electoral events. There is no reason to assume that human societies must parallel biological ecosystems in this respect. On the other hand, there is no reason to assume the reverse either. One must simply be aware of the possibilities in different settings.

Of course, human societies are not frog ponds, and there are many factors that lead to stability in electoral systems. Some of these factors, and only some, have been explored thoroughly here. Additional factors not mentioned here have been discussed by A. J. Milnor (1969) and others. Certainly, the total mix in the electoral environment is a crucial determinant in this respect. Yet the explorations presented in this volume are offered as a partial inventory of many of the most important mechanisms by which political systems are dominated by electoral volatility. In this way, I hope my investigations enhance our understanding of the democratic evolution of our societies.

Estimation

The linkage between the models and the parameter estimations that are reported in this volume is substantially different from much of what is typical in the social sciences. In social scientific research, models are often written isomorphically to correspond to "off-the-shelf" statistical formulations that are available in the major statistical software packages. In fact, a great deal of effort is often used to reduce a mathematical representation of a theory to some simplified form that corresponds to a preexisting statistical model. The preexisting statistical models are usually linear in their parameters and, although they need not be, in their variables as well. Indeed, the existence and ease-of-use of statistical models seductively encourages users to utilize such models at the expense of their own attempts at freewheeling theory construction. In general, it is easy to inhibit one's creative instincts when those instincts lead to models that cannot be handled by available software.

It is necessary to point this out since the departure from statistical modeling leads directly to the philosophy underlying the estimation strategies used here. It is easy to understand why modelers would want to expand their algebraic specifications to match their theories more closely. This is particularly true with regard to functional and longitudinal nonlinear specifications. But the question remains of why they should want to do this if the price they have to pay is so often so great, namely, to have to write from scratch much of their own statistical software. The answer, of course, rests in what is gained by doing so.

Nonmutilative Estimation

The estimation procedures used in my analyses are examples of what is called "nonmutilative estimation," or NME (pronounced like *enemy*). These procedures differ philosophically from standard statistical approaches in the sense that the estimation of the parameters takes a subordinate role to the construction of the model. The model is to reflect a theory of society, and concern for estimation conveniences are not weighed too heavily during the model-building process. The general philosophy of NME is, ideally, to construct a model that is sufficiently rich in theory that it captures all of the systematic components of the data while leaving the data in as "virgin" a form as possible. "Mutilations" of the model or data to employ a convenient statistical model for estimation purposes is avoided.

The NME characteristics of the current analyses are apparent in the way the models are evaluated with respect to the "natural" condition of the data. For example, pooling of data from different time periods is generally avoided. Instead, the data are separated sequentially in correspondence with the natural historical record during the entire estimation process. The models interact with the sequentially separated data in a parallel sequential fashion. Also, differencing is typically avoided in two-election analyses to preserve the potential for the reconstruction of longitudinal nonlinearities. Multiple objects moving simultaneously in time (e.g., following 3,000 counties across elections) are not averaged during the estimation process to produce one trajectory. Trajectories are calculated for each object, regardless of the number of objects. To average before computing the trajectories would erase contextual variation in the data's dynamics. Averaging can occur for other reasons, as in the computation of statistical measures, but trajectory variation is not sacrificed.

On a statistical level, statistical irregularities (such as autocorrelation in an error term) in NME models are seen as evidence of specification inadequacy, in the sense that something systematic has escaped into the error term that an improved model—and thus an improved theory—should capture. Specification repairs may typically require more than merely adding another variable in a linear fashion. Often functional rearrangement is required, depending on the substance of the problem.

Thus, the examination of residuals and other statistical diagnostics are used more as aids in the model-building process, rather than as automatic switches that kick in fixes that seek to preserve the statistical properties of poorly specified but commonly available statistical models. Such fixes, in general, are avoided by ensuring that model specifications are sufficiently adequate to eliminate statistical problems (as determined by the appropriate statistical diagnostics). Fixes that distort the original data through variable substitution or draconian transformations are particularly avoided, especially in the absence of diagnostic evidence of their need.

What to do is a choice each researcher has to make, and in truth there is no clear single answer. NME modeling is one approach; traditional statistical strategies are another. If one can accurately represent a social theory using a traditional approach, there is no reason not to use it.

The problem with NME is that, once a model is constructed, it is often impossible to use standard regression packages to estimate it. NME models are often unique in their estimation requirements, and no standard statistical package could hope to cope with all of the requirements of models with such functional variation. This means that NME modelers often have to write their own estimation routines. (In a related fashion, this is a point that has also been raised by King [1989] with regard to some approaches to maximum likelihood estimation.) Moreover, it means that NME modelers may have to write different routines for each model to correctly reflect all of the social theory specified in the model in the estimation procedure. Statistical diagnostics, always necessary as a safeguard as well as a check on the model construction and social theory linkage, complicate this since they often have to be individually programmed as well.

The Calculations

The remainder of this appendix describes how the models in this volume were estimated. Computer code (abbreviated in terms of bells and whistles and statistical diagnostic routines, but thoroughly annotated and explained) is offered at the end of this appendix to help clarify the procedures. While the estimation of each model is unique in some ways, there are, nonetheless, many similar components in all of the estimations conducted here. Many readers should find that these components can be incorporated into their own work, should they wish to use them. Also, there is much guiding literature on such algorithms.

The iterative parameter estimation procedure used in this analysis has its roots in a broad literature spanning diverse disciplines. While these numerically intensive techniques have recently been productively employed in the social sciences, they have long been a standard workhorse in other disciplines such as engineering, chemistry, and physics. In the social sciences, these techniques have been used to estimate continuous time systems of differential equations (C. Brown 1987 and 1988; Ward 1984) as well as discrete time systems of difference equations (e.g., Przeworski and Sprague 1986). Perhaps the most lucid description of the general procedure can be found in Hamming 1971. The focus of the related literature is the merger of standard numerical approximation techniques with least squares unconstrained optimization procedures. Much of the relevant literature is identified in Dennis and Schnabel 1983 (364–70; see also Hamming 1973). Interested readers might also find useful Dennis, Gay, and Welsh 1981a and 1981b; Fletcher 1965; Powell 1964; and Sorenson 1980.

The description of the estimation technique used in these analyses is necessarily brief. But this description should be sufficient to explain the essential ingredients to those who are interested. In general, the investigated models employ both continuous and discrete time specifications. The mapping of these models to the data requires a numerically intensive iterative form of maximum likelihood estimation that demands a significant use of computer resources. In total, the amount of CPU time that was expended on an IBM 3090 computer to perform the estimations presented in this volume exceeded 800 hours (running without competition). The estimations required a real time of a number of years running almost continuously due to the needs of other computer users at Emory University. In short, the estimation of the type of model specifications presented here using such large bodies of data could not have been accomplished before the arrival of fast, large-scale mainframes. If, as I believe, the real world is well reflected in the specifications I have explored, then it has been worth the effort both theoretically and substantively. This, at least, has been the expectation, and the hope, that has quided these inquiries.

The estimation process begins by computing a trajectory using guessed (but plausible) values of the parameters (a process to be repeated often with different values). A Runge-Kutta approximation to definite integration is then used to compute an over-time trajectory for each partisan population. An initial step of this higher order approximation takes the familiar form of the Euler,

$$DNEXT = D + h(dD/dt),$$

where h is a small number, and D stands for the Democrats (used for the purpose of the example). The Runge-Kutta is repeated for a fixed number of iterations (typically 10) to yield the next election's predicted partisan total.

For the discrete type model used in chapter 7, the Runge-Kutta approximation described above is, of course, not used. Calculation over a set number of time periods (i.e., elections) is all that is required. For the analysis of congressional voting, recall that there is a "data cloud" of county election information for each of the elections spanning four decades. Each county represented in each "cloud" is also represented in all the other "clouds" (similar to respondents in a panel survey with a certain number of waves of interviews). Rather than pooling all of the data, the system of difference equations uses the data for each county sequentially (i.e., each election following the last) to produce a dynamic trajectory for each county, thereby reconstructing each county's congressional mobilization history.

The predicted values for each of the parties and the nonvoters are then evaluated for the fit to the actual data. The fit is calculated as

$$FIT = 1 - (RSS/TSS),$$

where RSS is the residual sums of squares between the predicted and actual values for each group, and TSS is the total sums of squares measuring the total variation for each group between the two elections. For the discrete case, this involves computing residuals for each county and each election separately before totaling to produce the measure of fit.

The partial derivatives of the fit surface with respect to all parameters are then computed as

(change in fit / change in parameter).

This is accomplished by disturbing each parameter around its present value and evaluating the concomitant change in fit. All of this is done for one parameter at a time.

The estimated parameter values are then moved through the parameter space in order to maximize the fit based on the directional information contained in the vector of partials for the fit surface. This movement is accomplished iteratively using the relation

$$BNEXT = B + z(P),$$

where the vector of partials for the fit surface is P, the vector of parameter values is B, and z is a small number. The value of z can vary, depending on the steepness of the overall fit surface and the proximity of the maximum to that surface. Movement in the parameter space continues until the maximum to the surface has been reached, as indicated by an evaluation of the partials to the fit surface.

With any one attempt at arriving at the maximum of the fit surface, there is no guarantee that the achieved maximum is the global maximum of the surface. This is characteristic of all nonsmooth problems of this sort. The usual practice of varying the initial parameter values as a safeguard has been followed here. This was done both by repeatedly choosing initial conditions randomly from within a specified range and by using a systematic grid of initial conditions.

Figure A1.1 has been prepared to give a visual interpretation to the movement in the parameter space. In this figure, two parameter dimensions—one for parameter b and the other for parameter f—are represented on the "floor" of the figure. The model's fit for the 1928–32 period (from chap. 4), here averaged for presentational purposes across the fits for the model's three equations, is represented on the vertical axis. The iterative estimation procedure "climbs" up the fit surface by progressively moving the parameter values to maximize this surface, that is, "to climb to the top of the mountain."

The chi-square statistics for the parameters test the impact of each parameter on the predicted values for each group (i.e., Democrats, Republicans, and nonvoters) from which the measures of fit are derived. First, predicted values for each group are calculated using the optimal values for each parameter. Second, new predicted values are calculated after setting each parameter to zero (one at a time). The differences between the two population sets are used to compute the chi-square statistics. Thus, a low chi-square value indicates that an estimate has little impact on the predicted surface (and thus the model) and that the null hypothesis that the parameter equals zero should not be rejected.

The estimation procedure described above was written in SAS IML (version 5.18), a matrix language. It was run on an IBM 3090 computer under MVS/ESA. A greatly shortened and simpler version of such a program is

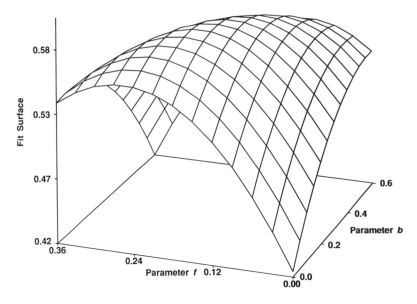

Fig. A1.1. Model fit surface near parameter optima

presented below. While this program is not the exact version used in the analyses presented in this volume (due to normal printing limitations), the basic ingredients of the estimation routine are the same, and interested readers will be able to follow the logic of what was done without too much difficulty. Building on this program, it will be possible for others to construct similar estimation routines relatively easily. Unfortunately, I know of no simple-to-use "plug and chug" program that can handle multiple object trajectories (e.g., the 3,000 county trajectories moving simultaneously). Again, each new empirical setting requires special modifications to the code to allow for the exact evaluation of the original theory-driven formal model.

A Program

```
PROC IML;

    USE POLIDATA;
    READ ALL;
    SHOW NAMES;

*In this program, R and C stand for the state variables,
    such as Republican and Democratic mobilization.
    RNEXT and CNEXT are the same variables for the
    next time period.;
```

```
*The variables var1, var2, etc. are the original names of
  the state variables in the POLIDATA SAS data set.;

R=var1;RNEXT=var1next;
C=var2;CNEXT=var2next;

*********************************************************.
                                                         ;
***This Counts The Number of Cases****;
CASES=NROW(R);
*********************************************************.
                                                         ;

YEAR=1930;
*P1 and P2 are population weights that can be assigned.;
P2=P1932;
P1=P1930;

*********************************************************.
                                                         ;
  *Now the mean and variance stuff.;

TOTPOP=P2(|+,|);TOTPOP1=P1(|+,|);TOTPOP2=P2(|+,|);
RSUM=(P1#R)(|+,|);CSUM=(P1#C)(|+,|);
RMEAN=RSUM/TOTPOP1;CMEAN=CSUM/TOTPOP1;
RNEXTSUM=(P2#RNEXT)(|+,|);CNEXTSUM=(P2#CNEXT)(|+,|);
CNEXMEAN=CNEXTSUM/TOTPOP2;RNEXMEAN=RNEXTSUM/TOTPOP2;
RSQDEV=P2#((RNEXT-R)##2);RSSDEV=RSQDEV(|+,|);
CSQDEV=P2#((CNEXT-C)##2);CSSDEV=CSQDEV(|+,|);
PRINT RMEAN, RNEXMEAN, CMEAN, CNEXMEAN, TOTPOP, CASES;

*********************************************************.
                                                         ;
START;
****Initial Parameter Guesses*;

  F=  0  ;
  B=  0  ;

*********************************************************.
                                                         ;
*Below are special counters and small numbers used
  to monitor the program and for numerical integration.;
Some of these small numbers, especially Z1, have to be changed
  frequently on a trial and error basis, depending
  on the data characteristics.;
      Y99 = 1;GCOUNT=0;
      I = 0.000001;h = 0.1 ;
      Z1 = |0.1 0.1|;
      Z1 = Z1 / 1000;
      TESTLIST=0;ITCOUNT = 0;TE = 0 ; TE2=0;
      TIMEUP=0;
      E1=0;DP1=0;D1=1;D2=1;D3=1;
```

```
*********************************************************.
                                                        ;
GOTO ESTIMATE;
*********************************************************.
                                                        ;

MODELFIT:

    *This section iterates and fits the model, DRDT and DCDT.
        A simple model (with two equations and two parameters)
        and a second order Runge Kutta (Heun's method) is
        presented here just as an example.
        A fourth order Runge Kutta is more precise and is
        the method of choice for the final estimation. The second
        order method is useful from a programming
        standpoint if the model is tentative, long, complicated,
        and still being changed frequently.;


IF DP1=1 THEN DO;
PRINT 'MODELFIT BEGINNING';
END;
R=var1;C=var2;

DO U1=1 TO 10;
*The next two lines are the model.;
DRDT1= (F#R);
DCDT1= (B#C);

m2=R+(h#DRDT1);
m1=C+(h#DCDT1);

DRDT2= (F#m2);
DCDT2= (B#m1);

RNEW=R+((h/2)#(DRDT1 + DRDT2));
CNEW=C+((h/2)#(DCDT1 + DCDT2));

R=RNEW;C=CNEW;

END;

R2=P2#R;C2=P2#C;
PRED=R2||C2;
PREDIC=PRED(|+,|);
PREDICT=PREDIC/TOTPOP;
IF DP1=1 THEN DO;
PRINT 'PREDICTED R and C MEANS';
PRINT PREDICT;
```

```
END;
LINK RSQ;

RETURN;
*******************************************************.
                                                      '
******   The following are the subroutines
******   for the R-squares and the saving
******   of the best parameter estimates.;
*******************************************************.
                                                      '
RSQ:
RESIDR=(P2#((RNEXT−RNEW)##2))(|+,|);
RESIDC=(P2#((CNEXT−CNEW)##2))(|+,|);
RRSQUARE=1−(RESIDR/RSSDEV);
CRSQUARE=1−(RESIDC/CSSDEV);
RSQUARE=(RRSQUARE+CRSQUARE)/2;
IF DP1=1 THEN DO;
PRINT 'RRSQUARE CRSQUARE RSQUARE';
RSQFITS=RRSQUARE||(CRSQUARE||RSQUARE);
PRINT RSQFITS;
END;
RETURN;


*******************************************************.
                                                      '
BESTPAR:
   BESTF = F;BESTB = B;
   BESTRSQ = RSQUARE;
   BESTRRSQ = RRSQUARE;
   BESTCRSQ = CRSQUARE;
PARMS=F||B;
   IF DP1 = 1 THEN DO;
PRINT 'F' 'B';
      PRINT , PARMS;
      END;
   RETURN;


*******************************************************.
                                                      '
***This next section computes the partials of the fit surface
***with respect to the parameters.:

SURFACE:
*   DP1 = 0 ;
   PRINT 'SURFACE' 'BEGINNING';
   PRINT 'SURFACE' 'BEGINNING';
*   PRINT 'FFFFFFFFFFFFFFFFFFFFFFFFFFFFFFFFFFFFFFFFFFFFF';
   F = F − I;
   LINK MODELFIT;
   LINK PUTFIT;
```

```
   F = F + ( 2 # I );
   LINK MODELFIT;
   DFFIT = ( RRSQUARE - FIT2 );
   F = F - I;
*  PRINT 'BBBBBBBBBBBBBBBBBBBBBBBBBBBBBBBBBBBBBBBBBB';
   B = B - I
   LINK MODELFIT;
   LINK PUTFIT;
   B = B + ( 2 # I );
   LINK MODELFIT;
   DBFIT = (CRSQUARE - FIT3);
   B = B - I;

   PARMFIT=DFFIT‖DBFIT;
   PARTIALS = PARMFIT / ( 2 # I );
   TEST = SSQ(PARTIALS);
   TESTLIST=(TESTLIST//TEST);
   PARM=F‖B;
   PRINT 'F' 'B';
   PRINT , PARM , PARTIALS;
   LINK MODELFIT;
   PRINT 'RRSQUARE' 'CRSQUARE' 'RSQUARE';
   RSQFITS=RRSQUARE‖(CRSQUARE‖RSQUARE);
   PRINT , RSQFITS;
   PRINT 'SURFACE' 'ENDING';
   DP1 = 0 ;
   RETURN;
*Save the fits for future comparisons;
PUTFIT:
   FIT1 = RSQUARE;
   FIT2 = RRSQUARE;
   FIT3 = CRSQUARE;
   RETURN;
*Saves the predicted values of the model for future comparisons;

PUTPRED:
   PREDIC1 = PREDIC;
   RETURN;
*The chi-square statistics;
CSFITS:
   CHSQALL1 = ((PREDIC1 - PREDIC)##2) / (PREDIC1);
   CHSQALL = SUM(CHSQALL1);
   PRINT CHSQALL;
   RETURN;
```

```
***********************************************************.
                                                        ;
*This next section guides the program through
  all of the subroutines.;
ESTIMATE:
  DP1 = 1;TE = 1;E1 = 0;
  LINK MODELFIT;TE = 0;E1 = 0;

  LINK BESTPAR;
  DP1 = 0 ;
  DO Y99 = 1 TO 10;
    Z2 = Z1;
    ZCOUNT = 0 ;
    ITCOUNT = 0 ;
    LINK SURFACE;
    PRINT 'ESTIMATE' 'BEGINNING';
    E1 = 0 ;
    LINK MODELFIT;
    E1 = 0 ;
BEGIN:
    FIT1 = RSQUARE;
    NEWPARM = PARM + ( PARTIALS # Z2 );
    F = NEWPARM(| 1 , 1 |);
    B = NEWPARM(| 1 , 2 |);
    LINK MODELFIT;
    IF RSQUARE > FIT1 THEN DO;
      LINK BESTPAR;
      PARM = NEWPARM;
      END;
    ITCOUNT = ITCOUNT + 1 ;
    IF RSQUARE > FIT1 THEN GOTO BEGIN;
    IF ZCOUNT < 2 THEN DO; PRINT ITCOUNT; END; = 0 ;
    ITCOUNT = 0;
    ZCOUNT = ZCOUNT + 1 ;
*     PRINT , ZCOUNT;
    Z2 = Z2 / 10 ;
    IF ZCOUNT > 4 THEN GOTO JUMP1;
    F = BESTF;
    B = BESTB;
    GOTO BEGIN;
JUMP1:
    F = BESTF;
    B = BESTB;
    END;
  PRINT 'ESTIMATE' 'ENDING';
TE = 1 ;LINK MODELFIT;TE = 0;
```

```
***********************************************************.
                                                          ,
*Global maximum check;
CHECK=0;CHECK2=0;GCOUNT=GCOUNT+1;
IF GCOUNT = 2 THEN GOTO SKIP2;
PRINT GCOUNT;

CHECKFIT=RSQUARE;
STEP=0.2;
DO F=-3 TO 3 BY STEP;
LINK MODELFIT;IF RSQUARE > CHECKFIT THEN DO;
CHECKFIT=RSQUARE;
BESTF=F;CHECK=1;CHECK2=1;
PRINT 'GLOBAL F CONDITION ENCOUNTERED' F
   RRSQUARE CRSQUARE RSQUARE;END;END;
IF CHECK2=0 THEN DO;PRINT 'F GLOBAL CHECK OK';END;CHECK2=0;
F=BESTF;LINK MODELFIT;
CHECKFIT=RSQUARE;

STEP = 0.2;
DO B=-3 TO 3 BY STEP;
LINK MODELFIT;IF RSQUARE > CHECKFIT THEN DO;
CHECKFIT=RSQUARE;
BESTB=B;CHECK=1;CHECK2=1;
PRINT 'GLOBAL B CONDITION ENCOUNTERED' B
   RRSQUARE CRSQUARE RSQUARE;END;END;
IF CHECK2=0 THEN DO;PRINT 'B GLOBAL CHECK OK';END;CHECK2=0;
B-BESTB;LINK MODELFIT;
CHECKFIT=RSQUARE;

Z1=Z1/100;
IF CHECK=1 THEN GOTO ESTIMATE;
SKIP2:

*Global check finished;
GOTO CHISQUAR;
***********************************************************.
                                                          ,
*This organizes the calculation of the chi-square
   statistics;

CHISQUAR:
TE2=1;
   CSF = F;LINK MODELFIT;LINK PUTPRED;
   F = 0 ;LINK MODELFIT;LINK CSFITS;
   CHISQF = CHSQALL;F = CSF;
***********************************************************.
                                                          ,
   CSB = B;LINK MODELFIT;LINK PUTPRED;
   B = 0 ;LINK MODELFIT;LINK CSFITS;
   CHISQB = CHSQALL;B = CSB;
```

```
************************************************************;
****   Preparation for output;   ********************;
************************************************************;
   DP1 = 1 ;
   LINK MODELFIT;
   DP1 = 0 ;
   ALLFIT1 = ( RRSQUARE || CRSQUARE );
   SYSPAR=F||B;
   SYSCHI=CHISQF||CHISQB;
   ALLFITS = SHAPE( ALLFIT1 ,0 , 1 );
   SYSCHISQ = SHAPE( SYSCHI ,0 , 1 );
   SYSPARMS = SHAPE( SYSPAR ,0 , 1 );
   SYSEST = SYSPARMS || SYSCHISQ;
   PRINT , C44 , SYSPARMS , SYSCHISQ , SYSEST , TESTLIST;

STUFF={PARMS CHISQ};
ROW = {'F' 'B'};
CREATE BETAS FROM SYSEST (|COLNAME=STUFF ROWNAME=ROW|);
APPEND FROM SYSEST (|ROWNAME=ROW|);
CLOSE BETAS;

FIT={'FITS'};
ROWW = {'R' 'C'};
CREATE FITS FROM ALLFITS (|COLNAME=FIT ROWNAME=ROWW|);
APPEND FROM ALLFITS (|ROWNAME=ROWW|);
CLOSE FITS;

FINISH;RUN;
QUIT;

PROC PRINT DATA=BETAS;VAR ROW PARMS CHISQ;
PROC PRINT DATA=FITS;VAR ROWW FITS;
```

References

Abramowitz, Alan I., Albert D. Cover, and Helmut Norpoth. 1986. The President's Party in Midterm Elections: Going from Bad to Worse. *American Journal of Political Science* 30:563–76.

Andersen, Kristi. 1979a. *The Creation of a Democratic Majority 1928–1936.* Chicago: University of Chicago Press.

Andersen, Kristi. 1979b. Generation, Partisan Shift, and Realignment: A Glance Back to the New Deal. In *The Changing American Voter*, ed. Norman H. Nie, Sidney Verba, and John Petrocik, 74–95. Cambridge, Mass.: Harvard University Press.

Arsenau, R. B., and R. E. Wolfinger. 1973. Voting Behavior in Congressional Elections. Paper presented at the annual meeting of the American Political Science Association, New Orleans.

Asher, Herbert B. 1988. *Presidential Elections and American Politics: Voters, Candidates, and Campaigns since 1952.* Chicago: Dorsey Press.

Bagg, Robert. 1978. *Introduction to The Bakkhai by Euripides.* Amherst, Mass.: University of Massachusetts Press.

Bard, Y. 1974. *Nonlinear Parameter Estimation.* New York: Academic Press.

Barrilleaux, Charles J. 1986. A Dynamic Model of Partisan Competition in the American States. *American Journal of Political Science* 30:822–40.

Beck, Paul Allen. 1974. Environment and Party: The Impact of Political and Demographic County Characteristics on Party Behavior. *American Political Science Review* 68:1229–44.

Berelson, Bernard R., Paul F. Lazarsfeld, and William N. McPhee. 1954. *Voting: A Study of Opinion Formation in a Presidential Campaign.* Chicago: University of Chicago Press.

Bill, James A., and Robert L. Hardgrave, Jr. 1973. *Comparative Politics: The Quest for Theory.* Columbus, Ohio: Charles E. Merrill Publishing.

Black, Earl, and Merle Black. 1987. *Politics and Society in the South.* Cambridge, Mass.: Harvard University Press.

Blau, Peter M. 1977. *Inequality and Heterogeneity.* New York: Free Press.

Blum, Terry C. 1985. Structural Constraints on Interpersonal Relations: A Test of Blau's Macrosociological Theory. *American Journal of Sociology* 91:511–21.

Brown, Courtney. 1982. The Nazi Vote: A National Ecological Study. *American Political Science Review* 76:285–302.

Brown, Courtney. 1987. Voter Mobilization and Party Competition in a Volatile Electorate. *American Sociological Review* 52:59–72.

Brown, Courtney. 1988. Mass Dynamics of U.S. Presidential Competitions, 1928–36. *American Political Science Review* 82:1153–81.

Brown, Thad. 1981. On Contextual Change and Partisan Attributes. *British Journal of Political Science* 11:427–47.

Brown, Thad. 1988. *Migration and Politics*. Chapel Hill, N.C.: University of North Carolina Press.

Burnham, Walter Dean. 1970. *Critical Elections and the Mainsprings of American Politics*. New York: Norton.

Butler, David and Donald Stokes. 1969. *Political Change in Britain*. New York: St. Martin's Press.

Campbell, Angus. 1960. Surge and Decline: A Study of Electoral Change. *Public Opinion Quarterly* 24:397–418.

Campbell, Angus. 1964. Voters and Elections: Past and Present. *Journal of Politics* 26:745–57.

Campbell, Angus, Philip E. Converse, Warren Miller, and Donald E. Stokes. 1960. *The American Voter*. New York: Wiley.

Campbell, Angus, Philip E. Converse, Warren Miller, and Donald E. Stokes. 1966. *Elections and the Political Order*. New York: Wiley.

Campbell, James E. 1986. Presidential Coattails and Midterm Losses in State Legislative Elections. *American Political Science Review* 80:45–63.

Campbell, James E. 1987. The Revised Theory of Surge and Decline. *American Journal of Political Science* 31:965–79.

Carmines, Edward G., and James A. Stimson. 1989. *Issue Evolution: Race and the Transformation of American Politics*. Princeton, N.J.: Princeton University Press.

Chappell, Henry W., Jr. and William R. Keech. 1985. A New View of Political Accountability for Economic Performance. *American Political Science Review* 79:10–27.

Chubb, John E. 1988. Institutions, the Economy, and the Dynamics of State Elections. *American Political Science Review* 82:133–54.

Clubb, Jerome M. 1978. Party Coalitions in the Early Twentieth Century. In *Emerging Coalitions in American Politics*, ed. Seymour Martin Lipset, 61–79. San Francisco: Institute for Contemporary Studies.

Clubb, Jerome M., William H. Flanigan, and Nancy H. Zingale. 1980. *Partisan Realignment: Voters, Parties, and Government in American History*. Beverly Hills, Calif.: Sage.

Coleman, James S. 1964. *Introduction to Mathematical Sociology*. New York: Free Press.

Coleman, James S. 1981. *Longitudinal Data Analysis*. New York: Basic Books.

Conover, Pamela Johnston, and Stanley Feldman. 1986. Emotional Reactions to the Economy: I'm Mad as Hell and I'm Not Going to Take It Anymore. *American Journal of Political Science* 30:50–78.

Converse, Philip. 1975. Public Opinion and Voting Behavior. In *The Handbook of Political Science*, ed. Fred A. Greenstein and Nelson Polsby, 4:75–169. Reading, Mass.: Addison-Wesley.

Converse, Philip E., and Gregory B. Markus. 1979. Plus ça Change . . . : The New CPS Election Study Panel. *American Political Science Review* 73:32–49.

Cortez, Fernando, Adam Przeworski, and John Sprague. 1974. *Systems Analysis for Social Scientists*. New York: Wiley.

Cover, Albert D. 1986. Presidential Evaluations and Voting for Congress. *American Journal of Political Science* 30:786–801.

Danby, J. M. A. 1985. *Computing Applications to Differential Equations: Modelling in the Physical and Social Sciences.* Reston, Va.: Reston Publishing Company.

Degler, Carl N. 1971. American Political Parties and the Rise of the City. In *Electoral Change and Stability in American Political History,* ed. Jerome M. Clubb and Howard Allen, 122–47. New York: Free Press.

DeNardo, James. 1980. Turnout and the Vote: The Joke's on the Democrats. *American Political Science Review* 74:406–20.

Dennis, John E., D. M. Gay, and R. E. Welsh. 1981a. An Adaptive Nonlinear Least Squares Algorithm. *ACM Transactions on Mathematical Software* 7:348–68.

Dennis, John E., D. M. Gay, and R. E. Welsh. 1981b. Algorithm 573 NL2SOL—An Adaptive Nonlinear Least Squares Algorithm. *ACM Transactions on Mathematical Software* 7:369–83.

Dennis, John E., and Robert B. Schnabel. 1983. *Numerical Methods for Unconstrained Optimization and Nonlinear Equations.* Englewood Cliffs, N.J.: Prentice-Hall.

Duvall, Raymond D., and John R. Freeman. 1983. The Techno-Bureaucratic Elite and the Entrepreneurial State in Dependent Industrialization. *American Political Science Review* 77:569–87.

Eldersveld, Samuel J. 1982. *Political Parties in American Society.* New York: Basic Books.

Eisenstadt, S. N. 1964. Institutionalization and Change. *American Sociological Review* 29:235–47.

Eisenstadt, S. N. 1966. *Modernization: Protest and Change.* Englewood Cliffs, N.J.: Prentice-Hall.

Erikson, Robert S., and Kent L. Tedin. 1981. The 1928–1936 Partisan Realignment: The Case for the Conversion Hypothesis. *American Political Science Review* 75:951–62.

Ferejohn, John A., and Randall L. Calvert. 1984. Presidential Coattails in Historical Perspective. *American Journal of Political Science* 28:127–46.

Fiorina, Morris P. 1977. *Retrospective Voting in American National Elections.* New Haven: Yale University Press.

Fletcher, R. 1965. Function Minimization Without Evaluating Derivatives—A Review. *Computing Journal* 8:33–41.

Flexner, E. 1975. *Century of Struggle.* Cambridge, Mass.: Harvard University Press.

Franklin, M. N. 1971. A "Non-election" in America? Predicting the Results of the 1970 Mid-term Election for the U.S. House of Representatives. *British Journal of Political Science* 1:508–13.

Gans, Herbert J. 1962. *The Urban Villagers: Group and Class in the Life of Italian-Americans.* New York: Free Press.

Garfinkel, Harold. 1967. *Studies in Ethnomethodology.* Englewood Cliffs, N.J.: Prentice Hall.

Gillespie, John V., Dina A. Zinnes, Philip A. Schrodt, G. S. Tahim, and R. Michael Rubinson. 1977. An Optimal Control Model of Arms Races. *American Political Science Review* 71:226–44.

Glaser, William A. 1962a. Fluctuation in Turnout. In *Public Opinion and Congressional Elections,* ed. W. N. McPhee and W. A. Glaser, 19–51. New York: Free Press.

Glaser, William A. 1962b. Intention and Turnout. In *Public Opinion and Congressio-*

nal Elections, ed. W. N. McPhee and W. A. Glaser, 225–39. New York: Free Press.

Goldberg, Samuel. 1958. *Introduction to Difference Equations*. New York: Wiley.

Goodwin, Grace Duffield. 1913. *Anti-Suffrage: Ten Good Reasons*. New York: Duffield and Company.

Gosnell, Harold F. 1927. *Getting Out the Vote: An Experiment in the Stimulation of Voting*. Chicago: University of Chicago Press.

Gurwitsch, Aron. 1962. The Common-sense World as Social Reality—A Discourse on Alfred Schultz. *Social Research* 29:50–72.

Haberman, Richard. 1977. *Mathematical Models: Mechanical Vibrations, Population Dynamics, and Traffic Flow*. Englewood Cliffs, N.J.: Prentice-Hall.

Hamming, Richard W. 1971. *Introduction to Applied Numerical Analysis*. New York: McGraw-Hill.

Hamming, Richard W. 1973. *Numerical Methods for Scientists and Engineers*. 2d ed. New York: McGraw-Hill.

Hanushek, Eric A., and John E. Jackson. 1977. *Statistical Methods for Social Scientists*. New York: Academic Press.

Hesseltine, William B. 1948. *The Rise and Fall of Third Parties: From Anti-Masonry to Wallace*. Washington, D.C.: Public Affairs Press.

Hesseltine, William B. 1962. *Third-Party Movements in the United States*. New York: Van Nostrand.

Hibbing, John R. 1988. Legislative Institutionalization with Illustrations from the British House of Commons. *American Journal of Political Science* 32:681–712.

Hinckley, Barbara. 1967. Interpreting House Midterm Elections: Toward a Measurement of the In-Party's "Expected" Loss of Seats. *American Political Science Review* 61:694–700.

Hirsch, Morris W., and Stephen Smale. 1974. *Differential Equations, Dynamical Systems, and Linear Algebra*. New York: Academic Press.

Holmberg, Sören. 1981. *Svenska Väljare*. Stockholm: Lieber.

Huckfeldt, R. Robert. 1983. The Social Context of Political Change: Durability, Volatility, and Social Influence. *American Political Science Review* 77:929–44.

Huckfeldt, R. Robert, and Carol Weitzel Kohfeld. 1989. *Race and the Decline of Class in American Politics*. Urbana: University of Illinois Press.

Huckfeldt, R. Robert, Carol Weitzel Kohfeld, and Thomas W. Likens. 1982. *Dynamic Modeling: An Introduction*. Beverly Hills, Calif.: Sage.

Huckfeldt, R. Robert, and John Sprague. 1987. Networks in Context: The Social Flow of Political Information. *American Political Science Review* 81:1197–1216.

Huckfeldt, R. Robert, and John Sprague. 1988. Choice, Social Structure, and Political Information: The Informational Coercion of Minorities. *American Journal of Political Science* 32:467–82.

Huckfeldt, R. Robert, and John Sprague. 1989. Social, Political, and Behavioral Bases of Partisanship: The Relationships between Parties and Citizens. Paper presented at the annual meeting of the American Political Science Association, Atlanta.

Huntington, Samuel P. 1968. *Political Order in Changing Societies*. New Haven: Yale University Press.

Irwin, Laura, and Allan J. Lichtman. 1976. Across the Great Divide: Inferring Individual Level Behavior from Aggregate Data. *Political Methodology* 3:411–39.

Jackson, John E. 1987. Variable Coefficient Models and Analyis of Electoral Change. Paper presented at the annual meeting of the Midwest Political Science Association, Chicago.

Jacobson, Gary C. 1987a. The Marginals Never Vanished: Incumbency and Competition in Elections to the U.S. House of Representatives, 1952–82. *American Journal of Political Science* 31:126–41.

Jacobson, Gary C. 1987b. *The Politics of Congressional Elections*. Boston: Little, Brown.

Jacobson, Gary C. 1989. Strategic Politicians and the Dynamics of U.S. House Elections, 1946–86. *American Political Science Review* 83:774–93.

Jacobson, Gary C., and Samuel Kernell. 1982. Strategy and Choice in the 1982 Congressional Elections. *PS* 15:423–30.

Johnston, J. 1972. *Econometric Methods*. New York: McGraw-Hill.

Judge, George G., R. Carter Hill, William Griffiths, Helmut Lutkepohl, and Tsoung-Chau Lee. 1982. *Introduction to the Theory and Practice of Econometrics*. New York: Wiley.

Katz, Daniel, and Samuel J. Eldersveld. 1961. The Impact of Local Party Activities upon the Electorate. *Public Opinion Quarterly* 25:1–24.

Kawato, Sadafumi. 1987. Nationalization and Partisan Realignment in Congressional Elections. *American Political Science Review* 81:1235–50.

Kernell, Samuel. 1977. Presidential Popularity and Negative Voting: An Alternative Explanation of the Midterm Congressional Decline of the President's Party. *American Political Science Review* 71:44–66.

Key, V. O. 1949. *Southern Politics in State and Nation*. Knoxville: University of Tennessee Press.

Key, V. O. 1955. A Theory of Critical Elections. *Journal of Politics* 17:3–18.

Key, V. O. 1959. Secular Realignment and the Party System. *Journal of Politics* 21:198–210.

Key, V. O. 1964. *Politics, Parties, and Pressure Groups*. 5th ed. New York: Crowell.

Kinder, Donald R., and D. Roderick Kiewiet. 1981. Sociotropic Politics: The American Case. *British Journal of Political Science* 11:129–61.

King, Gary. 1989. *Unifying Political Methodology: The Likelihood Theory of Statistical Inference*. Cambridge: Cambridge University Press.

Kleppner, Paul. 1979. *The Third Electoral System, 1853–1892*. Chapel Hill, N.C.: University of North Carolina Press.

Kleppner, Paul. 1982. *Who Voted: The Dynamics of Electoral Turnout, 1870–1980*. New York: Praeger.

Kleppner, Paul. 1987. *Continuity and Change in Electoral Politics, 1893–1928*. New York: Greenwood.

Kocak, Huseyin. 1989. *Differential and Difference Equations through Computer Experiments*, 2d ed. New York: Springer-Verlag.

Koppstein, Peter E. A. 1983. Parameterized Dynamical Systems: Perspectives on Collective Action with Special References to Political Protest and Civil Violence. Ph.D. diss., Department of Political Science, Yale University.

Kramer, Gerald H. 1970–71. The Effects of Precinct-Level Canvassing on Voter Behavior. *Public Opinion Quarterly* 34:560–72.

Kramer, Gerald H. 1971. Short-term Fluctuations in U.S. Voting Behavior, 1896–1964. *American Political Science Review* 65:131–43.

Kramer, Gerald H. 1983. The Ecological Fallacy Revisited: Aggregate versus

Individual-Level Findings on Economics and Elections and Sociotropic Voting. *American Political Science Review* 77:92–111.

Ladd, Everett Carll. 1982. *Where have all the Voters Gone? The Fracturing of America's Political Parties*. New York: Norton.

Ladd, Everett Carll, and Charles D. Hadley. 1978. *Transformations of the American Party System: Political Coalitions from the New Deal to the 1970s*. New York: Norton.

Lamar, Mrs. Walter D. N.d. *The Vulnerability of the White Primary*. Macon, Ga.: Georgia Association Opposed to Woman Suffrage.

Langton, Kenneth P., and Ronald Rapoport. 1975. Social Structure, Social Context, and Partisan Mobilization: Urban Workers in Chile. *Comparative Political Studies* 8:318–44.

Lewis-Beck, Michael S. 1985. Pocketbook Voting in U.S. National Election Studies: Fact or Artifact? *American Journal of Political Science* 29:348–56.

Lipset, Seymour Martin. 1981. *Political Man: The Social Bases of Politics*. New York: Doubleday.

Lowenberg, Gerhard. 1973. The Institutionalization of Parliament and Public Orientation to the Political System. In *Legislatures in Comparative Perspective*, ed. Allan Kornberg, 41–72. New York: McKay.

Luardini, Christine A., and Thomas J. Knock. 1980–81. Woodrow Wilson and Woman Suffrage: A New Look. *Political Science Quarterly* 95:655–71.

Lubell, Samuel. 1965. *The Future of American Politics*. New York: Harper.

Luenberger, David G. 1979. *Introduction to Dynamic Systems: Theory, Models, and Applications*. New York: Wiley.

MacKuen, Michael, and Courtney Brown. 1987. Political Context and Attitude Change. *American Political Science Review* 81:42–56.

MacKuen, Michael, Robert S. Erikson, and James A. Stimson. 1989. Macropartisanship. *American Political Science Review* 83:1125–42.

McDonagh, Eileen L., and H. Douglas Price. 1985. Woman Suffrage in the Progressive Era: Patterns of Opposition and Support in Referenda Voting. *American Political Science Review* 79:415–35.

McPhee, William N. 1963. *Formal Theories of Mass Behavior*. New York: Macmillan.

McPhee, William N., and Jack Ferguson. 1962. Political Immunization. In *Public Opinion and Congressional Elections*, ed. William N. McPhee and William A. Glaser, 155–79. New York: Free Press.

McPhee, William N., and Robert B. Smith. 1962. A Model for Analyzing Voting Systems. In *Public Opinion and Congressional Elections*, ed. William N. McPhee and William A. Glaser, 123–54. New York: Macmillan.

McRae, Duncan, Jr., and James A. Meldrum. 1960. Critical Elections in Illinois: 1888–1958. *American Political Science Review* 54:669–83.

Mann, Thomas E., and Raymond E. Wolfinger. 1980. Candidates and Parties in Congressional Elections. *American Political Science Review* 74:617–32.

Markus, Gregory B. 1988. The Impact of Personal and National Economic Conditions on the Presidential Vote: A Pooled Cross-Sectional Analysis. *American Journal of Political Science* 32:137–54.

Marra, Robin F., and Charles W. Ostrom. 1989. Explaining Seat Change in the U.S.

House of Representatives, 1950–86. *American Journal of Political Science* 33:541–69.

May, Robert M. 1974. *Stability and Complexity in Model Ecosystems.* Princeton, N.J.: Princeton University Press.

Mazmanian, Daniel A. 1974. *Third Parties in Presidential Elections.* Washington, D.C.: Brookings Institute.

Merriam, Charles Edward, and Harold Foote Gosnell. 1924. *Non-Voting: Causes and Methods of Control.* Chicago: University of Chicago Press.

Mesterton-Gibbons, Michael. 1989. *A Concrete Approach to Mathematical Modeling.* New York: Addison-Wesley.

Miller, Warren E. 1956. One-Party Politics and the Voter. *American Political Science Review* 50:707–25.

Miller, William L. 1977. *Electoral Dynamics.* London: Macmillan.

Milnor, A. J. 1969. *Elections and Political Stability.* Boston: Little, Brown.

Mishler, William, and Anne Hildreth. 1984. Legislatures and Political Stability: An Exploratory Analysis. *Journal of Politics* 46:25–59.

Molotch, Harvey L., and Deirdre Boden. 1985. Talking Social Structure: Discourse, Domination and the Watergate Hearings. *American Sociological Review* 50:273–88.

Nachmias, David, and Chava Nachmias. 1987. *Research Methods in the Social Sciences.* 3d ed. New York: St. Martin's.

Nash, Howard P., Jr. 1959. *Third Parties in American Politics.* Washington, D.C.: Public Affairs Press.

Nie, Norman H., Sidney Verba, and John R. Petrocik. 1979. *The Changing American Voter.* Enl. ed. Cambridge, Mass.: Harvard University Press.

Niemi, Richard G., Richard S. Katz, and David Newman. 1980. Reconstructing Past Partisanship: The Failure of the Party Identification Recall Questions. *American Journal of Political Science* 24:633–51.

Niemi, Richard G., and Herbert F. Weisberg. 1984. *Controversies in Voting Behavior.* 2d ed. Washington, D.C.: CQ Press.

Nisbet, R. M., and W. S. C. Gurney. 1982. *Modelling Fluctuating Populations.* New York: Wiley.

Ostrom, Charles W., Jr. 1990. *Time Series Analysis: Regression Techniques.* 2d ed. Newbury Park, Calif.: Sage.

Parent, T. Wayne, Calvin C. Jillson, and Ronald E. Weber. 1987. Voting Outcomes in the 1984 Democratic Party Primaries and Caucuses. *American Political Science Review* 81: 67–84.

Patterson, Samuel C., and Gregory Caldeira. 1983. Getting Out the Vote: Participation in Gubernatorial Elections. *American Political Science Review* 77:675–89.

Petrocik, John R. 1981a. *Party Coalitions: Realignments and the Decline of the New Deal Party System.* Chicago: University of Chicago Press.

Petrocik, John R. 1981b. Voter Turnout and Electoral Oscillation. *American Politics Quarterly* 9:161–80.

Piereson, James E. 1975. Presidential Popularity and Midterm Voting at Different Electoral Levels. *American Journal of Political Science* 19:683–94.

Polsby, Nelson W. 1968. The Institutionalization of the U.S. House of Representatives. *American Political Science Review* 62:144–68.

Powell, G. Bingham, Jr. 1986. American Voter Turnout in Comparative Perspective. *American Political Science Review* 80:17–43.

Powell, M. J. D. 1964. An Efficient Method for Finding the Minimum of a Function of Several Variables without Calculating Derivatives. *Computer Journal* 7:155–62.

Przeworski, Adam, and John Sprague. 1986. *Paper Stones: A History of Electoral Socialism.* Chicago: University of Chicago Press.

Przeworski, Adam, and Glaucio A. D. Soares. 1971. Theories in Search of a Curve: A Contextual Interpretation of Left Vote. *American Political Science Review* 65:51–65.

Przeworski, Adam. 1975. Institutionalization of Voting Patterns, or is Mobilization the Source of Decay. *American Political Science Review* 69:49–67.

Putnam, Robert D. 1966. Political Attitudes and the Local Community. *American Political Science Review* 60:640–54.

Rapoport, Anatol. 1963. Mathematical Models of Social Interaction. In *Handbook of Mathematical Psychology*, ed. R. Duncan Luce, Robert R. Bush, and Eugene Galanter, 2:145–85. New York: Wiley.

Rapoport, Anatol. 1983. *Mathematical Models in the Social and Behavioral Sciences.* New York: Wiley.

Reiter, Howard L. 1980. The Perils of Partisan Recall. *Public Opinion Quarterly* 44:385–88.

Rockwood, D. Stephen, Cecelia Brown, Kenneth Eshleman, and Deborah Shaffer. 1985. *American Third Parties Since the Civil War: An Annotated Bibliography.* New York: Garland.

Rosen, R. 1970. *Stability Theory and Its Application.* Vol. 1 of *Dynamical System Theory in Biology.* New York: Wiley.

Rosenstone, Steven J., Roy L. Behr, and Edward H. Lazarus. 1984. *Third Parties in America: Citizen Response to Major Party Failure.* Princeton, N.J.: Princeton University Press.

SAS Institute. 1990. *SAS/ETS Users Guide*, Version 6. Cary, N.C.: SAS Institute, Inc.

Schelling, Thomas C. 1978. *Micromotives and Macrobehavior.* New York: Norton.

Shively, W. Philip. 1971–72. A Reinterpretation of the New Deal Realignment. *Public Opinion Quarterly* 35:621–24.

Simmel, Georg. 1955. *The Web of Group Affiliations.* Glencoe, Ill.: Free Press.

Simon, Herbert A. 1957. *Models of Man: Social and Rational.* New York: Wiley.

Sorenson, Harold W. 1980. *Parameter Estimation: Principles and Problems.* New York: Marcel Dekker.

Sprague, John. 1976. Estimating a Boudon Type Contextual Model: Some Practical and Theoretical Problems of Measurement. *Political Methodology* 3:333–53.

Sprague, John. 1980. Two Variants of Aggregation Processes and Problems in Elementary Dynamic and Contextual Causal Formulations. Political Science Paper no. 50, Department of Political Science, Washington University, St. Louis.

Sprague, John. 1981. One-Party Dominance in Legislatures. *Legislative Studies Quarterly* 6:259–85.

Stanley, Harold W. 1987. *Voter Mobilization and the Politics of Race: The South and Universal Suffrage.* New York: Praeger.

Stokes, Donald E., and Warren E. Miller. 1962. Party Government and the Saliency of Congress. *Public Opinion Quarterly* 26:531–46.

Sundquist, James L. 1983. *Dynamics of the Party System: Alignment and Realignment of Political Parties in the United States*. Washington, D.C.: Brookings Institution.

Thomassen, Jacques. 1976. Party Identification as a Cross-National Concept: Its Meaning in the Netherlands. In *Party Identification and Beyond*, ed. Ian Budge, Ivor Crewe, and Dennis Farlie, 97–121. London: Wiley.

Tufte, Edward R. 1975. Determinants of the Outcomes of Midterm Congressional Elections. *American Political Science Review* 69:812–26.

Tuma, Nancy Brandon, and Michael T. Hanna. 1984. *Social Dynamics: Models and Methods*. New York: Academic Press.

Walton, Hanes, Jr. 1969. *The Negro In Third Party Politics*. Philadelphia: Dorrance.

Walton, Hanes, Jr. 1972. *Black Political Parties*. New York: Free Press.

Ward, Michael Don. 1984. Differential Paths to Parity: A Study of the Contemporary Arms Race. *American Political Science Review* 78:297–317.

Weatherford, M. Stephen. 1982. Interpersonal Networks and Political Behavior. *American Journal of Political Science* 26:117–43.

Weisberg, Herbert F. 1980. A Multidimensional Conceptualization of Party Identification. *Political Behavior* 2:33–60.

White, William Allen. 1965. *A Puritan in Babylon: The Story of Calvin Coolidge*. New York: Capricorn Books.

Index